*From*
*the wisdom of*
MISHLÉ

# SAMSON RAPHAEL HIRSCH

*From*

*the wisdom*

*of*

# MISHLÉ

FELDHEIM PUBLISHERS

Jerusalem    New York

Rendered into English by

KAREN PARITZKY-JOSHUA

First published 1976
Reprinted 1984, 1991
ISBN 0-87306-040-7

Philipp Feldheim Inc.
200 Airport Executive Park
Spring Valley, NY 10977

Feldheim Publishers Ltd
POB 35002/Jerusalem, Israel

*Printed in Israel*

# CONTENTS

◉

# FOREWORD

This commentary on *Mishlé* (the Book of Proverbs) is an illuminating explanation of King Shlomo's wise guidelines to life. It is an invaluable contribution in our constant fight against the moral decay and confusion of ideals of every age. The lucid words of Rabbi Shamshon Rephoel Hirsch will inspire those who read them in their quest for guidance and solutions to the social and ethical problems of our times.

It appears that the *p'sukim* (verses) in Mishlé are arranged in the chronological order in which they were expressed by the wise King Shlomo. Shamshon Rephoel Hirsch has explained Mishlé in twenty-two chapters, each chapter bearing the title of a principal idea of the Book of Proverbs. In this essay form the philosophical teachings of Mishlé became most effective. Rabbi Hirsch published his commentary on Mishlé in installments entitled "Salomonische Spruchweisheit" in the Jewish-German weekly periodical *Jeschurun*. The work appeared in the years 1883 to 1885, at a time when my grandfather Isaac Hirsch (Shamshon Rephoel's son), a businessman in Hanover, took over the publication of *Jeschurun* upon the request of his illustrious father. My mother, Sara, assisted her father in compiling and editing the journal. She considered it a *z'chus,* a great privilege, to be instrumental in the publication of the works of Rabbi Shamshon Rephoel Hirsch. Both my father and my mother fervently advocated the philosophy of Rabbi Shamshon Rephoel Hirsch in the education of their children. It is thus a memorable occasion for me to see the appearance of this volume, which I gratefully dedicate to the memory of my parents, William and Sara Moller ז״ל.

I would like to express my thanks to Mrs. Karin Paritzky of Bayit Vegan, Israel, who so ably translated the original German text into the English language, and I am most grateful to Rabbi Shlomo Danziger for editing the English text. I also owe thanks to the Samson Raphael

Hirsch Society and to Mr. Jacob Breuer for his constant good advice. My appreciation goes to Mr. Max Nussbaum for inserting the Hebrew *p'sukim* (verses) and, last but not least, my gratitude goes to Mr. Philipp Feldheim and his staff for arranging and printing this text.

Dr. Raphael Moller

# INTRODUCTION

As indicated by the title and table of contents of this newly translated work, Rav S.R. Hirsch זצ"ל has not provided us with a complete and consecutive translation and commentary of *Sefer Mishlé*.

Mishlé contains a wealth of fundamental themes, some of which recur at various places in the Séfer. In the present volume, the author groups together the texts and translations of certain parts of Mishlé dealing with a particular theme and follows them up with a treatise pertaining to this theme. These treatises first appeared in the German-language publication *Der Neue Jeschurun*.

During a period of fourteen years, S. R. Hirsch edited a monthly under the title *Jeschurun*. After his death his son, Dr. Naftali Hirsch, compiled the rich literary work contained in *Jeschurun* in six volumes, which he published as the "Collected Writings" *(Gesammelte Schriften)*.

When advanced age and the pressure of other literary tasks (such as the Commentary to the Psalms) forced S. R. Hirsch to cease publication of *Jeschurun,* his son Isaac, of Hanover, began to issue a new monthly under the title *Der Neue Jeschurun*. He was eminently qualified for this difficult literary undertaking. Inspired by the spiritual impact of the ideology expounded by his great father, and endowed with a brilliant pen (which S. R. Hirsch, as reported by my father זצ"ל, characterized as "extraordinary"), Isaac Hirsch, by profession a businessman, was able to apply his extensive Jewish and secular knowledge in the evaluation and clear analysis of the problems which beset the Judaism and Jewry of his time. The treatises contained in the present volume were written by S. R. Hirsch for *Der Neue Jeschurun*.

Raphael Moller, the grandson of Isaac Hirsch, has taken a special interest in the master's writings on Mishlé. He left no stone unturned until he located the issue containing the first article which, together with the remaining work, he arranged to have translated in preparation for this publication.

These treatises are brilliant rays of light, seeds sown in prolific abundance by the great leader in Israel during a rich lifetime graced by Divine Providence. They are seeds which will blossom and ripen in ever greater beauty in the future. More than ever, their timeless message is designed to illuminate our contemporary scene.

Rav Dr. Joseph Breuer

# I

## RIGHTEOUS AND UNRIGHTEOUS

In describing people who do or do not obey the Torah's commandments, Mishlé divides them into two distinct groups, under the general
classification of צדיקים and רשעים. The *tzaddik* is the law-abiding man,
who subordinates himself to God's commandments and fulfils His requirements, both inward (in belief and thought) and outward (in action).
He is also called *yashar*, upright, because of the straight course of his
striving, since he steadfastly proceeds towards the aim determined by
God, unimpeded by any external or internal disturbance. Or he is called
*tam*, because of the surrender of all his·emotions, thinking and volition
to this one aim; *tam* actually means the whole person, complete within
himself.

The opposite of *tzaddik* is רשע (related to רשה), the lawless man, who
lives and acts utterly by whim.

The Proverbs portray these contrasting characters for us by their different conceptions, tendencies and aspirations; by the difference in their
respective influences on the welfare of their fellow-men; and, most of all,
by their respective relationship to God and the consequences of their
behavior on their own well-being. The basic thoughts in this respect may
well be expressed by these sentences:

בְּטַח אֶל־ד׳ בְּכָל־לִבֶּךָ
וְאֶל־בִּינָתְךָ אַל־תִּשָּׁעֵן׃
בְּכָל־דְּרָכֶיךָ דָעֵהוּ
וְהוּא יְיַשֵּׁר אֹרְחֹתֶיךָ׃

*Trust in God with your whole heart,*
*and do not lean upon your own understanding.*
*In all your ways acknowledge Him,*
*and He will direct your paths aright.*

13

אַל־תְּהִי חָכָם בְּעֵינֶיךָ
יְרָא אֶת־ד' וְסוּר מֵרָע:

*Be not wise in your own eyes;*
*fear God and desist from evil.* (3, 5−7)

Note that this passage begins not 'בטח בד' but 'בטח אל ד' — not to have reliance on whatever God has already granted, but to trust God, be confident about what He has in store for us. It means to build our entire future upon God, to be unshakeable in our conviction that we can reach our goal in life only with God, from God and by God's help. Hence we should ask ourselves at every step whether the aims we seek and the means by which we try to attain them are in keeping with God's will, to such an extent that we may hopefully expect His assistance. This is the attitude which, according to Mishlé, is fundamental to the *tzaddik*'s thinking.

Contrastingly, we are shown how faith can sunder on the cliff of arrogance, how it can be misled and misleading by its over-reliance on human understanding and by the thought that God's knowledge, teachings and guidance — and consequently also His assistance — can be dispensed with.

רוּם־עֵינַיִם וּרְחַב־לֵב
נִר רְשָׁעִים חַטָּאת:

*Raised eyes, wide with heart's desire,*
*the tilled soil of the wicked is sin.* (21, 4)

A lawless person thinks that his own intelligence and calculations make him able to do virtually anything at all; he "lifts high his eyes"; and by raising, "lifting high" his eyes, by putting his confidence entirely on his own cleverness and qualifications, he lets his heart's desires roam far and wide. Only what is physically unattainable does not exist for him as a possible acquisition by his undaunted arrogance. His field, *nir*, his area of activity, is therefore sin; he believes that transgression of the sacred commandments is the soil on which he will reap success.

כָּל־דֶּרֶךְ אִישׁ יָשָׁר בְּעֵינָיו
וְתֹכֵן לִבּוֹת ד':

*Every way of a man is rightful in his own eyes,*
*but [only] God examines the heart. (21, 2)*

כָּל־דַּרְכֵי־אִישׁ זַךְ בְּעֵינָיו
וְתֹכֵן רוּחוֹת ד':
גֹּל אֶל־ד' מַעֲשֶׂיךָ
וְיִכֹּנוּ מַחְשְׁבֹתֶיךָ:

*All the ways of a man are pure in his own eyes,*
*but [only] God examines the spirits.*
*Commit your actions unto God*
*and your thoughts will be the right ones. (16, 2—3)*

Not even the most devious way will be taken by any human being unless he is convinced that he is not mistaken and that he is moving in
the right direction. What he is forgetting, however, is that right or wrong
are determined not by man, but by God. If we want to take the road that
leads us to our true destination, we must realize that yielding to our
heart's cravings will not get us there; we can reach this aim only by
those actions which are in keeping with God's approval. Hence, before
we can consider the desires of our heart justified and assume that our
convictions are the right ones, we must test them by the standard of
God's demands and God's decrees. In other words, our actions should
be directed, from the start, toward God! (The Hebrew word *gol* means a
movement, involving exertion, in the direction of a goal.) Once we make
our actions subject to God's approval and His sanction, then our very
thoughts will become the right thoughts and we shall be protected from
going astray anywhere in our thinking and volition.

תַּאֲוַת צַדִּיקִים אַךְ־טוֹב
תִּקְוַת רְשָׁעִים עֶבְרָה:

*The desire of the righteous is only [for the] good,*
*but the expectation of the wicked is [God's] wrath. (11, 23)*

Whatever situations and happenings a righteous person may wish for, the misfortune of others is never among them. He will never agree to become a tool for the destruction of others. Indeed, he would rather deny his own desires than have others suffer because of them. The desires of the lawless man, however, if we look closely, are based on his hope that some trouble will come up, of which he would like to become the instrument. This is pointed out by another adage of Mishlé:

כֹּל פָּעַל ד׳ לַמַּעֲנֵהוּ
וְגַם־רָשָׁע לְיוֹם רָעָה:

*God has made all things for His own purpose,*
*and even the wicked for a day of evil.* (16, 4)

Adversity and suffering are an integral part of God's methods — either punitive or probationary — to educate us. It is His way of leading individuals or a group to betterment if they are still amenable to improvement, or, if they are incorrigible, to destruction, for the sake of rescuing their surroundings from them. Ultimately, these methods of His aim at the salvation of the world. Yet once it has been ordained by His paternal guidance that such a period of suffering shall come to pass, He allows the madness and evil of men to become its instruments. He uses the folly and wickedness of people who speculate on such a period of 'evrah, Divine wrath, to carry out their own evil schemes and to cause destruction. In the end, however, they become a tool in God's design for the good of the world.

נֶפֶשׁ רָשָׁע אִוְּתָה־רָע
לֹא־יֻחַן בְּעֵינָיו רֵעֵהוּ:

*The soul of the wicked wishes for evil;*
*in his view, no comrade should be pardoned.* (21, 10)

תּוֹחֶלֶת צַדִּיקִים שִׂמְחָה

*The anticipation of the righteous is joy,*

וְתִקְוַת רְשָׁעִים תֹּאבֵד:

*but the hope of the wicked — may it never be fulfilled!* (10, 28)

מַחְשְׁבוֹת צַדִּיקִים מִשְׁפָּט
תַּחְבֻּלוֹת רְשָׁעִים מִרְמָה:

*The thoughts of the righteous are toward justice,*
*but the schemings of the wicked, to deceit.* (12, 5)

The mental process needed to penetrate to truth and justice is straightforward and uncomplicated. Therefore the thoughts, מחשבות, of truthful
and just people are equally straightforward and artless. They are
directed toward justice and only justice. The thoughts of the unrighteous, on the other hand, are likened to חבל, a rope spun out of
many threads and a net tied out of many ropes. Their thoughts are
forever directed toward deception and trickery.

◉

שִׂמְחָה לַצַּדִּיק עֲשׂוֹת מִשְׁפָּט
וּמְחִתָּה לְפֹעֲלֵי אָוֶן:

*To the righteous it is a pleasure to exercise justice,*
*but to those used to violence, it is terrifying.* (21, 15)

A law-abiding person never has to be forced in the direction of justice.
He gladly and obligingly fulfills the call of duty. But to people who are
used to acting arbitrarily, it seems terrifying if, for once, they must fulfill
the demands of justice.

יֹדֵעַ צַדִּיק דִּין דַּלִּים
רָשָׁע לֹא־יָבִין דָּעַת:

*The just man knows the rights of the poor;*
*the wicked one knows no such consideration.* (29, 7)

A just man knows that everyone is entitled to justice, and that this includes the poor as well, even though a poor man, because of his impecunity and subordinate station in life, might perhaps be unable to look after his interests, uphold his rights, or bring to justice those who have harmed him. Someone who has no respect for justice, however, has no such consideration. For him there is only one law: the law of the strongest, the law which can be enforced vengefully by power. A law which can be easily broken, such as the right of the poor, means nothing to him. Hence it follows that true respect for justice shows itself in a man's respect for the rights of the poor.

אַנְשֵׁי דָמִים יִשְׂנְאוּ־תָם
וִישָׁרִים יְבַקְשׁוּ נַפְשׁוֹ:

*Men of violence hate one who has moral integrity;*
*under the disguise of honesty they seek his soul.* (29, 10)

In Mishlé the word דמים does not correspond to actual murder. It denotes a disaster caused by the undermining of a person's life and happiness. The *tam*, who has no other thoughts than the fulfillment of his task, who is completely absorbed in following the call of duty and never suspects others of having any different intentions, who himself never thinks of deception, is the one most easily deceived; he is the easiest victim of crime. There is no more welcome object for the criminal intentions of אנשי דמים, men of violence, than the *tam;* they are his sworn antagonists. Under the guise of honesty they approach the unsuspecting *tam*, only to bring about his destruction.

הֵעֵז אִישׁ רָשָׁע בְּפָנָיו
וְיָשָׁר הוּא יָבִין דַּרְכּוֹ:

*However bold an evil man may be in his presence,*
*the just man, let him watch his ways.* (21, 29)

מַעְיָן נִרְפָּשׂ וּמָקוֹר מָשְׁחָת
צַדִּיק מָט לִפְנֵי־רָשָׁע:

*A troubled fountain and a contaminated well,*
*such is a righteous man flinching before the wicked.* (25, 26)

A man of moral rectitude should not allow himself to be led astray; he
should not even be guilty of a momentary vaccillation, no matter how
brashly he is being faced. His obligation is to remain resolute in his convictions. His words and actions should remain a pure fountain and an
unpolluted well of truth and Godliness. When adherence to justice and
right have disappeared, when contempt and mockery of observance of
law have become the order of the day, then the words and deeds of the
uncorruptible, righteous person should reveal such truth which by itself
will testify to human dignity and Divine approbation. Even a momentary irresolution, however, would reveal that this well, too, is clean no
longer; it has not been able to resist the penetration of impurities. This
source too has lost its adamantine strength as a last refuge of the Divine
presence within humanity. Hence, the smallest inconsistency in a man of
integrity strengthens the lawless in their aberration and constitutes, according to our Sages, חילול השם, a desecration of His name.

The disparity between the righteous and the unrighteous is evident not
only when their respective social behavior is compared. They form a
decided contrast also in the physical sphere of human behavior. The one
who observes God's law elevates himself by fulfilling its physical requirements, to the standard of human morality. On the other hand, one
who defies God's law degrades himself, by his sensuality, to the level of
an animal, or even lower.

This thought is concisely expressed in the following adage:

צַדִּיק אֹכֵל לְשֹׂבַע נַפְשׁוֹ
וּבֶטֶן רְשָׁעִים תֶּחְסָר:

*The righteous eats for the satisfaction of his soul,*
*but the body of the wicked is never satisfied.* (13, 25)

The person who observes Divine law allows himself the enjoyment of food and the satisfaction of other physical needs only inasmuch as this is necessary for the maintenance of his body as the receptacle of his soul on earth and for the fulfillment of his obligations in this connection. Accordingly, even when attending to his physical needs, the righteous man remains within the sphere of the spiritual. To a person without any law, on the other hand, sensual satisfaction is purely a demand of his body; and while animals find their proper limit in the fulfillment of their natural needs and restrain themselves at that, a sensual person knows neither limit nor satiety in the gratification of his senses.

We have noted that the man of integrity abhors social injustice and violence. He has the same aversion towards immorality and backs away from the very thought of immoral behavior. Conversely, the man outside Divine law abhors not only social justice; he loathes moral dignity too, to such an extent that even the thought of controlling one's own desires and leading a life of unfailing moral conduct is repugnant to him.

תּוֹעֲבַת צַדִּיקִים אִישׁ עָוֶל
וְתוֹעֲבַת רָשָׁע יְשַׁר־דָּרֶךְ:

*Just as a violent person is an abomination to the just,*
*so is the morally straight person to the wicked.* (29, 27)

Our highest vocation in life is the faithful observance of the Divine commandments; and our relationship to God must have as its only objective the fulfillment of this vocation. Everything else must be relative and subordinate to this as a means toward the end.

עֲשׂה צְדָקָה וּמִשְׁפָּט
נִבְחָר לַד' מִזָּבַח:

*To do righteousness and justice*
*is more acceptable to God than sacrifices.* (21, 3)

True, God has chosen sacrificial offerings as an act of expression of our relationship to Him; but this refers only to the honest sacrifice, called in the Psalms כרתי בריתי עלי זבח (Ps. 50, 5); i.e. the offering is always a renewal of our covenant with God. "To do righteousness and justice," however, is more than a renewal of the covenant; it is living up to the terms of the covenant. In other words, it is the fulfillment of the vows which are the essential part of a sacrificial offering, which give the sacrifice its intrinsic value.

אֱוֵלִים יָלִיץ אָשָׁם
וּבֵין יְשָׁרִים רָצוֹן:

*For the unwise, a guilt-sacrifice must intercede [by promising better-ment],*
*but among these who retain their moral rectitude dwells [God's] goodwill. (14, 9)*

Those who have been foolish enough to stray from the right path need a guilt-offering to vow betterment and so restore them into God's favor. However, for those who have remained ישרים, such a sacrifice is not needed. God's benevolence stays at their side at every step.

כִּי תוֹעֲבַת ד׳ נָלוֹז
וְאֶת־יְשָׁרִים סוֹדוֹ:

*For an abomination to God is one who divests himself of moral ties,*
*while the upright enjoy His invisible, intimate closeness. (3, 32)*

נלוז is from לוז, to abandon, to leave. סוד denotes an intimate relationship known only to the person involved.

יִצְפֹּן לַיְשָׁרִים תּוּשִׁיָּה
מָגֵן לְהֹלְכֵי תֹם:

*In hidden ways He grants energy to the upright,*
*being a shield to those who walk in integrity. (2, 7)*

People of integrity are aware of God's proximity, for He grants them both additional energy, enabling them to carry out their good intentions, and protection against perils which might hinder them in their striving to fulfil their duty.

תּוֹעֲבַת ד׳ דֶּרֶךְ רָשָׁע
וּמְרַדֵּף צְדָקָה יֶאֱהָב:

*The way of the wicked is an abomination to God,*
*but He loves him who eagerly strives to fulfil his obligation.* (15, 9)

רָחוֹק ד׳ מֵרְשָׁעִים
וּתְפִלַּת צַדִּיקִים יִשְׁמָע:

*God remains far from the wicked,*
*but to the prayers of the righteous He listens.* (15, 29)

From people who shun His commandments, God remains distant. But to the righteous He is close; and by their prayer they can gain from Him clarity of thought, purity of intention, and strength for fulfillment of good purposes. On the other hand,

זֶבַח רְשָׁעִים תּוֹעֲבַת ד׳
וּתְפִלַּת יְשָׁרִים רְצוֹנוֹ:

*The sacrifice of the wicked is an abomination to God,*
*while He favors the prayer of the upright.* (15, 8)

זֶבַח רְשָׁעִים תּוֹעֵבָה
אַף כִּי־בְזִמָּה יְבִיאֶנּוּ:

*The sacrifice of the wicked is an abomination;*
*how much more if he brings it with sinful intention.* (21, 27)

God accepts with favor not only what we show and express to Him by sacrificial offerings, but also what we convey to Him by mere words. He abhors, however, sacrifices brought by those who defy His law, when they do not change their sinful thoughts; when the person offering the sacrifice not only makes no resolve to observe His commandments in the future, but even offers it with the thought of bribing God so as to obtain a dispensation for future disregard of His law. Such a sacrifice is simply a reprehensible blasphemy.

⊙

The life of a man who is truly faithful in observing His law is filled with a richly rewarding happiness: the certainty of God's nearness in his striving for fairness and purity of actions. God's order is directed toward the preservation and promotion of the good, and the righteous person is assured of God's protection and salvation as well as the continuity and prosperity of his descendants in the future.

However, over and above this recompense, the truly faithful observance of the Torah is rewarded by a feeling of joyousness; the very fact of following in the path of justice instills serenity. The world judges by appearances, never suspecting how much bliss and peace can dwell in the heart and hearth of a righteous man, even at a time when poverty and misfortune may be visited upon him. An unrighteous man, on the other hand, even though favored by circumstances and living in the most resplendent magnificence, may harbor in his heart exactly opposite feelings.

הֵן צַדִּיק בָּאָרֶץ יְשֻׁלָּם
אַף כִּי־רָשָׁע וְחוֹטֵא:

*Behold, the righteous is repaid while yet on earth;*
*how much more the wicked and the sinner!* (11, 31)

We only have to survey the histories of our greatest personages (in the past), shining in their faithful observance of God's law and justice, in order to see that not even the slightest deviation from the path of duty, the slightest foible, to which, like any mortal, they for once fell victim, remained uncensured. On the contrary, they had to atone for every sin yet בארץ, while on earth. If such is the case with *tzaddikim,* whose entire lives otherwise shone like a beacon of observance of Divine law and duty, can a life of levity and disobedience to duty then stay uncondemned and unexpiated?

פְּעֻלַּת צַדִּיק לְחַיִּים
תְּבוּאַת רָשָׁע לְחַטָּאת׃

*The deeds of the righteous are for life;*
*the acquisitions of the wicked, for expiation.* (10, 16)

For a righteous man, not only the results of his actions are meaningful, but also the actions themselves. By allowing his psyche to unfold in accordance with its vocation, i.e. to strive in singleness of purpose and faithful fulfillment of its duty towards an aim of purity, he gains life and exaltation of his being, morally and spiritually; these are his progress and his profit. For the wicked, however, even his successes, his earnings and his accomplishments will ultimately prove to be his undoing and become an expiation for his sins and dereliction. (חטאת has the same meaning here as in Zechariah 14, 19.)

מְגוֹרַת רָשָׁע הִיא תְבוֹאֶנּוּ
וְתַאֲוַת צַדִּיקִים יִתֵּן׃
כַּעֲבוֹר סוּפָה וְאֵין רָשָׁע
וְצַדִּיק יְסוֹד עוֹלָם׃

*That which the wicked man dreads, that shall come upon him,*
*and shall contribute toward the fulfillment of the righteous' wishes.*
*When a whirlwind passes [over the world] the wicked one is no more,*
*but the righteous one remains as the foundation of the everlasting future.*
(10, 24—25)

What is it the lawless man (without any Torah in his life) fears most? It is poverty, a lowly station in life, being denied the possibility to gratify his sensual cravings. In order to escape from this fear, he permits himself every defiance of the Divine law, every transgression of the Divine commandments; he becomes a רשע, divesting himself of any bonds imposed by duty. But what he fears most, what he believes to be able to escape by disregarding God's law — this is exactly what *will* befall him. For just as surely as God's plans do not have as their aim the prospering and continued thriving of evil, so — without their knowledge and against their will—all the events caused by the lawless will ultimately frustrate their intentions and contribute toward the Divine purpose of healing and blessing.

This purpose is directed to shaping the conditions of humanity in such a way that truth, integrity, and goodness will be revealed, to be acknowledged in the future — a future toward which the hopes and desires of all the righteous are confidently pointed.

As long as all is quiet and everything seemingly proceeds routinely, to all appearances the lawless man too is prospering; he too enjoys the fulfillment of his desires. At a time, however, when God ordains a purifying storm to pass through human circumstances, then everything rotten, all that was built on unlawful foundations, will reveal itself and collapse, and the lawless shall disappear from the scene of the world. Justice and the just, however, will be able to withstand any storms. They shall remain as the solid foundation for the future of humanity, which rests in God's hands.

⊙

יִרְאַת ד' תּוֹסִיף יָמִים
וּשְׁנוֹת רְשָׁעִים תִּקְצֹרְנָה:

*The fear of God prolongs days,*
*while the years of the wicked are too short.* (10, 27)

The God-fearing man lives in terms of days, and the lawless one in terms of years; yet even years are not sufficient to bring him the fulfillment of his schemes. The God-fearing man's endeavor, his faithful com-

pliance with the Divine commandments, can be successfully accomplished on each and every day. Each day that has been lived
through in faithful observance of the Torah is a gain, a profit for him.
Having accomplished this, he can have it entered on the life-calendar of
his sojourn upon earth; he has not lived in vain. He counts days, not
years (see Psalms 90, 12).

The lawless person, however, sees the value of his life only in external
acquisitions. Such acquisitions, though, come to maturity (reach their
full value) under the rays of the earthly sun and need years for their
development. Mere days, therefore, are meaningless to the lawless man;
he can count only years. But even years are not sufficient to bring him
fulfillment of his forever-increasing wishes. This is what our Sages
meant when they said: No man departs from this world having attained
half of his desires (Koheleth Rabbah 1, 13).

בְּמוֹת אָדָם רָשָׁע תֹּאבַד תִּקְוָה
וְתוֹחֶלֶת אוֹנִים אָבָדָה:

*When a lawless man dies, his hope is at an end,*
*and his expectation of /material/ increase of his strength has perished.*
(11, 7)

הָפוֹךְ רְשָׁעִים וְאֵינָם
וּבֵית צַדִּיקִים יַעֲמֹד:

*Overthrow the wicked, and they are no longer;*
*but the house of the righteous shall stand.* (12, 7)

When the lawless lose their fortune and fall from the proud pinnacle on
which their fortune stands. nothing remains of them. The sum of such
a man's own person plus his fortune comprise a grand total of superficialities. As soon as these façades have collapsed, such people
themselves become buried under the ruins.

For the righteous man however, all externals are only means toward the one end which he never loses sight of. "Home" to him is not represented by the measure of comfort with which his house was built and is now maintained.

To him, home denotes striving and accomplishing aims favorable in God's eyes, through the means granted him and the human beings entrusted into his care. His circumstances may change, his prosperity may vanish, but his task always remains the same. Those of God's demands which he has already fulfilled will never be lost; they are his — into eternity. In adversity it only remains for him to prove, serene and undaunted, that his and his family's faithfulness and striving toward God are unshaken even though his fortunes have turned and the circumstances of his life have changed. His "home" remains.

In truth, while the lawless collapses when his fortune is doomed, the righteous man retains his confidence even in death, for his existence and his accomplishments go beyond the span of his sojourn upon earth.

בְּרָעָתוֹ יִדָּחֶה רָשָׁע
וְחֹסֶה בְמוֹתוֹ צַדִּיק:

*In his adversity, the wicked is thrown over;*
*but the righteous, even in dying, keeps trusting.* (14, 32)

As long as his luck holds, the lawless man [without faith or Torah] may be bold and brash; but as soon as his fortunes seem to turn, he becomes cowardly and discouraged, because apart from his external |wordly| fortunes he possesses no internal, inner steadiness. The righteous man, however, remains courageously upright even in extreme distress.

It is in such times of distress that we see most clearly the difference between those who are led by God's guidance in both auspicious and inauspicious circumstances, and those who have withdrawn from His

guiding hand, taking both their conduct and their fate into their own
hands. It is in such times of distress that the strength inherent in true
trust in God proves itself most conclusively.

נָסוּ וְאֵין־רֹדֵף רָשָׁע
וְצַדִּיקִים כִּכְפִיר יִבְטָח:

*They flee though there is no persecutor — those /who know themselves to
be/ lawless;*
*the righteous, however, are confident as a young lion. (28, 1)*

מִגְדַּל־עֹז שֵׁם ד׳
בּוֹ־יָרוּץ צַדִּיק וְנִשְׂגָּב:

*The name of God is a strong tower;*
*the righteous one strives forth in it and feels himself elevated. (18, 10)*

Conscientious observance of God's Law provides, in itself, protection
from many an evil. The conscientiously devout person rejects enticement to evil, while a lawless man lets himself be allured, by seemingly
dazzling advantages, into a course of action which very often necessarily leads to ruin. This may well be the idea expressed by the following
verses:

צְדָקָה תִּצֹּר תָּם־דָּרֶךְ
וְרִשְׁעָה תְּסַלֵּף חַטָּאת:

*Righteousness guards him that walks in integrity,*
*but wickedness, /by its/ crooked ways, incurs expiation. (13, 6)*

יָתֵר מֵרֵעֵהוּ צַדִּיק

*The righteous excels above his neighbor,*

וְדֶרֶךְ רְשָׁעִים תַּתְעֵם:

*but the way of the wicked leads them astray.* (12, 26)

תֻּמַּת יְשָׁרִים תַּנְחֵם
וְסֶלֶף בֹּגְדִים יְשָׁדֵּם:

*The integrity of the upright shall guide them,*
*while the crookedness of the faithless shall destroy them.* (11, 3)

צִדְקַת תָּמִים תְּיַשֵּׁר דַּרְכּוֹ
וּבְרִשְׁעָתוֹ יִפֹּל רָשָׁע:

*The righteousness of a sincere person shall smooth his way,*
*but by his lawlessness the wicked one shall fall.* (11, 5)

צִדְקַת יְשָׁרִים תַּצִּילֵם
וּבְהַוַּת בֹּגְדִים יִלָּכֵדוּ:

*Observance of duty shall save the upright,*
*but the faithless shall be trapped in their own schemings.* (11, 6)

מְסִלַּת יְשָׁרִים סוּר מֵרָע
שֹׁמֵר נַפְשׁוֹ נֹצֵר דַּרְכּוֹ

*The ascending course of the upright is avoidance of evil;*
*he who watches his way protects his soul.* (16, 17)

מַשְׂכִּיל צַדִּיק לְבֵית רָשָׁע
מְסַלֵּף רְשָׁעִים לָרָע:

*The righteous man understands the house of the lawless one,*
*how it brings, by crookedness, ruin to the lawless.* (21, 12)

שֹׁד־רְשָׁעִים יְגוֹרֵם
כִּי מֵאֲנוּ לַעֲשׂוֹת מִשְׁפָּט:

*The violence of the wicked shall drag them on,*
*because once they refused to do what is right.* (21, 7)

(The word יגורם is from גרר, as in יגורהו בחרמו, "they drag them into
their net" — Habakkuk 1, 15.)

צַדִּיק מִצָּרָה נֶחֱלָץ
וַיָּבֹא רָשָׁע תַּחְתָּיו:

*The righteous man remains spared from trouble,*
*and the wicked one comes in his stead.* (11, 8)

כֹּפֶר לַצַּדִּיק רָשָׁע
וְתַחַת יְשָׁרִים בּוֹגֵד:

*The lawless person is a ransom for the righteous one,*
*and the faithless one comes instead of the upright.* (21, 18)

It seems to us that these last two proverbs reflect on a situation where
an attractive and advantageous, but evil, scheme might have been of-
fered initially to a righteous man, whose integrity, however, forbade him
to enter upon it. Instead of him, lawless and faithless men will carry it
out, thereby causing their own destruction — from which fate the
righteous man has escaped unharmed.

◉

As we have learned, observance of the Divine Law by itself preserves
the righteous from going astray towards ruin. However, beyond this, a
righteous person has God's direct, individual protection. Beyond any
doubt there are educational forces in his life which, in order to allow him
to perfect himself, have the purpose of elevating and ennobling him by

trials and tests, showing in these very situations [that try him] the fatherly love of God. Just as surely, though, God will not let a righteous man
be destroyed, and He will ordain for him (even if but a modest one) an
ever re-flowering future. Evil, however, unfailingly ends in ruin.

This, now, is the Book of Mishlé's further advice to the Lawless: It is no
use to plot an ambush.

אַל־תֶּאֱרֹב רָשָׁע לִנְוֵה צַדִּיק

אַל־תְּשַׁדֵּד רִבְצוֹ:

כִּי שֶׁבַע יִפּוֹל צַדִּיק וָקָם

וּרְשָׁעִים יִכָּשְׁלוּ בְרָעָה:

*Do not lie in wait, O wicked man, at the dwelling of the righteous;*
*do not pillage his place of rest.*
*For a righteous man may fall seven times, and he will rise up again,*
*but the wicked stumble under adversity. (24, 15—16)*

צַדִּיק לְעוֹלָם בַּל־יִמּוֹט

וּרְשָׁעִים לֹא יִשְׁכְּנוּ־אָרֶץ:

*The righteous shall not be toppled forever,*
*but the wicked shall never find rest on earth. (10, 30)*

לֹא־יִכּוֹן אָדָם בְּרֶשַׁע

וְשֹׁרֶשׁ צַדִּיקִים בַּל־יִמּוֹט:

*A man shall not be firmly established by lawlessness,*
*but the root of the righteous shall never waver. (12, 3)*

A tree may seem to move to and fro, but the root within and below remains firm. Upon it the tree will steady itself again. So, too, the
righteous man. In the midst of the storms of life, a righteous person has

an inner, invisible support, holding him firm and straight. It is this *shoresh*, this root, which the lawless lack and are unable to replace, in spite of all artificial, man-made, contrived superficialities.

חָמַד רָשָׁע מְצוֹד רָעִים
וְשֹׁרֶשׁ צַדִּיקִים יִתֵּן:

*The wicked one desires the prey of evil men,*
*yet contributes to the root of the righteous. (12, 12)*

By example and lucky chance, a lawless person entices as many companions as possible to his evil deeds. But his bitter end only serves to strengthen the righteous in their purpose.

רָשָׁע עֹשֶׂה פְעֻלַּת־שָׁקֶר
וְזֹרֵעַ צְדָקָה שֶׂכֶר אֱמֶת:

*The lawless' actions end in deceiving,*
*but he who sows righteousness earns true reward. (11, 18)*

לֹא־יַרְעִיב יְהֹוָה נֶפֶשׁ צַדִּיק
וְהַוַּת רְשָׁעִים יֶהְדֹּף:

*God will not let the soul of the righteous famish,*
*But He thrusts away the scheming of the wicked. (10, 3)*

בּוֹטֵחַ בְּעָשְׁרוֹ הוּא יִפּוֹל
וְכֶעָלֶה צַדִּיקִים יִפְרָחוּ:

*He who relies on his riches shall fall,*
*but the righteous shall flourish like a leaf. (11, 28)*

חַטָּאִים תְּרַדֵּף רָעָה
וְאֶת־צַדִּיקִים יְשַׁלֶּם־טוֹב:

*Sinners are pursued by evil,*
*but to the righteous, good shall be repaid. (13, 21)*

בֵּית רְשָׁעִים יִשָּׁמֵד
וְאֹהֶל יְשָׁרִים יַפְרִיחַ:
יֵשׁ דֶּרֶךְ יָשָׁר לִפְנֵי־אִישׁ
וְאַחֲרִיתָהּ דַּרְכֵי־מָוֶת:
גַּם־בִּשְׂחֹק יִכְאַב־לֵב
וְאַחֲרִיתָהּ שִׂמְחָה תוּגָה:
מִדְּרָכָיו יִשְׂבַּע סוּג לֵב
וּמֵעָלָיו אִישׁ טוֹב:

*The lawless man's house shall not escape destruction,*
*but the tent of the upright shall always produce blossoms.*
*Sometimes a road seems straight to a man,*
*yet it ends in the ways of death.*
*Yes, even in merriment the heart aches,*
*and its end is a mirth of sadness.*
*He who is of a straying heart seeks satisfaction from his ways,*
*but a good man, from his own [person]. (14, 11–14)*

A lawless man is deceived in his expectations from the possessions he strives to acquire while evading and ignoring the Divine commandments. One who faithfully observes the Divine law, however, may expect genuine fulfillment of his aims. For the wishes of the righteous stand in relationship to the desires of the lawless as רעב (hunger) to הות (scheming, craving; 10, 3). The wishes of a righteous person do not go beyond the natural and necessary. He is therefore entitled to hope that they will ultimately be granted. The lawless man, however, "schemes" and forever thinks of new contrived, excessive pleasures, which in the end become a necessity to him — a necessity whose satisfaction God rejects.

Anything which centers on mere external gratification collapses and crumbles, just as external prosperity itself is transitory. The contentment of the righteous man, however, grows from inner divinely-blessed roots. Not prominently, perhaps, like tall cedars, or pompously like an ornamental tree, but humbly, always fresh like a new leaf, he flowers and flourishes over and over again.

The evil perpetrated by an unrighteous man becomes his own enemy, just as the righteous person actually finds his reward in the good actions that he performs. True, the lawless man may enjoy a stately house, while a man who "goes straight" has to be satisfied with a humbler dwelling. Yet the lawless one proceeds toward destruction, while the good person goes in the way of constantly reviving youthful blossoming. Some people may think they are on the road leading directly to fortune, never noticing that it ends in many paths, all terminating in ruin. But even before the ultimate ruin, the "merry-making" itself — as far removed as possible from שמחה של מצוה, the joy of a *mitzvah*—even בשחוק in the midst of gaiety, this "merry-making" leaves the better, nobler feelings in a man unsatisfied. Once the exhilaration has died down, one does not know what it should be called: שמחה or תוגה, exhilaration or sorrow.

In short, the contrast can be summarized thus: A person whose heart is not morally sound, who does not follow the straight path, looks for satisfaction only in attaining exterior goals; while the good person looks for fulfillment to his inner achievements, which by his efforts become part of his spiritual and moral character. Whatever he has harvested there remains his own in ever satisfying, serenely rewarding awareness.

כֵּן־צְדָקָה לְחַיִּים
וּמְרַדֵּף רָעָה לְמוֹתוֹ:

*Righteousness leads to life as surely*
*as he who pursues evil goes to his death.* (11, 19)

בְּאֹרַח צְדָקָה חַיִּים
וְדֶרֶךְ נְתִיבָה אַל־מָוֶת:

*In the pathway of righteousness there is life,*
*and a road directed to immortality.* (12, 28)

The very God who, in the form of His Law (Torah), has given us a task to accomplish, is the One who has shaped our spiritual and physical being for the purpose of such accomplishment. Our being was created for the Law, and the Law for our being. Abiding by it, all our spiritual and physical forces, talents and capabilities are brought to the deployment and employment for which they have been destined; they come alive, and our existence becomes Life.

If, however, the energy which has been granted us is directed to evil, to matters that are "bad" in God's eyes, then all the positive potential within us remains dead; we pursue aims and create objects whose *non-existence* God desires. Moreover, our own existence is then worse than non-existence, since it stays in the service of evil and is thus objectionable to God. Our life then spells death to goodness, and so leads us to death.

The path of Law-abidance is Life, and not only here on earth. It elevates our entire sojourn on earth above transitoriness, into the domain of the everlasting. Our earthly thinking, volition and action become one with the substance of immortality. Though our being, created in the divine image, was vested in a mortal frame, it will not be allowed to turn into the dust of the grave. And thus the path of truly faithful Law-abidance upon earth, through which we are in constant relation to God, always turned towards Him and remaining close to Him, becomes the road which guides us to immortality.

⊙

בֵּית צַדִּיק חֹסֶן רָב
וּבִתְבוּאַת רָשָׁע נֶעְכָּרֶת:

*The house of the righteous is a rich treasure,*
*but by the revenues of the wicked trouble comes.* (15, 6)

אוֹר־צַדִּיקִים יִשְׂמָח
וְנֵר רְשָׁעִים יִדְעָךְ:

*The light of the righteous remains joyful,*
*but the lamp of the wicked shall be dimmed out.* (13, 9)

בְּפֶשַׁע אִישׁ רָע מוֹקֵשׁ
וְצַדִּיק יָרוּן וְשָׂמֵחַ:

*In the crime of a wicked man there is a snare,*
*but the righteous one may sing and remain happy.* (29, 6)

When a righteous man succeeds in founding a home, no matter how rich
or humble his sum of possessions may be, his home is always full of
treasures. The smallest gain which the righteous acquires in keeping
with the Law and — again in keeping with the Law — spends in his home
and for his home, is transmuted into meaningful lasting values, through
its use for purposes and aims which meet with Divine approval. His
domestic gains do not rise or fall with the stock market; they are not exposed to devaluation and bring no curse to the home.

But that which has been acquired in defiance of the Divine commandments and is used in defiance of the commandments — no matter how
resplendent its appearance may be—causes the home to become
troubled, נעכרת. The joy which might have ruled in it becomes troubled
by lawlessness and is transformed into sorrow.

The happiness of the righteous compares to that of the lawless as
natural light compares to artificial illumination. Natural light always remains shining; the artificial kind becomes constantly dimmer, until it
goes out. A man may have earned fortunes by means which are displeasing to God, and then he can look at them only in fear. Consciously
trespassing the Law is a crime against God, in whose hands rests the
fate of mankind. A way of crime which has "luckily" succeeded should
fill him with fear, for in its very success may lurk the snare which will
trap him. But as for the fortune that has come to the righteous in his
compliance with the Law, and which he enjoys in compliance with the
Law — with this he may indeed rejoice. In such a fortune, acquired in integrity and used in purity, no snare lurks; he is allowed to rejoice and exult, ירון ושמח, and remain serenely happy even after the rejoicing.

מִתְהַלֵּךְ בְּתֻמּוֹ צַדִּיק
אַשְׁרֵי בָנָיו אַחֲרָיו:

*He that walks in his integrity, a just man,*
*happy are his children after him.* (20, 7)

יָד לְיָד לֹא־יִנָּקֶה רָּע
וְזֶרַע צַדִּיקִים נִמְלָט:

*Hand to hand, no evil shall remain unpunished;*
*but the descendants of the righteous shall escape.* (11, 21)

טוֹב יַנְחִיל בְּנֵי־בָנִים
וְצָפוּן לַצַּדִּיק חֵיל חוֹטֵא:

*A good man leaves an inheritance to his children's children,*
*and the wealth of the sinner is laid up for the righteous.* (13, 22)

Abiding by the Law bears fruit — not only for one's personal existence but even for his children. If parents follow the path of the Law, the Torah, in moral integrity, then their children will enjoy everlasting progress. For God has given His promise to reward the children and grandchildren of those who love him and prove their love in faithfully obeying His commandments.

Evil is avenged from "hand to hand": the hand which sows it is repaid with evil. But if a child of sinful parents does not follow their evil way, he does not pay and atone for their sin. By contrast, the merit of good parents can sometimes become the salvation of a guilty descendant — so that while usually "hand to hand, no evil shall remain unpunished," a guilty man who comes from righteous parents may be saved. For after all, righteous people do transmit to their descendants, by heredity, instruction, and example, some natural tendencies, influences and impressions which, although smothered or suppressed by evil and baseness, still remain as a potential seed for the good, waiting for some re-awakening of inherent nobility. This possibility can make him worthy of salvation.

And so, the good person lives not only for himself. His merit and the beneficial impressions gained from him will surely remain an everlasting heritage bequeathed to his children and grandchildren. On the other hand, what a transgressor of the Law has gathered during a lifetime of sin shall benefit his children only if they become as unlike their parent as possible, if they observe the Torah's commandments with the same assiduity that their parent transgressed them.

בְּטוּב צַדִּיקִים תַּעֲלֹץ קִרְיָה
וּבַאֲבֹד רְשָׁעִים רִנָּה:
בְּבִרְכַּת יְשָׁרִים תָּרוּם קָרֶת
וּבְפִי רְשָׁעִים תֵּהָרֵס:

*When it goes well with the righteous, the city rejoices,*
*and when the wicked perish, there is joy.*
*By the blessing of the upright a community is exalted,*
*but by the mouth of the wicked it is destroyed.* (11, 10—11)

בַּעֲלֹץ צַדִּיקִים רַבָּה תִפְאָרֶת
וּבְקוּם רְשָׁעִים יֵחָפֵשׂ אָדָם:

*When the righteous exult, the glory increases,*
*but when the wicked rise, the image of man becomes masked.* (28, 12)

בְּקוּם רְשָׁעִים יִסָּתֵר אָדָם
וּבְאָבְדָם יִרְבּוּ צַדִּיקִים:

*When the wicked rise, men hide themselves,*
*but when they perish, the righteous increase.* (28, 28)

בִּרְבוֹת צַדִּיקִים יִשְׂמַח הָעָם
וּבִמְשֹׁל רָשָׁע יֵאָנַח עָם:

*When the righteous increase, the people rejoice,*
*But when the wicked come to rulership, the people sigh.* (29, 2)

בִּרְבוֹת רְשָׁעִים יִרְבֶּה־פָּשַׁע
וְצַדִּיקִים בְּמַפַּלְתָּם יִרְאוּ:

*When the wicked are increased, transgression increases,*
*but the righteous shall witness their downfall.* (29, 16)

זֵכֶר צַדִּיק לִבְרָכָה
וְשֵׁם רְשָׁעִים יִרְקָב:

*The renown of the righteous remains as a blessing,*
*but the name of the wicked will rot.* (10, 7)

According to these adages, the righteous man's life and acts are salutary not only for his own existence and for the progress of his descendants; through his actions and his good fortune the whole community gains benefit and honor. The actions and prospering fortune of the lawless, however, undermine the well-being of the entire community; they do not let goodness and human dignity raise their heads. Therefore a community is glad not only about the happiness of the just but also about the downfall of the lawless.

If someone who follows the straight and decent path of unswerving fulfillment of his task in life becomes prosperous, he will use this prosperity only in such a way as to bring blessing also to his surroundings. Consequently, through his blessed state the community is improved, both ethically and socially.

The lawless, however, undermine social welfare — not only by their deeds but also, and mainly, by their mouths. The damage they cause by "the mouth of the wicked," by talking and spreading their opinions, principles and viewpoints, cannot be undone, even if they were to spend thousands.

When a righteous person attains happiness, then all that is virtuous and just gains esteem and respect in the world — a world in whose opinion exterior appearances are, after all, not without influence. On the other hand, at times when the Law-defying succeed, society will show no respect for humaneness. Then, a person whose claim to esteem derives from his humanitarian qualities does not dare stand up, and he simply withdraws from public life. Only upon the lawless men's downfall do the virtuous again win followers and "the just multiply."

People are glad when the number of the righteous increases. They sigh when the lawless get the upper hand. The majority of the people in a community know by experience what they stand to benefit by the ascendance of the righteous, and what they stand to lose by a rise of the lawless.

One great consolation is reserved for society: evil, by its excesses, causes its own downfall. Through an increase in evil, criminals abound; and then, through the steady increase of crime, cultivated by their words and example, the criminals themselves are destroyed. Their ruin can be confidently expected by the righteous, as they remain on the side.

When life's final accounting has to be made, and death draws up the balance sheet — then Divine Law-abidance and Law-defiance stand far apart. The life of the righteous man shows an eternally enduring credit balance; the lawless man departs from this world with a never-to-be-repaid deficit. The sum total of the value or non-value of one's life remains in the reputation, in the name he leaves behind. Long after the righteous person's departure, his memory, the example of his faithfulness to the Torah's commandments, remains as a model to those near and far who knew him — people who, in turn, will leave in the minds of their descendants the image of his good example.

When a person who has not lived according to the Law dies, however, then his reputation too is buried. It is good for him and for the world that his name rots and is no longer recalled, and none follows in his footsteps of Law-defiance.

All that the Book of Mishlé has taught us about the joy of observing God's Law is summarized in this Proverb:

$$\text{רֹדֵף צְדָקָה וָחָסֶד}$$
$$\text{יִמְצָא חַיִּים צְדָקָה וְכָבוֹד:}$$

*He who strives for righteousness and mercy*
*shall find life, prosperity and honor.* (21, 21)

He will find life through his own existence, prosperity from God, and honor from mankind. (When it applies to people, צדקה denotes a dutiful life; when to God — beneficial rule, that grants a man at all times what he needs for his true happiness; see Genesis 15, 6.)

# II

## WISE MEN AND FOOLS

Parallel to the contrasting personalities of צדיקים and רשעים in the area of action, we have חכמים and כסילים as opposite characters in the area of the abilities and improvement of the mind.

Our Proverbs are inexhaustible in their labor to praise the advantages of wisdom, constantly advising us to obtain it. On the other hand, they bring home to us the pitiable condition of unwise and foolish people.

The mental faculty needed to acquire and keep wisdom is called in the Proverbs שכל, intellect; or sometimes, more generally, לב, the heart. The sphere of intellect, ruled by חכמה (wisdom), is further subdivided into תבונה and בינה, understanding and insight; דעת, knowledge; עצה, plan or design; מזימה, consideration, reflection; ערמה, shrewdness; and תחבולה, contrivance.

As an example, let us say I have learned the prohibition of לא תחמד, "You shall not covet". I have thus gained a precept of חכמה. Then I may try to penetrate deeper into its motives and consequences; for instance, I may reflect that lusting for forbidden things in itself tarnishes moral purity, and in the end it will lead a person to appropriate, use and enjoy forbidden goods and pleasures. Therefore I should be guilty of transgressing לא תחמד even if I pay for the desired goods [that are not permissible]. To reach this conclusion, I have exercised בינה and gained תבונה. Suppose I now try to identify the nature and kind of the various attractions which tempt me, as well as my reactions to them. I will then exercise דעה and gain דעת. If all this results in making me seriously determined to fulfil the precept of לא תחמד, this determination is called עצה. Planning the manner of my conduct in order to remain faithful to this determination is מזימה.

Now I may well become convinced that if I am to remain faithful to my determination, it is not sufficient to merely repress the desire for something forbidden, but I shall also have to avoid those temptations which are bound to awaken my craving. Or I may even have to practice denying myself some allowed pleasures in order to bolster my self-control and conquer my convetous inclination. This is ערמה, ethical shrewdness, to teach me self-control and self-limitation.

Suppose now that some desire in me is so strong that I have to think of several combinations in order to arrange my life in such a manner as to vanquish my desire and not let it become a passion. In such a case, I have devised תחבולות, stratagems for victorious endurance in inner battle, just as one plans and executes an attack on an enemy by תחבולות. The character which is formed in this process is חכם, נבון and ערום.

To describe the opposite of חכמה, we find only one expression in Mishlé: אולת. Individuals who turn away from wisdom are called אוילים, כסילים, פתיים; but the trait they have in common, lack of wisdom, lack of knowledge, has only one definition: אולת. This word is related to אולי, "perhaps," and to אפל, darkness. It accordingly refers to a (mental) state which has remained unenlightened by wisdom, an inability to "see the light." A כסיל, translated as "fool," is not feeble-minded, but rather a person prejudiced by an erroneous view of things, one who blindly follows his opinions in utter disregard of rational conclusions. On the other hand, פתי is a person who, for lack of experience and learning, is exposed to all kinds of exterior impressions and influences. He is the inexperienced, untaught one. Then there still are: the לץ, the enemy of חכמה, the one who sarcastically sneers at wisdom, moral sensibility and nobility; and בער, whose mental development has remained on a very low, almost animal-like level.

All these characteristics are by no means incurable or congenital defects of the mind; rather, because of their inadequacy they are subject to moral stricture.

Interestingly enough, the expressions סכל and סכלות, which are frequently used in *Koheleth* (Ecclesiastes) to describe a fool, never appear in

Mishlé (the Book of Proverbs). The word סכל, which is very similar to
שכל, probably describes someone of a speculative turn of mind who has
gone astray, and is thus not relevant to the particular sphere of morality
with which the Proverbs deal.

The terms חכמה, תבונה and דעת are found also as applied to God. In
fact, they can be applied in their truest, deepest, and fullest sense *only* to
God. The share which human beings get from this spiritual essence of
wisdom, understanding and knowledge — emanating from it and made
possible by it — is merely an infinitely faint echo of the Divine חכמה,
תבונה and דעת.

Now, we might define wisdom as knowledge about the nature and function of objects and entities, including the nature and function of men;
but human nature and functions derive from God, as through them He
manifests His wisdom. Thus it is He who has infused into man, from His
spirit, spiritual faculties; it is He who has bestowed on him mental
abilities; it is He who has awakened in him the curiosity to pursue by
mental processes the traces of His wisdom. These traces, as regards the
nature and function of things, can be discerned through our observation
of the *world;* and as regards the nature and function of men, through
His spoken *word.* The Divine wisdom that speaks to us through the
work of His Creation or through the words of His Law is ever one
and the same:

ד׳ בְּחָכְמָה יָסַד־אָרֶץ

כּוֹנֵן שָׁמַיִם בִּתְבוּנָה:

בְּדַעְתּוֹ תְּהוֹמוֹת נִבְקָעוּ

וּשְׁחָקִים יִרְעֲפוּ־טָל:

*God by wisdom founded the earth,*
*by understanding has directed the heavens.*
*By His knowledge, floods broke forth out of the depths,*
*and the skies drop down the dew. (3, 19—20)*

Man's spirit urges him to find out what is at the basis of the earth and its
development. He tries to gain understanding into the Divine thought

that has regulated the inter-relationships of the cosmic system, its position and the course on which it is maintained. He feels elated by the thought of the higher knowledge, which, mindful of specific needs, causes water to break forth from the depths, in springs, brooks or rivers, and causes dew-drops to fall from the clouds in order to create fertile regions. In trying to comprehend all this, man strives to penetrate by his mental efforts into God's wisdom, God's insight, and God's knowing care. This wisdom of the Creation is considered by the Book of Proverbs as one and the same as the wisdom which, through His Law, regulates our life and our personal relationships and needs — so much so that the verses cited above are immediately followed by this admonition:

בְּנִי אַל־יָלֻזוּ מֵעֵינֶיךָ
נְצֹר תֻּשִׁיָּה וּמְזִמָּה:
וְיִהְיוּ חַיִּים לְנַפְשֶׁךָ
וְחֵן לְגַרְגְּרֹתֶיךָ:
אָז תֵּלֵךְ לָבֶטַח דַּרְכֶּךָ
וְרַגְלְךָ לֹא תִגּוֹף:
אִם־תִּשְׁכַּב לֹא תִפְחָד
וְשָׁכַבְתָּ וְעָרְבָה שְׁנָתֶךָ:
אַל־תִּירָא מִפַּחַד פִּתְאֹם
וּמִשֹּׁאַת רְשָׁעִים כִּי תָבֹא:
כִּי־ד' יִהְיֶה בְכִסְלֶךָ
וְשָׁמַר רַגְלְךָ מִלָּכֶד:

*My son, do not let them [the Divine wisdom, insight and knowing care]*
*depart from your sight;*
*[through them] keep your energy and resolution,*
*so that they shall be Life to your soul and grace to your neck.*
*Then you will walk securely on your way*
*and shall not bash your foot.*
*When you lie down you shall not be afraid,*
*and when you repose your sleep shall be sweet.*
*Be not afraid of sudden terror*
*or of devastation by the lawless, which might come;*
*for in God rests your unreserved confidence,*
*who will protect your foot from entrapment. (3, 21—26)*

In other words, the Torah — whose directions guide your life, your relationships and your endeavors — derives from the same supernal wisdom, insight, and knowing care which guides by its laws the relationships of the heavens above you and the earth under your feet. It follows that by conducting yourself in keeping with the Torah, by letting yourself be guided solely by it, you fit into a harmonious accord with the world which surrounds you. Not having to depend on your own wisdom, you may then be confident that you are fulfilling your Divinely ordained vocation. Your God and the God of the universe is the One who directs both you and the world around you. Since it is His will by which you are acting, from it, too, will emanate the energy and the resolution that you need. Your soul will gain life, as well as God's and man's goodwill toward your entire thinking, volition and range of activity (גרגרותיך; see above).

Wisdom is more ancient than the world. It was God's at the time He shaped the universe and consecrated it, as eternal sovereign of His creation, even before He brought it into its final state of being. He used His wisdom in all His arrangements and plans. According to that wisdom, He produced the laws which are at the basis of nature, by whose principles nature unfailingly progresses to this day. In the days of the creation of the world, God's thoughts were directed upon His wisdom, and His wisdom found its employment in His care. So too it finds joy and occupation in His government of the world—joy in mankind's development of the earth, and occupation by awakening the spiritual life and mental endeavors of the sons of man.

"I" — thus speaks the Divine wisdom in the Book of Proverbs:

ד׳ קָנָנִי רֵאשִׁית דַּרְכּוֹ
קֶדֶם מִפְעָלָיו מֵאָז:
מֵעוֹלָם נִסַּכְתִּי

*I belonged to God in the beginning of His volition,*
*in the beginning of His causation of time;*
*from eternity, from the beginning I was consecrated,*

מֵרֹאשׁ מִקַּדְמֵי־אָרֶץ׃
בְּאֵין־תְּהֹמוֹת חוֹלָלְתִּי
בְּאֵין מַעְיָנוֹת נִכְבַּדֵּי־מָיִם׃
בְּטֶרֶם הָרִים הָטְבָּעוּ
לִפְנֵי גְבָעוֹת חוֹלָלְתִּי׃
עַד־לֹא עָשָׂה אֶרֶץ וְחוּצוֹת
וְרֹאשׁ עַפְרוֹת תֵּבֵל׃
בַּהֲכִינוֹ שָׁמַיִם שָׁם אָנִי
בְּחֻקוֹ חוּג עַל־פְּנֵי תְהוֹם׃
בְּאַמְּצוֹ שְׁחָקִים מִמָּעַל
בַּעֲזוֹז עִינוֹת תְּהוֹם׃
בְּשׂוּמוֹ לַיָּם חֻקּוֹ
וּמַיִם לֹא יַעַבְרוּ־פִיו
בְּחוּקוֹ מוֹסְדֵי אָרֶץ׃
וָאֶהְיֶה אֶצְלוֹ אָמוֹן
וָאֶהְיֶה שַׁעֲשׁוּעִים יוֹם יוֹם
מְשַׂחֶקֶת לְפָנָיו בְּכָל־עֵת׃

*from the start, the very origin of the earth.*
*When floods were still to be, I was brought forth;*
*when yet there were no fountains, water-rich,*
*before the mountains were settled,*
*before the hills, I was brought forth.*
*When yet He had not shaped the earth and its surface,*
*prior to the dust-formations of the world,*
*when He planned the heavens—there was I.*
*As He circumscribed the surface of the floods,*
*when He was bracing the cloudy heights*
*and fortifying fountains of the deep;*
*when He was decreeing His law to the sea,*
*and waters were charged not to transgress His command;*
*when He was decreeing the laws for earth's foundation —*
*then I was by Him, in His care.*
*And [just] as he directed His thoughts upon me on each day [of the creation]*
*I disport myself before Him at all times.*

מְשַׂחֶקֶת בְּתֵבֵל אַרְצוֹ

וְשַׁעֲשֻׁעַי אֶת־בְּנֵי אָדָם:

וְעַתָּה בָנִים שִׁמְעוּ־לִי

וְאַשְׁרֵי דְּרָכַי יִשְׁמֹרוּ:

שִׁמְעוּ מוּסָר וַחֲכָמוּ

וְאַל־תִּפְרָעוּ:

אַשְׁרֵי אָדָם שֹׁמֵעַ לִי

לִשְׁקֹד עַל־דַּלְתֹתַי יוֹם יוֹם

לִשְׁמֹר מְזוּזֹת פְּתָחָי:

כִּי מֹצְאִי מָצָא חַיִּים

וַיָּפֶק רָצוֹן מֵד':

וְחֹטְאִי חֹמֵס נַפְשׁוֹ

כָּל־מְשַׂנְאַי אָהֲבוּ מָוֶת:

*I disport myself in the habitable world of His earth*
*and have my occupation with the sons of man.*
*And now, children, listen to me:*
*Only those stride toward happiness who watch my ways.*
*Hear instruction and become wise,*
*and do not become unruly.*
*The man who listens to me strides towards happiness,*
*attentively standing at my gates day after day,*
*watching the doorposts of my entrances.*
*For whoever finds me finds life*
*and has obtained favor from God.*
*Whoever misses me, though, wrongs his own soul;*
*all those who hate me, love death.* (8, 22–36)

Only one way leads to fulfillment: obedience to the teachings of this Divine wisdom. As for the human wisdom which results from these teachings, it consists of only one conclusion: ואל תפרעו, do not be unruly! The call of אל תפרעו reverberates from heaven to earth, and resounds back from earth to the heavens. The deeper and·more penetrating our quest for knowledge becomes, exploring the secrets of Creation, the more distinctly comes back to us the echo of אל תפרעו. Do not be unruly; do not go against the rules! Do not take pride in unrestrained behavior, and do not let that be your aim.

When you observe nature, you will never find transgression of the natural laws. Look around you: only by unswerving obedience to a higher law has everything in nature become what it is and everything is what it has become. Whether you observe the multiplication of the tiniest cell or calculate the orbit of the mightiest galaxy, everything in the world testifies to this. Only by obeying the laws which govern them can every item and entity in nature find the energy needed for its existence and perpetuation.

This elementary wisdom speaks to us through everything in the world, whether large or small, calling out to us: אל תפרעו. Of all things created, you alone have been ennobled by spirit and will, bestowed upon you so that you might gain the wisdom of God's Law; and while everything else follows God's law automatically and unconsciously, you can fulfill it by the free determination of your will. The understanding and the senses that we have been given were not intended to create just any rules or truths. The very words "understanding" and "senses" point to the fact that truth is a given factor, something which is external, outside ourselves; it must therefore be understood and sensed.

It is for this purpose that God has endowed us with the shrines of wisdom, law and instruction, to whose gates we should betake ourselves day after day in order to receive instruction for our daily work. Only there can be found the wellspring of life. Only there can God's goodwill be obtained. Whoever misses that direction wrongs himself, and at the moment when he believes he is grasping life, he actually embraces death.

הֲלֹא־חָכְמָה תִקְרָא
וּתְבוּנָה תִּתֵּן קוֹלָהּ׃
בְּרֹאשׁ־מְרֹמִים עֲלֵי־דָרֶךְ
בֵּית נְתִיבוֹת נִצָּבָה׃

*For does not wisdom call,*
*and understanding raise its voice*
*upon high places on the way,*
*established at the crossroads!*

לְיַד־שְׁעָרִים לְפִי־קָרֶת
מְבוֹא פְתָחִים תָּרֹנָּה:
אֲלֵיכֶם אִישִׁים אֶקְרָא
וְקוֹלִי אֶל־בְּנֵי אָדָם:
הָבִינוּ פְתָאיִם עָרְמָה
וּכְסִילִים הָבִינוּ לֵב:
שִׁמְעוּ כִּי־נְגִידִים אֲדַבֵּר
וּמִפְתַּח שְׂפָתַי מֵישָׁרִים:
כִּי־אֱמֶת יֶהְגֶּה חִכִּי
וְתוֹעֲבַת שְׂפָתַי רֶשַׁע:
בְּצֶדֶק כָּל־אִמְרֵי־פִי
אֵין בָּהֶם נִפְתָּל וְעִקֵּשׁ:
כֻּלָּם נְכֹחִים לַמֵּבִין
וִישָׁרִים לְמֹצְאֵי דָעַת:
קְחוּ־מוּסָרִי וְאַל־כָּסֶף
וְדַעַת מֵחָרוּץ נִבְחָר:
כִּי־טוֹבָה חָכְמָה מִפְּנִינִים
וְכָל־חֲפָצִים לֹא יִשְׁווּ־בָהּ:

Beside the gates, at the entry of a city,
at the entrance of gates, it speaks out aloud:
To you, O men, I call out,
and my voice goes out to the sons of man.
You, O inexperienced ones, understand shrewdness;
and fools, understand your heart.
Listen, for I say [words which call for] serious attention,
and the utterances of my lips are honesty.
For my palate speaks truth,
and lawlessness is abomination to my lips.
All the words of my mouth are righteousness;
nothing in them is twisted and distorted.
All are plain to the understanding,
and right to those who strive for knowledge.
Take my ethical teachings and not silver;
knowledge is better than fine gold.
For wisdom is better than pearls,

אֲנִי־חָכְמָה שָׁכַנְתִּי עָרְמָה
וְדַעַת מְזִמּוֹת אֶמְצָא:
יִרְאַת ד' שְׂנֹאת רָע
גֵּאָה וְגָאוֹן וְדֶרֶךְ רָע
וּפִי תַהְפֻּכוֹת שָׂנֵאתִי:
לִי־עֵצָה וְתוּשִׁיָּה
אֲנִי בִינָה לִי גְבוּרָה:
בִּי מְלָכִים יִמְלֹכוּ
וְרֹזְנִים יְחֹקְקוּ צֶדֶק:
בִּי שָׂרִים יָשֹׂרוּ
וּנְדִיבִים כָּל־שֹׁפְטֵי אָרֶץ:
אֲנִי אֹהֲבַי אֵהָב
וּמְשַׁחֲרַי יִמְצָאֻנְנִי:
עֹשֶׁר־וְכָבוֹד אִתִּי
הוֹן עָתֵק וּצְדָקָה:
טוֹב פִּרְיִי מֵחָרוּץ וּמִפָּז
וּתְבוּאָתִי מִכֶּסֶף נִבְחָר:

and all endeavors cannot meet its value.
I, wisdom, am neighbor to shrewdness;
I find knowledge which leads to reflection.
Since fear of God means hating evil,
I hate pride and haughtiness,
evil things and a crooked mouth.
Mine is advice and vigor,
I am insight and courage.
Through me kings exercise their kingship,
and princes understand justice in law.
Through me sovereigns reign,
and judges are dedicated to the good.
I love those who love me,
and those who seek me shall find me.
Riches and honor are with me,
enduring wealth and benevolence.
My fruit is better than gold and jewellery,
and my produce than choice silver.

בְּאֹרַח־צְדָקָה אֲהַלֵּךְ
בְּתוֹךְ נְתִיבוֹת מִשְׁפָּט:
לְהַנְחִיל אֹהֲבַי יֵשׁ
וְאֹצְרֹתֵיהֶם אֲמַלֵּא:

*I walk in the ways of law-abidance,*
*in the midst of the paths of justice,*
*to bequeath things of substance to those who love me,*
*and to fill their treasuries.* (8, 1—21)

The knowledge which in our Proverbs is called "wisdom" is not the
heritage of a privileged or "educated" class. Neither is it intended to offer a substitute to those whom fate has denied a share of material fortunes, and so — once the fortune has been attained — to withdraw into a
corner, having again become dispensable and superfluous. No more is it
a science, an academic subject, far removed from the strivings and actions of ordinary life on earth. Quite to the contrary: it relates directly to
the entire fullness of life on earth, including every internal and external
relationship of the individual and of society as a whole. This is what
wisdom—by illumination, penetration, and formulation through its
challenging spirit—wishes to direct. This is why wisdom goes out, right
into the middle of the vitality and activity of life, right up to the eleva-
tions which overlook the ways of mortals, and right onto the centers
where paths of life meet and cross. This is why it looks for disciples at
the gates of public life, at the entrance of a city's community and at the
doorstep of the home, in the domesticity of individuals and families.

This is why it invites everybody to drink from its fountain before trying
to solve problems and fulfill tasks in public and social life, or in the circle
of his family, or even by himself. If anyone tries to fulfill his duties,
whether in the role of husband, citizen, human being, or member of a
family, without previously arming his mind with the lessons of wisdom,
he will ultimately find his lot as a dismal failure, a פתי or a כסיל.

If he is a פתי, untaught, unenlightened about the realities and truths of
human conditions and the inalienable Divine laws of conduct for each

and every human relationship — he is in danger of succumbing to any momentary impression or influence and ultimately violating his most sacred duties by omission or transgression. Given any subconscious impulse, any dazzling enticement, any alluring example, or even some mistaken and misleading pronouncement made by some self-important personality — a פתי is bound to be influenced by any or all of those. In order that פתאים may protect themselves from such deceptive influences and resulting aberrations, wisdom offers them ערמה, "moral shrewdness" telling them plainly and undisguisedly (ערום) how to act in any given circumstance. As a first step, however, a פתי is invited להבין ערמה, to become aware of the importance and necessity for such "moral shrewdness," since lacking it our entire conduct remains exposed to chance and vulnerable to sin.

A כסיל, on the other hand, will have had opportunities to gain knowledge. Having disdained them, however, and still disdaining them, because he overestimates man's intelligence in general and his own in particular, in foolish conceit he allows himself to form opinions and hold on to them by sheer force (גזל — כסל), never heeding objections from a higher source—not even from the Highest one. So, wisdom bids such arrogant fools, who consider themselves so wise: הבינו לב, first of all, try to gain some insight into your own capacity for understanding, before you grant unlimited confidence to your own intelligence and to human intelligence in general; before you form an authoritative opinion about things and matters; before you spurn any superior advice. Get to know your "heart," the narrow range of its understanding, and the impact that sensual desires have upon it. Only then can you ultimately become open, accessible to the Divine wisdom.

And now, שמעו listen! Once the פתאים (naive) and כסילים (fools) have reached the stage where they can discern the need for advice, let them listen to wisdom's instructions. All its words are called נגידים. A *nagid* is a prince after he has assumed his lordly position. Having taken up his post as leader of the people, he stands up *neged*, facing them; and upon him all eyes are focused to find their direction. Comparably, each word of the Torah is called a נגיד, and its teachings are נגידים, both commanding attention and meriting it. They are right here, on earth — neither far away nor supernatural. All they want is to reveal to us, to our spirit and our mind, our words and our deeds, how to fulfill our task. Their status is נגידים, princely. Their directives are מישרים, straight, right for our vocation and for the requirements of every being, including ourselves. Their contents are אמת. This is אמת as opposed to רשע, lawlessness, meaning therefore moral integrity. Their stamp is צדק, engraved upon all their utterances; *tzedek*, the highest ideal of justice. Their character is simplicity and integrity, אין בהם נפתול ועקש; crooked lies and violent assertions are alien to them.

If anyone is not satisfied with a superficial knowledge of this wisdom and makes an effort to penetrate into its reasons and consequences, he will be rewarded by the revelation of its convincing evidence and its realism about all things and concerns. Moreover, the instruction of our wisdom does not mean to remain a barren, academic subject; it wishes to become מוסר, to contain all of our desires, actions, and emotions within its framework of divinely directed truth and virtue, integrity and sanctity; and thus it will lead our lives toward closeness to God. This is what gives our wisdom its unique value and makes it preferable to acquire it above every other attainment.

Now wisdom calls itself "a neighbor of cleverness." It would not like to be mistaken for this bright neighbor, that is a master in looking for its own advantage and is, consequently, admired by the masses as the greatest of mental qualities. Cleverness is not wisdom; it is merely its neighbor. Yet wisdom makes use of this brilliance for itself and its own aims by employing cleverness to serve the true advantage of mankind — moral purity and virtue. In this way, wisdom redeems cleverness from the meanness of base calculations for the sake of expediency, by sublimating it and raising it to the pure heights of moral sagacity. In this way, too, דעת מזימות, the "knowing which leads to reflection", must be mobilized into the service of any person who intends to walk the path of righteousness and does not intend to leave any of his steps to chance. Such "cleverness," ערמה, and "knowing considerations", דעת מזימות, are necessary for the attainment of even base goals. But neither can the ef-

fective arm of wisdom do without them. It therefore elevates and enno-
bles them to become tools for its highest moral purposes.

For when wisdom is practiced, not only the end is a moral one, but the
means which lead to this end must also be morally clean. True wisdom
rejects at the very start anything or anyone that is immoral. It is the
only science which demands from its disciples as its prerequisite a fear
of God and purity of morals. Other sciences may be satisfied with ade-
quate capabilities and a desire for knowledge, dispensing with proof of
moral probity, even celebrating as spiritual heroes men whose character
and behavior, once revealed, can only cause blushing. Indeed, where
mental genius is concerned, they would like to issue a veritable dispensation from observing morality. Not so our wisdom, which derives from
God's teaching. This can be attained only by men of purity, pure spirit
and a pure heart. Entrance into its hall of knowledge is dependent on
fear of God. And since fear of God entails hatred of evil, it follows that
wisdom hates haughtiness and pride, hates the path of immorality and
mouths dedicated to crookedness. Hence, only the humble and truthful
are allowed to discover its treasures in truth. Thus, too, even ערמה and
מזימה become morally ennobled in the service of חכמה.

The same can be said for all other properties of the mind. Such properties and their implementation can succeed in a beneficial way only
through wisdom. Wisdom says: "Mine is advice and vigor, I am insight,
courage is mine." She does not abandon her friends at the crossroads,
helpless for lack of advice, but shows them the direction that leads to
light and life. The discernment which wisdom teaches gives us confidence, which in turn generates the courage and energy needed to put
her teachings of truth and righteousness into practice. Deeper probing
into the reasons and effects of wisdom's teachings brings wisdom to a
higher and more mature level of our consciousness, invigorating us to
withstand the enemy within and opposition without.

Yet not only the task of the individual can be accomplished through
wisdom. Society too depends on wisdom in those who are highly-placed.
Only through wisdom do kings become true sovereigns, and leaders can

manifest leadership. Only in wisdom do princes gain authority, and
judges can remain objective and dedicated to truth and justice. Whoever
loves wisdom, wisdom loves in return, and it stays with him as his constant adviser. Whatever the nature of such goods as men strive for,
whatever the benefit they may try to obtain, it can be attained only at
the hand of wisdom. Only riches that are wisely acquired and wisely
spent make a man wealthy. Only fame that has been wisely won and is
wisely borne makes for honor. Only through wisdom does wealth endure and become a benefit to its owner and his surroundings. For true
benefit does not accrue from gold; it is the fruit of wisdom. Wisdom
goes in the ways of duty and justice, leading its friends to the one and
only valuable heritage, and filling their stores with treasures in truth.

קְנֵה חָכְמָה קְנֵה בִינָה
אַל־תִּשְׁכַּח וְאַל־תֵּט מֵאִמְרֵי־פִי:

*Acquire wisdom, acquire understanding;*
*never forget nor depart from the words of my mouth.* (4, 5)

רֵאשִׁית חָכְמָה קְנֵה חָכְמָה
וּבְכָל־קִנְיָנְךָ קְנֵה בִינָה:

*The beginning of wisdom: acquire wisdom,*
*and with all you have acquired, buy understanding.* (4, 7)

אֱמֹר לַחָכְמָה אֲחֹתִי אָתְּ
וּמֹדָע לַבִּינָה תִקְרָא:

*Say to wisdom: you are my sister,*
*and call understanding: friend.* (7, 4)

אֱמֶת קְנֵה וְאַל־תִּמְכֹּר
חָכְמָה וּמוּסָר וּבִינָה:

*Truth acquire and never sell it;*
*wisdom, too, discipline and understanding.* (23, 23)

Upon our coming into being, God bestowed on each one of us a valuable gift: the potential for acquiring wisdom. Furthermore, that part of His wisdom which is destined for our understanding — the truth about the creation and function of the world, about the existence and function of humanity, and about the existence and function of His people — has been set down by Him in the Torah, the Book of His instruction and His law. Moreover, He has entrusted the interpretation of this wisdom, for our comprehension and commitment, to the oral interpretation of our Sages. Our potential, however, can remain unused, the Book of Divine Wisdom sealed, and the wisdom entrusted to our Sages lost, unless we heed the admonition that challenges our spirit at the time of its first awakening to independent consciousness: *buy wisdom, buy insight*. Forget none of it, and keep away from anything which deviates from the straight line of truth that it teaches.

The beginning of wisdom: *acquire* wisdom. Its continuance: with your acquisition, *buy* insight. Wisdom needs to be acquired. It is something *given*, to be absorbed by us, not something to be invented by ourselves. The same is true for insight gained in the process of probing the deep meaning of wisdom, by not being content to remain at its surface, and by deriving from it the consequences in our actions. This insight too is not something to be improvised by us; this too is a *given* factor, and can be acquired only through the instruction of the Divine Scriptures and tradition of our Sages.

We are to call wisdom our "sister". She is the daughter of our Father. He has created her for us; and just as we are indebted to Him for our physical existence, so too are we indebted to Him for the existence of wisdom, which He put at our side for sisterly helpfulness. Hand in hand with this sister — like Moses' sister, who guided him to the right mother's milk (Exodus 2, 7—10) — we can stride towards Divine truth and be preserved from errors which might estrange us from God.

And insight we call "friend." Just as a true friend gives advice, help and comfort in every situation in life, being a faithful and likeminded partner in our fulfillment of the Divine task, so too constant occupation with the

Torah should provide us with advice, help and comfort in every situation, assisting us, till the end, in faithfully carrying out our vocation.

The truth we learn through God's wisdom is called a highly prized possession. In fact, it is more precious than anything. It therefore deserves
our greatest efforts to acquire and possess it at any price, and not to dispose of it under any circumstances, no matter what sacrifices we have to
make, whatever other knowledge, sciences and erudition we may have
to forego, and whatever status in life we may have to renounce in order
to remain faithful to our "sister" and our "friend." Nothing should be
able to make us deviate from the source of insight into Divine wisdom,
for nothing can offer a replacement for our closeness to it. If we lose this
truth, we lose wisdom, discipline, and understanding.

Yet this trade or exchange has been made in our times. Intimate acquaintance with our sources was crossed off the curriculum and deleted
from the plans of education — in order to leave time for many other
things. How regrettable is this replacement! Have these "many other
things" provided a substitute for wisdom, discipline, and understanding?

בְּנִי אִם־תִּקַּח אֲמָרָי
וּמִצְוֹתַי תִּצְפֹּן אִתָּךְ:
לְהַקְשִׁיב לַחָכְמָה אָזְנֶךָ
תַּטֶּה לִבְּךָ לַתְּבוּנָה:
כִּי אִם לַבִּינָה תִקְרָא
לַתְּבוּנָה תִּתֵּן קוֹלֶךָ
אִם־תְּבַקְשֶׁנָּה כַכָּסֶף
וְכַמַּטְמוֹנִים תַּחְפְּשֶׂנָּה:

*My son, if you would accept my words*
*and harbor my commands with you,*
*to have your ear attuned to wisdom,*
*incline your heart to understanding.*
*For if you will call out to insight,*
*and to understanding lift your voice;*
*if you explore for it as for silver,*
*and search for it as for treasures —*

אָז תָּבִין יִרְאַת ד'
וְדַעַת אֱלֹהִים תִּמְצָא:
כִּי־ד' יִתֵּן חָכְמָה
מִפִּיו דַּעַת וּתְבוּנָה:
יִצְפֹּן לַיְשָׁרִים תּוּשִׁיָּה
מָגֵן לְהֹלְכֵי תֹם:
לִנְצֹר אָרְחוֹת מִשְׁפָּט
וְדֶרֶךְ חֲסִידָיו יִשְׁמֹר:
אָז תָּבִין צֶדֶק וּמִשְׁפָּט
וּמֵישָׁרִים כָּל־מַעְגַּל־טוֹב:
כִּי־תָבוֹא חָכְמָה בְלִבֶּךָ
וְדַעַת לְנַפְשְׁךָ יִנְעָם:
מְזִמָּה תִּשְׁמֹר עָלֶיךָ
תְבוּנָה תִנְצְרֶכָּה:
לְהַצִּילְךָ מִדֶּרֶךְ רָע
מֵאִישׁ מְדַבֵּר תַּהְפֻּכוֹת:

*then you shall understand what is fear of God,*
*and will find knowledge of God.*
*For God shall give wisdom,*
*out of His mouth comes knowledge and understanding;*
*and He has energy in store for the upright,*
*is a shield to them who walk in integrity,*
*to guard the paths of justice*
*and protect the ways of those lovingly dedicated to Him.*
*Then you will gain understanding of justice and order,*
*how straight is every good way.*
*Once wisdom has entered your heart*
*and knowledge is sweet to your soul,*
*reflection shall watch over you,*
*understanding shall guard you,*
*to deliver you from the way of evil,*
*from any man who speaks perversely.* (2, 1–12)

Were every Jewish father to speak thus to his son, how different would
our growing generation look! The fact that wisdom and understanding

are at least as valuable as silver and treasures, and should be sought after at least as seriously and assiduously as today's society looks for money and wealth — this is what, through his own example, he should bring home to his son's mind and acknowledgment.

Would that our youth be again inspired by the desire and longing for the wisdom of the Torah and for understanding of its tenets. This is what our proverbs mean by "calling out" for insight and wisdom. Then we would witness the fulfillment of Amos' prophecy (8, 11) that "days will come when God will send a hunger on earth, not a hunger for bread, nor a thirst for water, but for the word of God." Then our youth would come to understand what "fear of God" means and would find the knowledge of God, because this thirst for wisdom and understanding (thus state our Proverbs) can be quenched more easily than the desire for silver and treasures. Just as surely as God helps the righteous by quietly increasing their energy, and protects those who are devoted to their duty, just as surely He assists those who seek wisdom and insight by granting them the faculties to penetrate into the profundity of justice and the order of life, and to recognize that only the way of virtue leads to the true aim and true happiness in life.

Once this wisdom has entered the hearts of our youths, once understanding will have become the sweetest pleasure to their souls, then this very wisdom and understanding will become their guardians and preserve them from false steps in civil life, and from the temptations of passion and sensuality.

לֹא־יֶאֱהַב לֵץ הוֹכֵחַ לוֹ
אֶל־חֲכָמִים לֹא יֵלֵךְ:

*A scoffer does not like to be reproved;*
*he will not go to the wise. (15, 12)*

לֵב נָבוֹן יְבַקֶּשׁ־דָּעַת
וּפִי כְסִילִים יִרְעֶה אִוֶּלֶת:

*A discerning heart looks for knowledge,*
*but the mouth of fools feeds on non-wisdom. (15, 14)*

לֹא־יַחְפֹּץ כְּסִיל בִּתְבוּנָה
כִּי אִם־בְּהִתְגַּלּוֹת לִבּוֹ:

*A conceited fool has no desire for understanding,*
*but only wants to express his own view.* (18, 2)

לָמָּה־זֶּה מְחִיר בְּיַד־כְּסִיל
לִקְנוֹת חָכְמָה וְלֶב־אָיִן:

*What good are the means in the hand of a conceited fool*
*to purchase wisdom, when his heart is not in it!* (17, 16)

Two characters, according to Mishlé, will hardly succeed in gaining
wisdom: לצים and כסילים. For the *létz* everything which transcends the
concrete and the sensual is fantasy; whatever is ethical, holy, relating to
God, is the target of his ridicule. A doctrine which demands sacrificing
palpable, sensual advantages and pleasures for ethical ideals, seems to
him an absurd pretension or conceit, and followers of such a doctrine,
who find serenity and happiness in its fulfillment, appear to him as
laughable fools. So how should such a *létz* approach the source of this
instruction, which to him looks like folly?

Yet all this is only on the surface of the man. No matter how able a
demagogue he may be in the circle of an attentive audience by indulging
in contemptuous irony, deadening every feeling of reverence in the
hearts of his companions (mainly the younger ones), his own confidence
is not quite so firmly established. He is afraid that some day he may be
taught better, and therefore he fears, indeed hates, to be reproved.
Therefore he never goes to the wise, for he cannot bear opposition to his
opinions, which he holds so dear and exhibits so proudly.

Another, perhaps even larger, group of people who are usually lost to
wisdom are the כסילים. A *k'sil* may possess a good mind. He may even
have had some education. However, he is so pleased with his own mental faculties and his smattering of learning that he is convinced of the absolute infallibility of his own views. Such people have not the slightest

doubt that by themselves they are able to form a judgment, and have no need for further instruction from anyone, let alone from a higher authority. While a person of insight is aware of the limits of his knowledge and of human intelligence in general, a prideful *k'sil* is fully satisfied with his own unwisdom; he never even tries to learn the facts. The only thing he is interested in is to "sell" his own opinion, which to him is the highest, most irrefutable one. Then of what value are the means to buy wisdom to such a one, if the vessel to contain it is lacking? His heart is so completely filled with his own vain pride that there is no room left for anything else.

⊙

אִם־חָכַמְתָּ חָכַמְתָּ לָּךְ
וְלַצְתָּ לְבַדְּךָ תִשָּׂא:

*If you have become wise, you are wise for yourself;*
*and if a scoffer, you alone shall bear it.* (9, 12)

There are people who look down in supreme contempt on all the values of truth and holiness which wisdom teaches and represents; they deride and mock its adherents. If just once they should stoop to give the slightest recognition to these values, to pay the smallest attention to their characteristics, then they immediately feel that they have made a great concession and that their "tolerance" entitles them to the gratitude of the adherents of truth and holiness.

This very common opinion is refuted by our Proverbs, which tell us: Whoever has become wise, has become so for himself; but if you have remained a scoffer, you alone must bear it. The truth, the sanctity of wisdom towers far above the opinions and illusions of men. Its value neither rises nor falls whether recognition is accorded it or withheld. Its truth remains true even if an entire generation should deny it, and its sanctity remains holy regardless of the number of our contemporaries who disregard it. Inherent truth and sanctity are assured of ultimate victory, for God, the First Source from whom they emanate, has assured their future: He shall make a generation come forth in which truth and virtue will be revered!

In other words, wisdom and the values inculcated by it are absolute, not conditional on any attention which is paid or denied them. Whoever goes to the source of this wisdom, to draw from it in purity and humility, and to faithfully follow its tenets, fulfills himself. He perfects his own spiritual and ethical being; he reaches temporal happiness and eternal salvation.

What, though, is the fate of one who rejects this wisdom, who derides it and holds it in contempt? For one thing, he will have to do without its blessing; and ultimately he will suffer a bitter curse, as his own spiritual essence of being wastes away. For another, he will witness the depravity and spiritual impoverishment of his surroundings; for by ridiculing every value, he has deprecated and degraded their entire existence and all the efforts of those around him. He has cut away the ground from under their feet in his evaluation, depriving them of any spiritual basis. No material successes, however brilliant they may seem, can make good this loss.

⊙

בַּעֲנָשׁ־לֵץ יֶחְכַּם־פֶּתִי
וּבְהַשְׂכִּיל לְחָכָם יִקַּח־דָּעַת:

*When the scoffer is punished, the thoughtless one becomes wise, and when turning to a sage for instruction, he shall gain knowledge.* (21, 11)

A scoffer is seldom reformed, even if calamity should befall him. However, a bystander, even if he is not generally a philosophical person, may be shocked into thinking, particularly if the misfortune was caused by the scoffer's own frivolousness. Under different circumstances, he might have been dangerously influenced by the scoffer's mockery, but now he may well come to different, more positive conclusions. If, at this point, he is fortunate enough to be near a wise man and pays attention to his advice and way of life, he will eventually gain insight into truth and goodness. In general, the examples we see and the things we hear have a decisive influence on ourselves; subconsciously they enter our thinking and modify our deeds:

הוֹלֵךְ אֶת־חֲכָמִים יֶחְכָּם
וְרֹעֶה כְסִילִים יֵרוֹעַ:

*He who goes with the wise becomes wiser,*
*but by association with fools one becomes worse.* (13, 20)

⊙

דֶּרֶךְ אֱוִיל יָשָׁר בְּעֵינָיו
וְשֹׁמֵעַ לְעֵצָה חָכָם:

*The way of a fool is straight in his own eyes,*
*but he who listens to counsel is wise.* (12, 15)

שְׁמַע עֵצָה וְקַבֵּל מוּסָר
לְמַעַן תֶּחְכַּם בְּאַחֲרִיתֶךָ:

*Listen to advice and accept instruction,*
*that you may be wise in the end.* (19, 20)

לֵב נָבוֹן יִקְנֶה־דָּעַת
וְאֹזֶן חֲכָמִים תְּבַקֶּשׁ־דָּעַת:

*An understanding heart acquires knowledge,*
*and the ear of the wise seeks knowledge.* (18, 15)

אַל־תּוֹכַח לֵץ פֶּן־יִשְׂנָאֶךָּ
הוֹכַח לְחָכָם וְיֶאֱהָבֶךָּ:
תֵּן לְחָכָם וְיֶחְכַּם־עוֹד
הוֹדַע לְצַדִּיק וְיוֹסֶף לֶקַח:

*Do not admonish a scoffer, lest he hate you;*
*admonish a wise man, and he will love you.*
*Offer to a wise man, and he will become even wiser;*
*teach a righteous man, and he will increase in learning.* (9, 8—9)

רָאִיתָ אִישׁ חָכָם בְּעֵינָיו
תִּקְוָה לִכְסִיל מִמֶּנּוּ:

*Do you see a man who is wise in his own eyes?*
*For a fool there is more hope than for him!* (26, 12)

Only the fool considers his own way infallible. Someone who has already acquired wisdom appreciates how much is needed to grasp the truth correctly and to distinguish between right and wrong. Moreover, such a person is aware that there are people who have greater wisdom and deeper understanding. He is glad to receive advice and likes to listen to the views of other people who stand on the same basis of Godly reverence. For:

תְּחִלַּת חָכְמָה יִרְאַת ד'
וְדַעַת קְדֹשִׁים בִּינָה:

*The prerequisite for wisdom is fear of God,*
*and /only/ the understanding of the sanctified is insight.* (9, 10)

Our Divine vocation is to become wise, to strive for wisdom. Our true Sages called themselves תלמידי חכמים ("students of the wise") and remained lifelong students in the school of wisdom. Obviously, it takes individual mental effort to penetrate and understand what wisdom teaches. Still, a true sage will never cease to listen attentively to the knowledge of others in order to enrich his own.

And so, should you ever come across a person who, having sipped from the wells of wisdom, already believes himself a wise man — in fact, has already endorsed his own חכם-certificate — you may conclude from this very arrogance that the man has either not drawn from the right well or has not done it in the right way. What he has gained is not instruction but intoxication through arrogance. Because of his conceit, wisdom is lost to him, even more hopelessly so than if he had remained far from its portals entirely. While a foolish person may yet, in a propitious hour, be struck by a word of wisdom and by a desire to learn, for him who has

tasted from its spring and found only arrogance there is no longer a cure
on earth.

⊙

חָכָם בְּעֵינָיו אִישׁ עָשִׁיר
וְדַל מֵבִין יַחְקְרֶנּוּ

*A rich man is wise in his own eyes,*
*but a poor, perceptive man shall see through him.* (28, 11)

This adage draws attention to a typical misconception: Because he possesses goods which so many others covet and vainly strive to obtain, a
wealthy man may easily come to think that these possessions are the
proof of his own superior חכמה. Yet many a poor man may far surpass
him in spiritual and mental goods, which are by no means dependent on
material ones.

"Not always do wise men have bread, nor the understanding riches,"
states Koheleth (Ecclesiastes 9, 11) with the wisdom of experience. On
the other hand, according to our Proverbs, a true sage can easily do
without a great many material possessions. His wisdom amply compen-
sates for wealth and the honor resulting from it. In fact, according to our
Proverbs, material goods become truly valuable only when they accompany wisdom; if wisdom is lacking, their worth diminishes. Hence a wise
man can forego material wealth, but riches cannot dispense with
wisdom. This is expressed in the following sentences:

עֲטֶרֶת חֲכָמִים עָשְׁרָם
אִוֶּלֶת כְּסִילִים אִוֶּלֶת:

*The crown of the wise is their wealth,*
*but the folly of fools remains unwisdom.* (14, 24)

What is the wise man's wealth? It is the crown which only wisdom can
give him: his spiritual and moral nobility. His life is filled with spiritual
and ethical riches, and all other material belongings are dispensable to

him; if necessary he can do without them. In summarizing the life of a fool, however, we can simply say that his lack of insight will in the end put every other pleasure and possession in the debit balance.

$$אוֹצָר נֶחְמָד וָשֶׁמֶן בִּנְוֵה חָכָם$$
$$וּכְסִיל אָדָם יְבַלְּעֶנּוּ׃$$

*In the dwellings of a wise man, treasure and oil are worthy of effort,*
*but a fool amongst men makes them vanish. (21, 20)*

Wealth and the benefits of comfort (symbolized by oil — *shemen*) have lasting value only when they are at the service of a wise person. In the hands of one who lacks wisdom, they disappear (the verb *bala* has the same meaning as in כבלע את הקודש, Num. 4, 20); his foolishness causes them to vanish for all intents and purposes, as he puts them to such poor use that they might as well not be there. Or, if the Hebrew is taken literally: he is unable to conserve them. To become rich, one does not always need wisdom; he may have had a stroke of luck. But to remain rich, to preserve the wealth, calls for wisdom and insight.

$$בְּחָכְמָה יִבָּנֶה בָּיִת$$
$$וּבִתְבוּנָה יִתְכּוֹנָן׃$$
$$וּבְדַעַת חֲדָרִים יִמָּלְאוּ$$
$$כָּל־הוֹן יָקָר וְנָעִים׃$$

*Through wisdom a house is built,*
*and established by understanding;*
*and through knowledge its chambers are filled*
*with all precious and beneficial riches. (24, 3–4)*

$$חַכְמוֹת נָשִׁים בָּנְתָה בֵיתָהּ$$
$$וְאִוֶּלֶת בְּיָדֶיהָ תֶהֶרְסֶנּוּ׃$$

*A woman's wisdom has built her house,*
*but foolishness will tear it down by its own hands. (14, 1)*

(From בנתה ביתה, which is singular, we assume that חכמות is substantive in stat. const., from חכמות in 9,1, the concept of a varied wisdom).

⊙

Wisdom, however, is not only treasure. Wisdom spells power and proves itself as such in private, communal and public life.

גֶּבֶר־חָכָם בַּעוֹז
וְאִישׁ־דַּעַת מְאַמֶּץ־כֹּחַ:
כִּי בְתַחְבֻּלוֹת תַּעֲשֶׂה־לְךָ מִלְחָמָה
וּתְשׁוּעָה בְּרֹב יוֹעֵץ:
רָאמוֹת לֶאֱוִיל חָכְמוֹת
בַּשַּׁעַר לֹא יִפְתַּח־פִּיהוּ

*A wise man stands in victorious might,*
*and a man of knowledge turns strength into power.*
*Even in private struggles, plan strategically;*
*and help comes through much advising.*
*But to the unwise, wisdom remains unscalable as the heights of Re'em;*
*at the community council he cannot open his mouth. (24, 5−7)*

עִיר גִּבֹּרִים עָלָה חָכָם
וַיֹּרֶד עֹז מִבְטֶחָה:

*A city of mighty men may be scaled by a wise man,*
*and an impressive, confident stronghold brought to submission. (21, 22)*

In short, wisdom proves itself to be an indispensable ally for the attainment of goals in every sphere of life:

כָּבוֹד חֲכָמִים יִנְחָלוּ
וּכְסִילִים מֵרִים קָלוֹן:

*The wise shall inherit honor,*
*but fools bring dishonor to the top. (3, 35)*

Whatever position a wise man may occupy, he brings honor even to the highest. The more opportunities he has to use his wisdom for the benefit of others, the more honor he will reap from them. A fool, however, can meet with no worse fate than to be called to public office. His ineptness, which in private life might have remained hidden, known only to his immediate surroundings, becomes exposed to all if he rises to an elevated position; and thus he can only bring dishonor on himself.

⊙

פְּרִי־צַדִּיק עֵץ חַיִּים
וְלֹקֵחַ נְפָשׁוֹת חָכָם:

*The fruit of the righteous is a tree of life;*
*but he who is wise wins souls.* (11, 30)

For the righteous person, everything he does is a *tree* of life. Out of his every deed grows something beneficial, life-giving to his surroundings. On the other hand, the wise man is directly effective. His words penetrate into the souls of his listeners, grip them and put them under their spell, making them wiser and more noble. His word is not only a tree of life; it is a wellspring of life.

תּוֹרַת חָכָם מְקוֹר חַיִּים
לָסוּר מִמֹּקְשֵׁי מָוֶת:

*The teaching of the wise is a source of life,*
*to remain far from the snares of death.* (13, 14)

The ranks of the wise are made up not only of the wise themselves; they include also the friends of wisdom, those who seek instruction and like to listen to teaching, even if it should be an admonition:

אֹזֶן שֹׁמַעַת תּוֹכַחַת חַיִּים
בְּקֶרֶב חֲכָמִים תָּלִין:

*The ear that hearkens to the admonition of life*
*may abide among the wise.* (15, 31)

True wisdom is essentially communicative. It is not an abstract contemplation, detached from the world. Wisdom is a beacon that seeks to show the way, to influence its object: life itself. A saying of our Sages expresses it thus: "More than a suckling wants to suck, its mother wants to feed it."

מְקוֹר חַיִּים שֵׂכֶל בְּעָלָיו
וּמוּסַר אֱוִילִים אִוֶּלֶת:

*Intellect is a source of life to those who use it,*
*but folly is the chastisement of fools. (16, 22)*

A keen mind is salutary only if its owner has it in his command. If he cherishes and develops it and makes proper use of it, then it will become a source of life to him. The dire reward of the foolish, however, will come to them by their own lack of insight. They will eventually be brought to better understanding — or at least be moved to look for such understanding — only by the inevitable penalization brought upon them by their own foolishness.

⊙

זִמַּת אִוֶּלֶת חַטָּאת
וְתוֹעֲבַת לְאָדָם לֵץ:

*Evil perpetrated by folly is sin,*
*but in a sinner it becomes abomination to every man. (24, 9)*

(The word תועבת is in the possessive — literally "the abomination of" — but it is not connected to any noun; it is thus a general attribute: an abomination to both God and mankind.)

Committing a sin even from lack of knowledge incurs guilt. Even עושה בשגגה, someone who has sinned unwittingly, must bring a חטאת — sacrifice, because not-knowing in itself is an omission, a fault. No one should — and in Judaism no one needs to — remain uninstructed about anything regarding the fulfillment of his purpose in life. But if someone has stayed remote from knowledge about his task because he is counted among the *létzim,* those who show total contempt for anything sacred — then even the sins he commits because he lacks the knowledge cannot be atoned for. In that case they become more than sin; they become an abomination before God and man. In other words, technically he may have lacked the knowledge and sinned, but it is not the lack of knowledge primarily which *caused* his sinning. He would have trespassed even in the full and conscious awareness of his wrongdoing. In the terms of our Code of Law: he would not have been שב מידיעתו; better knowledge would not have deterred him from the wrong deed.

⊙

מַיִם עֲמֻקִּים דִּבְרֵי פִי־אִישׁ
נַחַל נֹבֵעַ מְקוֹר חָכְמָה:

*Deep waters are words spoken by a man's mouth;*
*a brook welling from the depth, the source of wisdom.* (18, 4)

חָכְמַת עָרוּם הָבִין דַּרְכּוֹ
וְאִוֶּלֶת כְּסִילִים מִרְמָה:

*The wisdom of the shrewd man is [to make] his ways understandable,*
*but the unwisdom of fools wants deception.* (14, 8)

The speech of the average person does not arise from his innermost core. His talk frequently has no sound basis; often he himself is barely aware of the origin, meaning and purpose of his words. At times he may even express himself obscurely on purpose, wanting to make himself seem important by keeping to himself the reasons for his words. People who, in their conceit, have remained aloof from the lessons of wisdom, find satisfaction in diplomatically deceiving others about the reasons and purposes of their doings so as not to be seen through. Such words are compared to deep waters which cannot be fathomed. The wise man's wisdom however, arises from his innermost depth, and yet his words are open and crystal-clear. He may not speak often or with volubility, but once he does speak, his words well up from the depth of his being; in each of his words his soul is reflected.

And just as his words are clear, so are his deeds. His actions are open to the eyes of the world; those around him understand his manner of action and his motives; they are able to form a true judgment about him and his ways. It would be easy for him to mislead the people about him; but such deception is repulsive to him. His mind serves wisdom, and wisdom calls for הבין דרכו — the whole world should understand his way of life.

⊙

יִרְאַת ד׳ רֵאשִׁית דָּעַת
חָכְמָה וּמוּסָר אֱוִילִים בָּזוּ:

*The fear of the Lord is the beginning of knowledge,*
*but the foolish despise wisdom and discipline. (1, 7)*

תְּחִלַּת חָכְמָה יִרְאַת ד׳
וְדַעַת קְדֹשִׁים בִּינָה:

*The prerequisite of wisdom is fear of the Lord,*
*and |only| hallowed knowledge becomes insight. (9, 10)*

יִרְאַת ד׳ מוּסַר חָכְמָה
וְלִפְנֵי כָבוֹד עֲנָוָה:

*The fear of the Lord is the disciplining of wisdom,*
*and humility must precede honor. (15, 33)*

To know about God and, as a result of this knowledge, to subordinate ourselves to Him — this is what is meant by "fear of God"; and this is the beginning of all knowledge.

Assuming that the sum of all fields of study is knowledge about the essence of things, the cause of their origin and existence, and the laws which determine their phenomena, then the search for such knowledge begins with the assumption that all things are characterized by a permanent property; that all phenomena, in their very variety and changeability, are founded upon immutable laws; and that all forces are put into motion, all matter is formed, and everything is limited and regulated by lasting rules. Without this assumption, all striving for knowledge would be illusory. It would be a frenzied search for the non-existent.

If, however, our search for knowledge assumes that every phenomenon has a reason, a regulation, a purpose and a law that we are able to discern, then the premise which comes before all others must of necessity be the existence of a Divine Thinker Who has thought out these reasons, and Whose thoughts we try to follow. The greatest reward of honor which any thinking person can derive is to follow the lines of thought of this supremely wise Thinker, this omnipotent First Cause Who evoked all forces, created all matter, set all limits, planned all purposes, and made all laws.

Shall we say the world reflects thoughts which no one reasoned, purposes which no one planned, laws which no one established ? These are contradictions which cancel each other out to nullity! On the other hand, a world filled with thought, striving towards an aim, progressing according to laws — this calls with compelling necessity for the precognition of an omniscient, omnipotent Creator and Law-maker, Whose all-wise and all-powerful will is being executed in everything and by everything. This precognition is so obvious, and its opposite is such an obscuration of the truth-seeking human mind, that the illogical denial of it can be attributed to only one cause: this basic premise compellingly and conclusively calls for the recognition of the fact that man too is nothing but the creation of this all-knowing and all-powerful Creator. It confronts us with the fact that man too, his existence and his being, are subordinate and subject to the highest will of this Law-maker, and man too has to subject his actions and desires to His supreme will.

דעת presents us with an irrefutable claim: יראת ד', the fear of God; and this may well bring some inconveniences in its wake! Only thus could it come about that science thinks it can circumvent such self-evident but inconvenient truth. The explorations of science are forever opening new frontiers in the knowledge of nature, revealing the thoughts behind its manifestations, their purposes and the laws which govern them. And still science tries to deny the deduction which logically imposes itself upon us: the presence of an all-wise, all-powerful, law-making Creator and Master. It deceives itself by inventing intelligence-insulting rationalizations that are not rational, such as purposes without a reason, involuntary volition, knowledge of the unconscious, etc. (Incidentally, surely those things in nature which are faultlessly executed, our own un-awareness notwithstanding, are in themselves proof of a higher Knowledge.) Science invents such non-thoughts because it is frightened of one thing: knowledge and acknowledgement of God; דעת invents these thoughts because it is afraid of יראת ד'.

As far as our Proverbs are concerned, such non-reasoning too is called אולת, literally "obscuration," the obscuring of intelligence. The beginning of all knowledge, prerequisite for all wisdom, is the fear of God. It follows that not only those those who despise חָכְמָה are אֱוִילִים, but also those who disregard מוּסָר, For יראת ד' the knowledge and acknowledgment of God. must exist within the framework of מוּסָר; hence מוּסָר and חָכְמָה are conditional, dependent on one another. Upon the rejection of מוּסָר, חָכְמָה too loses its ground. Such science which intends to be constructive, which searches for truth and respects it, must depend not only on intelligence, but in the first place upon moral integrity. Only דעת קדושים leads to בינה.

And finally, לפני כבד ענוה. Who will win first place in the search for humanly attainable wisdom? Some never reach humble worship of God, no matter how deeply they penetrate into the secrets of nature. Instead of humbly aspiring to God, Whose greatness and wisdom radiate from the wonders of His Creation, their little bit of human knowledge — so fraught with doubt and leaving so many riddles unsolved — is filled with adulation of the human mind and with such haughtiness as to cloud their intelligence. These will never carry off the prize for wisdom, because wisdom cannot be obtained unless humility precedes it.

אִוֶּלֶת אָדָם תְּסַלֵּף דַּרְכּוֹ
וְעַל־ד׳ יִזְעַף לִבּוֹ:

*The foolishness of a man distorts his way,*
*and his heart fumes against the Lord.* (19, 3)

God has implanted His voice within man — as our conscience. Our conscience reminds us without fail to avoid evil and to practice virtue. What
this evil is and what is virtue, He has revealed to us through the Tradition [the great body of Written and Oral Torah]. Furthermore, He has
endowed us with the faculty to recognize the nature of things and the
circumstances that condition them, thus allowing us to look out and see
how we may avoid evil and practice goodness. True, in this way we
may find temptations and hindrances, but these should not deflect us
from the direction He has shown us. On the contrary, their purpose is to
strengthen us by spurring us to resist temptation and overcome the difficulties thereby increasing our mental and spiritual forces in the service
of goodness. The way that leads to avoidance of evil and practice of virtue, and which alone leads to the true sanctification of mankind, is called
the straight way, because it leads to the right aim without deviations and
detours. And so we are admonished:

עֵינֶיךָ לְנֹכַח יַבִּיטוּ
וְעַפְעַפֶּיךָ יַיְשִׁרוּ נֶגְדֶּךָ:
פַּלֵּס מַעְגַּל רַגְלֶךָ
וְכָל־דְּרָכֶיךָ יִכֹּנוּ:
אַל־תֵּט־יָמִין וּשְׂמֹאול
הָסֵר רַגְלְךָ מֵרָע:

*Let your eyes look right ahead,*
*and your eyelids focus straight towards your aim.*
*Estimate the path of your feet,*
*and let all your ways be accurately directed.*
*Diverge neither right nor left;*
*restrain your foot from evil.* (4, 25—27)

בְּכָל־דְּרָכֶיךָ דָעֵהוּ
וְהוּא יְיַשֵּׁר אֹרְחֹתֶיךָ:

*In all your ways direct your thoughts to Him,*
*And this will make your path straight. (3, 6)*

But if man does not attain recognition of the true aim through the voice
of conscience, or if he does not apply himself to recognize it, then his
spirit remains in the dark. This too is called אולת in our Proverbs, a
clouding of the spirit, which we render by "want of judgment" or "folly." Such a lack of judgment leads a person astray. His path becomes
twisting and winding, and a winding path holds a twofold danger: it does
not lead to the place where one should go, and it does lead to a place
where one should not go. Yet if, at the end of such a path, the expected
benefit is not forthcoming, and instead some unwelcome bane is
awaiting him, then the same folly which has led the man on this path
may well make him accuse God of granting man so little happiness and
so much sorrow and misery, as he is oblivious of this simple truth:

תֻּמַּת יְשָׁרִים תַּנְחֵם
וְסֶלֶף בּוֹגְדִים יְשָׁדֵּם:

*Complete devotion to Him guides the righteous,*
*And the falseness of the faithless shall despoil them. (11, 3)*

יֵשׁ דֶּרֶךְ יָשָׁר לִפְנֵי־אִישׁ
וְאַחֲרִיתָהּ דַּרְכֵי מָוֶת:

*A way may seem straight to a man,*
*yet its end is the way of death. (14, 12)*

צִדְקַת תָּמִים תְּיַשֵּׁר דַּרְכּוֹ
וּבְרִשְׁעָתוֹ יִפֹּל רָשָׁע:

*The righteousness of a dutiful man makes his way straight,*
*while it is the lawless man's lawlessness which causes his fall. (11, 5)*

Rather than fretting and being vexed at God if things do not go our way, we should be מפשפשים במעשינו, examine our own way of life and actions. We should ask ourselves whether we still are on the right way, and we should ask this question before God — according to the criterion of His given Law; for:

$$\text{כָּל דֶּרֶךְ־אִישׁ יָשָׁר בְּעֵינָיו}$$
$$\text{וְתֹכֵן לִבּוֹת ד':}$$

*Each way of a man is right in his own eyes,*
*but God analyzes the heart. (21, 2)*

Whatever way a man may take, he thinks it is the right one. He believes it leads to his aim; otherwise he would not follow it. Yet is this goal really the right one? Perhaps the goal itself is outside the direction prescribed by God? Perhaps this way which looks so straight to him is in fact a twisting and winding one, leading him astray from the only right direction? All this has to be examined before God and judged according to His Word, for it is God who decides between heart and heart — between the heart whose will is contained in God's will and the heart which subordinates God's will to his own willful one.

And if, after having undergone self-examination, a man absolves himself, he should not trust his own insight without further effort. He should look for advice and instruction at the hand of more understanding people. For:

$$\text{דֶּרֶךְ אֱוִיל יָשָׁר בְּעֵינָיו}$$
$$\text{וְשֹׁמֵעַ לְעֵצָה חָכָם:}$$

*The way of an unwise man is straight in his own eyes,*
*but he who listens to advice is wise. (12, 15)*

⊙

So all those who perceive the need for instruction are advised:

עִזְבוּ פְתָאִים וִחְיוּ
וְאִשְׁרוּ בְּדֶרֶךְ בִּינָה:

*Forsake the ignorant, so that you may live,*
*and stride towards happiness on the way of insight!* (9, 6)

Forsake the company of the ignorant who, as you have done, walk in oblivion of the right way. Life is contained not in ignorance but in knowledge, in true, clear recognition. Then you will gain courage to go forth in serious determination on the way to understanding, which alone leads to sanctification.

Neither should you let yourself be led astray by the haughty self-confidence of the lawless:

הֵעַז אִישׁ רָשָׁע בְּפָנָיו
וְיָשָׁר הוּא יָבִין דַּרְכּוֹ
(כתיב: יָכִין דְּרָכָיו):

*Insolently as a lawless man may express himself to his face,*
*the upright man remains careful of his way.* (21, 29)

Or, according to the *k'thiv,* the written text, the upright man gives his ways the right direction.

⊙

לֵךְ מִנֶּגֶד לְאִישׁ כְּסִיל
וּבַל־יָדַעְתָּ שִׂפְתֵי־דָעַת:

*Go away from the presence of a conceited fool,*
*and do not know him, say the lips of knowledge.* (14, 7)

פָּגוֹשׁ דֹּב שַׁכּוּל בְּאִישׁ
וְאַל־כְּסִיל בְּאִוַּלְתּוֹ:

*Let a bereaved bear meet a man*
*rather than a conceited fool in his folly.* (17, 12)

There is nothing more annoying than meeting a man who lacks proper perception, but still considers his own opinions as irrefutably correct, and thus is not open to any instruction. On the contrary, he imposes his own opinions and views on everyone else. A sensible person remains far from such a character, and the rejection or denial of his acquaintance is the best proof that he knows him well!

Woe if such a conceited fool becomes passionately excited! Then it is easier to find a defense against a furious animal than against such a frenziedly raging fool. A gleaming blade of steel may penetrate the thick fur of a bear, but the heart of a conceited fool is armored against the brightest truth and most sensible argument.

⊙

אִישׁ־חָכָם נִשְׁפָּט אֶת־אִישׁ אֱוִיל
וְרָגַז וְשָׂחַק וְאֵין נָחַת:

*If a wise man is drawn into an argument with a fool,*
*he may be angry or laugh, but he gets no satisfaction. (29, 9)*

It is impossible to quarrel with an unreasonable person! One may become angry or be amused by the senselessness of his retorts, but he never reaches a satisfying conclusion.

אִם־תִּכְתּוֹשׁ אֶת־הָאֱוִיל בַּמַּכְתֵּשׁ
בְּתוֹךְ הָרִיפוֹת בַּעֱלִי
לֹא־תָסוּר מֵעָלָיו אִוַּלְתּוֹ:

*You may pound a fool with a pestle*
*among groats in the mortar —*
*his foolishness will not depart from him. (27, 22)*

כְּכֶלֶב שָׁב עַל־קֵאוֹ
כְּסִיל שׁוֹנֶה בְאִוַּלְתּוֹ:

*Like a dog who returns to his own vomit*
*is a fool who repeats his folly. (26, 11)*

כָּל־רוּחוֹ יוֹצִיא כְסִיל
וְחָכָם בְּאָחוֹר יְשַׁבְּחֶנָּה:

*A fool speaks everything he has in his mind,*
*but a wise man improves upon it by discretion.* (29, 11)

בְּלֵב נָבוֹן תָּנוּחַ חָכְמָה
וּבְקֶרֶב כְּסִילִים תִּוָּדֵעַ:

*In the heart of an understanding man, wisdom rests;*
*but within conceited fools it is pressed to become known.* (14, 33)

A wise man knows how vulnerable the human mind is to error. He therefore keeps the result of his thinking to himself for a long time. He examines it again and again in order to improve upon it if possible (ישבחנו, from the root שבח, has the same sense as in Talmudic usage) before he expresses it. The conceited person, however, thinks that his thoughts cannot be improved upon, and he has no rest until he has told all.

⊙

פֶּתִי יַאֲמִין לְכָל־דָּבָר
וְעָרוּם יָבִין לַאֲשֻׁרוֹ:
חָכָם יָרֵא וְסָר מֵרָע
וּכְסִיל מִתְעַבֵּר וּבוֹטֵחַ:
קְצַר־אַפַּיִם יַעֲשֶׂה אִוֶּלֶת
וְאִישׁ מְזִמּוֹת יִשָּׂנֵא:
נָחֲלוּ פְתָאיִם אִוֶּלֶת
וַעֲרוּמִים יַכְתִּרוּ דָעַת:

*An inexperienced man believes every word,*
*but a clever man observes his own step.*
*A wise man is apprehensive and departs from evil,*
*but a fool oversteps himself and remains confident.*
*The quick-of-decision will act foolishly,*
*but a man of endless deliberations will be hated.*
*An untrained inheritance remains foolishness,*
*but the clever bring knowledge to the peak.* (14, 15—18)

Whoever has not reached the stage of thinking for himself is dependent on the examples and words of those about him. A clear mind, however, capable of evaluating his duties amid the circumstances of reality, makes a person independent and enables him to judge by his own understanding every step he takes.

On the other hand, if a person possesses true wisdom, he will not trust even his own independent judgment too quickly. He will not have unlimited confidence in his own recognition of the right, and will always be afraid of erring in his own choice. A conceited fool, though, will overstep his limits, for he is either unaware of them or inattentive. He is always confident, and it never occurs to him that he might be mistaken.

The Book of Mishlé advises us not to exaggerate to either extreme in the matter of judgment and decision. Someone who is קְצַר אַפַּיִם (literally short or quick of desire and endeavor, so that he does not consider things thoroughly; consequently it also means the impatient; see Exodus 6, 9) reflects too little; hence in the end he will carry out senseless action. On the other hand, אִישׁ מְזִמּוֹת, someone who never ends his deliberations and never arrives at a conclusion because of these considerations, not only will never get anywhere himself, but is useless also for others. His partnership should be avoided, since he will only hinder any undertaking with his lengthy contemplations.

To sum it up: פְּתָאִים, people lacking experience and instruction, will always be subject to senselessness and will never be able to escape from folly. But whoever combines lucidity of mind with comprehension and knowledge will be successful enough to earn such crowning recognition as mankind extends — more than to any other attainment — to the true wisdom of the spirit.

⊙

חָכְמוֹת בָּנְתָה בֵיתָהּ
חָצְבָה עַמּוּדֶיהָ שִׁבְעָה:

*The essence of all wisdom has built her house,*
*she has hewn out her seven pillars. (9, 1)*

טָבְחָה טִבְחָהּ מָסְכָה יֵינָהּ
אַף עָרְכָה שֻׁלְחָנָהּ׃
שָׁלְחָה נַעֲרֹתֶיהָ תִקְרָא
עַל־גַּפֵּי מְרֹמֵי קָרֶת׃
מִי־פֶתִי יָסֻר הֵנָּה
חֲסַר־לֵב אָמְרָה לּוֹ׃
לְכוּ לַחֲמוּ בְלַחְמִי
וּשְׁתוּ בְּיַיִן מָסָכְתִּי׃
עִזְבוּ פְתָאיִם וִחְיוּ
וְאִשְׁרוּ בְּדֶרֶךְ בִּינָה׃

*She has prepared her meat, has mixed her wine,*
*and also arranged her table.*
*She has sent forth her maidens through whom she calls,*
*upon the summits of the city's heights:*
*"Whoso is untaught, let him turn in here";*
*and whoso lacks heart (understanding), she speaks to him;*
*"Come eat my bread*
*and drink the wine which I have mixed.*
*Forsake the ignorant and you shall gain life,*
*and walk toward happiness upon the path of understanding." (9, 1—6)*

אֵשֶׁת כְּסִילוּת הֹמִיָּה
פְּתַיּוּת וּבַל־יָדְעָה מָה׃
וְיָשְׁבָה לְפֶתַח בֵּיתָהּ
עַל־כִּסֵּא מְרֹמֵי קָרֶת׃
לִקְרֹא לְעֹבְרֵי דָרֶךְ
הַמְיַשְּׁרִים אֹרְחוֹתָם׃

*The woman of foolish conceit is uproarious:*
*she is Ignorance and Non-knowledge,*
*and she sits at the entrance of her house*
*enthroned on the city's heights,*
*to call to the wayfarers,*
*who straighten their paths:*

מִי־פֶתִי יָסֻר הֵנָּה
וַחֲסַר־לֵב וְאָמְרָה לּוֹ:
מַיִם גְּנוּבִים יִמְתָּקוּ
וְלֶחֶם סְתָרִים יִנְעָם:
וְלֹא־יָדַע כִּי־רְפָאִים שָׁם
בְּעִמְקֵי שְׁאוֹל קְרֻאֶיהָ:

*"Whoso is untaught, let him come here";*
*and whoever lacks heart, she speaks to him:*
*"Stolen waters are sweet,*
*and the bread of secrecy is pleasant."*
*And he does not know that the shades are there,*
*that her guests are in the depths of the nether-world.* (9, 13–18)

Here we have two contrasting teachings trying to gain influence over an untaught and inexperienced mind. The first teaching leads to Life; the second, to Death. The first is the Divine teaching, the essence of all wisdom (חכמות). This teaching is not content to utter general truisms. She has "built her house," solidly based its entire edifice of individual and national existence upon "seven pillars" — the pillars of perfection. (According to the Talmud, tractate Shabbath 116a, this refers to the seven Books of the Law — the Pentateuch — the fourth Book being divided into three by פרשת ויהי בנסוע, Numbers 10:35–36 — considered in a sense a separate Book — so that the Pentateuch parallels God's other work of wisdom: the seven days of Creation; see Talmud, Sanhedrin 38a.)

This Divine teaching has worked out in every detail her instructions for the life to be led under her auspices. Her laws are "nurturing" and "blissfully refreshing," set out as a שלחן ערוך, an orderly prepared table offering those who come to it spiritual and moral nourishment. This teaching has sent out its "handmaids," teachers, prophets and Sages, to the summits which dominate human social existence. Through their mouths she calls those who are still ignorant, even those who are still unprepared mentally, to absorb the strengthening and joy-giving nourishment which she has prepared for their spirits and souls. She invites them to forsake the company and the example of the unwise, and to join her table in order to gain Life and to follow the ways of reason toward happiness.

The other teaching, the human one, has so far completed not even one whole building. It is likened to a noisy woman intoxicated by her own foolish conceit. She creates much noise about herself, and is yet the epitome of ignorance. She prides herself on her ignorance about everything which a person needs to know most of all, about anything "higher" or "ideal." On the contrary, she considers those who let such higher ideas spoil their sensual lives as silly, and thinks that such ideals are not matters for study and investigation, being merely dreams or fictions which prevent people from enjoying their lives.

This teaching too, this "noisy woman," seeks to make propaganda. True, she has never constructed a whole building nor even worked it out in its details; but this (she is certain) is far too difficult, and also superfluous. *Her* lessons are so simple and so easily understood, that they can be learned while standing on one foot, or in passing by. Neither does she speak from such august heights that tower above human social life. Such heights do not even exist for her. Nevertheless, she has taken up her quarters in the high echelons of human society, because that is where she can count on finding disciples. At the entrance of her dwelling she prepares a throne for herself, and from this throne she calls out to those who are innocently going their way or are even simply seeking the right and straight way.

She calls them "ignorant" and "senseless," people who know nothing of the right philosophy in life. Let them deviate just for once from the straight way to try out forbidden joys, to taste how sweet those stolen waters are, gaining even more sweetness from the fact that they are forbidden. Of course, for the masses, the laws of morality should stand. But in סתרים, in private, for himself (she insists), any reasonable person laughs at this so-called morality, intended for the "people" and knows how to indulge in agreeable, sensual pleasures.

Whoever listens to her instruction, however, does not know that her hand leads not to Life, but to Death. The followers in her circle have already departed from true Life; and those who are invited now to partake from her so-called Repast of Life are doomed to the depths of the earthly grave.

⊙

חָכְמוֹת בַּחוּץ תָּרֹנָּה
בָּרְחֹבוֹת תִּתֵּן קוֹלָהּ:
בְּרֹאשׁ הֹמִיּוֹת תִּקְרָא
בְּפִתְחֵי שְׁעָרִים בָּעִיר
אֲמָרֶיהָ תֹאמֵר:
עַד־מָתַי פְּתָיִם תְּאֵהֲבוּ־פֶתִי
וְלֵצִים לָצוֹן חָמְדוּ לָהֶם
וּכְסִילִים יִשְׂנְאוּ־דָעַת:
תָּשׁוּבוּ לְתוֹכַחְתִּי
הִנֵּה אַבִּיעָה לָכֶם רוּחִי
אוֹדִיעָה דְבָרַי אֶתְכֶם:
יַעַן קָרָאתִי וַתְּמָאֵנוּ
נָטִיתִי יָדִי וְאֵין מַקְשִׁיב:
וַתִּפְרְעוּ כָל־עֲצָתִי

*Wisdom, in the multiplicity of its contents, wants to be heard in the streets,*
*to lift her voice in the marketplace, to call out*
*where the surging masses are*
*at the entrance of the city's gates to speak her sayings:*
*"How long, you unwise ones, will you love ignorance,*
*and you scoffers, lust for ridicule,*
*and conceited fools, hate knowledge?*
*At my reproof, you should repent.*
*Behold, I shall let my spirit flow out to you,*
*shall let my words become known to you.*
*But because I have called and you have refused,*
*I have extended my hand and no one paid attention;*
*you have neglected all my advice*

וְתוֹכַחְתִּי לֹא אֲבִיתֶם:
גַּם־אֲנִי בְּאֵידְכֶם אֶשְׂחָק
אֶלְעַג בְּבֹא פַחְדְּכֶם:
בְּבֹא כְשׁוֹאָה פַחְדְּכֶם
וְאֵידְכֶם כְּסוּפָה יֶאֱתֶה
בְּבֹא עֲלֵיכֶם צָרָה וְצוּקָה:
אָז יִקְרָאֻנְנִי וְלֹא אֶעֱנֶה
יְשַׁחֲרֻנְנִי וְלֹא יִמְצָאֻנְנִי:
תַּחַת כִּי־שָׂנְאוּ דָעַת
וְיִרְאַת ד׳ לֹא בָחָרוּ:
לֹא־אָבוּ לַעֲצָתִי
נָאֲצוּ כָּל־תּוֹכַחְתִּי:
וְיֹאכְלוּ מִפְּרִי דַרְכָּם
וּמִמֹּעֲצֹתֵיהֶם יִשְׂבָּעוּ:
כִּי מְשׁוּבַת פְּתָיִם תַּהַרְגֵם
וְשַׁלְוַת כְּסִילִים תְּאַבְּדֵם:
וְשֹׁמֵעַ לִי יִשְׁכָּן־בֶּטַח
וְשַׁאֲנַן מִפַּחַד רָעָה:

*and would have none of my admonition –*
*I will likewise laugh at your calamity,*
*I will mock when your dread strikes,*
*when like a devastation your dread sets in,*
*and your calamity as a tempest,*
*when trouble and distress overcome you.*
*Then they will call me, but will not find me —*
*because they hated wisdom*
*and did not want the fear of God,*
*did not comply with my advice,*
*and despised all my admonitions.*
*Therefore they shall now eat of the fruit of their ways*
*and satisfy themselves with their own plans.*
*For the waywardness of the unwise shall slay them,*
*and the confidence of conceited fools shall lead them to destruction.*
*But whoever listens to me shall always remain calm*
*and undisturbed by fear of evil. (1, 20–33)*

The wisdom of God's teaching embraces all of life's phenomena, in their entire multiplicity. This wisdom is not some spiritual gift, awaiting its achievement and fruition in the seclusion of study and prayer. It rather seeks to animate the pulsating heartbeat of humanity and civilization. It endeavors to shape the lives of individuals and societies, and it therefore looks for disciples [as it were] in the marketplaces, the centers of living and striving. It looks for them — but does not find them.

The forces which influence the lives and striving of the masses are: ignorance, which praises and prides itself that the teachings of God's wisdom are remote from it; frivolous folly, which finds joy in mocking the teachings and requirements of His instruction; conceited foolishness, which in its hatred avoids any deeper understanding. These are the powers which rule the masses, but not to their best interest! As long as they are happy — in their sense of the word — they do not perceive what they are missing. But when they come upon darker times, even if they merely start becoming afraid of bad times, of a diminution or loss of material goods and pleasures — then they come to look for some consolation, some support and advice in their affliction, which they could have found once at the hand of Divine wisdom, but now can find no longer. And so those who have remained willfully ignorant go to their ruin as a result of their own willfulness, having remained fools in their own happy confidence.

The true followers of Divine wisdom, however, always remain calm. They do not know fear of misfortune. To them, both good times and bad are sent by the same loving Divine hand, providing tasks to be fulfilled, so that they can become yet more aware of the ever-loving closeness of God.

כִּשְׂחוֹק לִכְסִיל עֲשׂוֹת זִמָּה
וְחָכְמָה לְאִישׁ תְּבוּנָה:

*It is as play to the fool to carry out a thought,*
*but a thing of wisdom to a man of understanding.* (10, 23)

Wisdom and understanding are needed not only for getting the right idea, thought or plan, but also for its proper implementation. A conceited fool, however, does not reflect long before translating a thought into action (זמה as in the word זמתי, Job 17, 23).

⊙

אָדָם עָרוּם כֹּסֶה דָּעַת
וְלֵב כְּסִילִים יִקְרָא אִוֶּלֶת:

*A clever man keeps his knowledge discreet,*
*but the heart of fools proclaims its foolishness.* (12, 23)

כָּל־עָרוּם יַעֲשֶׂה בְדָעַת
וּכְסִיל יִפְרֹשׂ אִוֶּלֶת:

*Every clever man acts by knowledge,*
*but a conceited fool displays ignorance.* (13, 16)

Foolishness does not remain concealed, whether in a person's action or in speech. A clever man, though, generally knows more than he shows; and while a fool tells all, a clever man remains silent. However, when it comes to deeds, then the knowledge of a clever man can be seen; his intelligence is evident from his slightest action; while the unwisdom of a foolish person is revealed in whatever he does.

⊙

תַּאֲוָה נִהְיָה תֶּעֱרַב לְנָפֶשׁ
וְתוֹעֲבַת כְּסִילִים סוּר מֵרָע:

*Conquering a lust is a comfort to the soul,*
*but to depart from evil is abomination to fools.* (13, 19)

Fools have no inkling of the joyful bliss which rewards the soul for having suppressed an evil desire, for having overcome an unfortunate tendency, or even on having succeeded in a resolution for self-restraint

concerning a desire which is not forbidden. To fools, though, the mere
thought of abandoning the attainment of a goal of sensual satisfaction is
"abomination" (נהיה means to be suppressed while in the process of
coming into being, as in the phrase ישנתו נהיתה עליו, Daniel 2, 1).

⊙

אֶת־פְּנֵי מֵבִין חָכְמָה
וְעֵינֵי כְסִיל בִּקְצֵה־אָרֶץ:

*Whoever is able to understand finds wisdom wherever he turns,
but the eyes of a fool scan the ends of the earth. (17, 24)*

Whoever is able to connect cause and effect will find material for
enriching his mind right near and close to him. He does not have to look
for things far out of reach. Wisdom, חכמה, is right in front of his face,
את פניו; and that, too, is where he finds the implementation of the Divine
thought amid circumstances so shaped by Divine wisdom as to set the
tasks intended for his own individual fulfillment. To him it is important
to comprehend the events closest to him — because that is where he has
to act in his life and accomplish his endeavors.

For the uncomprehending, unwise person, however, events in his immediate vicinity look valueless, trivial and insignificant. His view glances
only over the surface of things, and so he feels in his foolish conceit that
he knows these things sufficiently. He may pride himself on knowing
what the vista is like at the poles, or even in heaven, yet he does not
know his own parents, or indeed even himself!

⊙

לֹא־נָאוֶה לִכְסִיל תַּעֲנוּג
אַף כִּי־לְעֶבֶד מְשֹׁל בְּשָׂרִים:

*Luxury is not seemly for a fool,
much less for a servant to rule over his masters. (19, 10)*

If we understand this proverb correctly, it would mean the following:
The way in which a well-to-do fool indulges himself in a life of luxury is

a repulsive spectacle for any reasonable onlooker. His pleasures are often unworthy of a human being, and certainly unreasonable or irrational. It is an even more revolting sight if, as often happens in the household of unwise masters spoilt by luxury, the servants become the real masters. The maid of an unwise, spoilt mistress and the servant of an unwise, spoilt master know very well how to discover the weak spots of their employers, while being obsequious to their face and providing them with satisfaction for their irrational and evil desires. Being cleverer than their masters, the servants know how to exploit their folly so well as to become indispensable to them and to completely dominate them.

⊙

כַּשֶּׁלֶג בַּקַּיִץ וְכַמָּטָר בַּקָּצִיר
כֵּן לֹא־נָאוֶה לִכְסִיל כָּבוֹד:

*As snow in the summer and rain in harvest,*
*So is honor not befitting a fool.* (26, 1)

כִּצְרוֹר אֶבֶן בְּמַרְגֵּמָה
כֵּן־נוֹתֵן לִכְסִיל כָּבוֹד:

*Like carefully wrapping a stone in a stone-heap,*
*so is giving honor to a fool.* (26, 8)

There is hardly a more laughable figure than a fool — and a כסיל, a conceited fool at that — who preens himself with undeserved honors. He does everything to display them in the most showy manner. If he deems himself an aristocrat, all his clothes, including his dressing-gown, must be adorned with the proper colored ribbon, and the lowliest vessel must bear his coat of arms. Not only is such honor as unseemly as snow in summer and rain at harvest-time, but it also does him harm, for it makes him even more vain. Hence, whoever bestows honor on a fool, makes it as worthless as a silly game, like someone who takes an ordinary stone from a stone-heap and carefully wraps it up as something of great value (or, if מרגמה is related to ארגמן, he wraps it up in a piece of fine velvet).

מְקַצֶּה רַגְלַיִם חָמָס שֹׁתֶה
שֹׁלֵחַ דְּבָרִים בְּיַד־כְּסִיל:

*He who sends a message by the hand of a fool*
*cuts off his own feet [and] will taste distortion.* (26, 6)

Whoever uses an intelligent messenger, adds, so to speak, to his own
feet, because the messenger's feet serve and benefit him. But if a man
sends out a fool, not only does he not gain feet, but he forfeits his own as
well, by having sent the fool rather than having gone himself. As to the
message, it does not merely remain undelivered; it will be transmitted in-
correctly. The recipient in turn will reply with a wrong, unjust answer,
which, again, will be distorted in the mouth of the foolish messenger. In
short, whoever sends a fool will suffer only annoyance.

◉

נֶזֶם זָהָב בְּאַף חֲזִיר
אִשָּׁה יָפָה וְסָרַת טָעַם:

*A golden ring in a swine's snout —*
*so a fair woman lacking understanding.*(11, 22)

This golden ring will not remain spared from dirt; on the contrary, the
animal will rub it in filth immediately. So too a woman's beauty: if she is
foolish, it will be the first to be dragged in the filth of immorality.

גַּם בְּלֹא־דַעַת נֶפֶשׁ לֹא־טוֹב
וְאָץ בְּרַגְלַיִם חוֹטֵא:

*Even in non-knowledge, a soul is not good,*
*and he who hastens sins with his feet.* (19, 2)

אֹרַח חַיִּים לְמַעְלָה לְמַשְׂכִּיל
לְמַעַן סוּר מִשְׁאוֹל מָטָּה:

*For one who uses his mind, the path of life is an ascending one,*
*that he may depart from the nether-world beneath.* (15, 24)

אֹהֵב מוּסָר אֹהֵב דָּעַת
וְשׂוֹנֵא תוֹכַחַת בָּעַר:

*He who loves instruction loves knowledge;*
*but he who hates admonition is senseless. (12, 1)*

הָבִיאָה לַמּוּסָר לִבֶּךָ
וְאָזְנֶךָ לְאִמְרֵי־דָעַת:

*Incline your heart toward instruction,*
*And your ears to the words of knowledge. (23, 12)*

אֱוִיל יִנְאַץ מוּסַר אָבִיו
וְשֹׁמֵר תּוֹכַחַת יַעְרִם:

*A fool despises his father's instruction,*
*But he who pays attention to admonition will become clever. (15, 5)*

בּוֹטֵחַ בְּלִבּוֹ הוּא כְסִיל
וְהוֹלֵךְ בְּחָכְמָה הוּא יִמָּלֵט:

*He who trusts his own heart is a fool,*
*but he who walks in wisdom shall escape. (28, 26)*

נֶזֶם זָהָב וַחֲלִי־כָתֶם
מוֹכִיחַ חָכָם עַל־אֹזֶן שֹׁמָעַת:

*As a ring of gold and precious adornment*
*is the admonition of a sage upon an attentive ear. (25, 12)*

If we commit a wrong deed out of ignorance and lack of knowledge, it
still remains a wrong deed. To have committed it through unawareness

does not make us virtuous, for the fact that we have remained ignorant about the character of our actions is a wrong in itself, and testifies to our lack of serious application. Moreover, whoever acts hurriedly, without considering whether his step is the correct one, sins.

Every step of our life on earth leads us on a road between two contrasts: on the one hand, materialistic sensuality, which belongs to temporality, our passing earthly life—its grave is earthly transitoriness, for with time it must end; and on the other hand, spiritual morality, which belongs in the sphere of the Divine, the eternal. At every moment of our lives we have to decide between the temporal grave and the sublime and eternal, between Life and Death. The *maskil,* who uses his mind properly, hestitates not for a moment to decide for the heights, no matter how powerful the attractions which entice him to the depths.

But prerequisite to the claim that one loves the meaning of truth and virtue is an ear attentive to admonition. Whoever lends his ear to the instruction of a wise person gains a valuable, spiritual adornment—the stamp of belonging to the service of truth and virtue.

# III

# SPEECH

מָוֶת וְחַיִּים בְּיַד־לָשׁוֹן
וְאֹהֲבֶיהָ יֹאכַל פִּרְיָהּ:

*Death and life are in the power of the tongue,*
*and according to one's love of it he shall enjoy its fruit.* (18, 21)

This adage shows the crucial importance that Mishlé attributes to our human word. On it depend the highest salvation and most abysmal misfortune. Among the faculties with which man is endowed for the fulfillment of his mission, none is so constantly available as human speech. None can so instantly augment or decrease the light of truth, justice, morality, peace and happiness as words. Therefore, our Book of Proverbs finds nothing more precious than שפתי דעת — lips at the service of understanding. Nothing can be better and more satisfying than a word spoken at the right time:

יֵשׁ זָהָב וְרָב־פְּנִינִים
וּכְלִי יָקָר שִׂפְתֵי־דָעַת:

*There is gold and a wealth of pearls,*
*but lips of knowledge are the most precious vessel.* (20, 15)

שִׂמְחָה לָאִישׁ בְּמַעֲנֵה־פִיו
וְדָבָר בְּעִתּוֹ מַה־טּוֹב:

*A man has joy in the utterance of his mouth,*
*and a word at the right time, how good it is!* (15, 23)

Not only because of its effect on the listener does Mishlé value the
spoken word so highly. Words are of prime importance for the clarifica-
tion and precision of our own thoughts as well. Our thoughts acquire
their exact meaning only when we try to express them. Only at that time
do they gain their exact structure and are tested by the standard of
truth.

לֵב חָכָם יַשְׂכִּיל פִּיהוּ
וְעַל־שְׂפָתָיו יֹסִיף לֶקַח:

*The heart of the wise man directs his mouth towards perception,*
*and even on his lips he gains understanding.* (16, 23)

שִׂפְתֵי חֲכָמִים יְזָרוּ דָעַת
וְלֵב כְּסִילִים לֹא־כֵן:

*The lips of the wise search for perception,*
*but not so the heart of the fool.* (15, 7)

לְשׁוֹן חֲכָמִים תֵּיטִיב דָּעַת
וּפִי כְסִילִים יַבִּיעַ אִוֶּלֶת:

*The tongue of the wise improves knowledge,*
*but the mouth of fools pours out foolishness.* (15, 2)

Even the knowledge and teachings transmitted to us become our personal, permanent property only if they remain not merely thoughts
within ourselves but are uttered by our lips and set into precise
sentences. None have held this principle in higher respect than our
חכמים, our wise Sages and scholars. This lies at the root of our entire
system and tradition of learning, תורה שבעל פה, our Oral Torah [trans-
mitted in precision by oral, spoken teaching].

בְּנִי לְחׇכְמָתִי הַקְשִׁיבָה
לִתְבוּנָתִי הַט־אׇזְנֶךָ׃
לִשְׁמֹר מְזִמּוֹת
וְדַעַת שְׂפָתֶיךָ יִנְצֹרוּ׃

*My son, listen to my wisdom,*
*incline your ears to my conclusions,*
*to retain considerations,*
*and that your lips may keep knowledge.* (5, 1–2)

הַט אׇזְנְךָ וּשְׁמַע דִּבְרֵי חֲכָמִים
וְלִבְּךָ תָּשִׁית לְדַעְתִּי׃
כִּי־נָעִים כִּי־תִשְׁמְרֵם בְּבִטְנֶךָ
יִכֹּנוּ יַחְדָּו עַל־שְׂפָתֶיךָ׃

*Incline your ear and hear the words of the wise,*
*direct your heart to my knowledge.*
*Though it is pleasant to keep them within yourself,*
*they should be established confluently upon your lips.* (22, 17–18)

According to Mishlé, apt use of speech determines not only our spiritual growth, but even our material welfare:

מִפְּרִי פִי־אִישׁ תִּשְׂבַּע בִּטְנוֹ
תְּבוּאַת שְׂפָתָיו יִשְׂבָּע׃

*From the fruit of a man's mouth, even his physical being is satisfied.*
*He satisfies himself with the harvest of his lips.* (18, 20)

מִפְּרִי פִי־אִישׁ יִשְׂבַּע־טוֹב
וּגְמוּל יְדֵי־אָדָם יָשִׁיב לוֹ׃

*From the fruit of a man's mouth, he gets good satisfaction,*
*as the recompense of a person's handiwork shall be rendered him.* (12, 14)

The effect of our speech in our communication with our fellow-men is particularly stressed in Mishlé, whose teachings are equally abundant in seriously cautioning us as in stimulating encouragement. In the first place, the proverbs warn against *too much* talk, in particular *quick, unthinking* speech. As against this, they praise the art of *listening* and *silence*. איש שומע לנצח ידבר — "The one who listens — *he* deserves to speak!" (21, 28).

בְּרֹב דְּבָרִים לֹא יֶחְדַּל־פָּשַׁע
וְחוֹשֵׂךְ שְׂפָתָיו מַשְׂכִּיל:

*Where there is much speaking, evil will not fail to appear;*
*but he who guards his lips is sensible.* (10, 19)

גַּם אֱוִיל מַחֲרִישׁ חָכָם יֵחָשֵׁב
אֹטֵם שְׂפָתָיו נָבוֹן:

*Even a fool when he keeps silent may be thought wise;*
*he who locks his lips is intelligent.* (17, 28)

שֹׁמֵר פִּיו וּלְשׁוֹנוֹ
שֹׁמֵר מִצָּרוֹת נַפְשׁוֹ:

*He who guards his mouth and his tongue [not to talk much in general,*
*or to be thoughtful about his utterances]*
*keeps his soul from suffering.* (21, 23)

מֵשִׁיב דָּבָר בְּטֶרֶם יִשְׁמָע
אִוֶּלֶת הִיא־לוֹ וּכְלִמָּה:

*He who answers before he hears*
*causes himself folly and shame.* (18, 13)

חָזִיתָ אִישׁ אָץ בִּדְבָרָיו
תִּקְוָה לִכְסִיל מִמֶּנּוּ:

*Did you see anyone rash in his speech? —*
*A fool has more hope than he.* (29, 20)

בְּכָל־עֶצֶב יִהְיֶה מוֹתָר
וּדְבַר שְׂפָתַיִם אַךְ לְמַחְסוֹר:

*For every effort there is a gain,*
*but the words of the lips are merely a loss.* (14, 23)

⊙

While an unnecessary word can be foolish and damaging, a wise and good word is beneficial. Indeed, the distinction between a conscientious and an unprincipled person can be made not only by their deeds, but mainly by their speech. For speech can cause either the greatest bliss or the greatest misfortune. Words can constitute the finest virtues or the most serious crimes.

Mishlé uses the expressions "mouth," "tongue" and "lips" to designate speech; "mouth" connotes speaking in general; "tongue," the specific contents of the spoken word; and "lips," the controlling guards of speech.

בְּרָכוֹת לְרֹאשׁ צַדִּיק
וּפִי רְשָׁעִים יְכַסֶּה חָמָס:

*Only blessings are about the head of a just man,*
*but the mouth of the wicked conceals injustice.* (10, 6)

מְקוֹר חַיִּים פִּי צַדִּיק
וּפִי רְשָׁעִים יְכַסֶּה חָמָס:

*A source of life is the mouth of the righteous,*
*but the mouth of the wicked conceals injustice.* (10, 11)

עֵד בְּלִיַּעַל יָלִיץ מִשְׁפָּט
וּפִי רְשָׁעִים יְבַלַּע־אָוֶן:

*As an unprincipled witness mocks justice,*
*so the mouth of the wicked conceals evil.* (19, 28)

אִישׁ בְּלִיַּעַל כֹּרֶה רָעָה
וְעַל־שְׂפָתוֹ כְּאֵשׁ צָרָבֶת:

*An unprincipled man prepares evil,*
*and on his lips there is a searing fire.* (16, 27)

A conscientious person tries with all his faculties to dispense blessing.
His mouth is a "fountain of life"; each word that springs from his innermost thoughts is life-giving; it is destined to implant the seed of blessing
within the listeners' minds and spirits. The unprincipled man, however,
uses his speech exactly to the contrary — not to express his thoughts,
but to conceal them, hiding his evil schemes.

הָסֵר מִמְּךָ עִקְּשׁוּת פֶּה
וּלְזוּת שְׂפָתַיִם הַרְחֵק מִמֶּךָ:

*Be you rid of a crooked mouth,*
*and undisciplined lips keep far from you.* (4, 24)

קֹרֵץ עַיִן יִתֵּן עַצָּבֶת
וֶאֱוִיל שְׂפָתַיִם יִלָּבֵט:

*He who winks an eye can cause distress,*
*and he who uses his lips unwisely shall stumble.* (10, 10)

חֲכַם־לֵב יִקַּח מִצְוֹת
וֶאֱוִיל שְׂפָתַיִם יִלָּבֵט:

*The wise in heart shall accept commandments,*
*but he who uses his lips unwisely shall stumble* (10, 8)

The best training for faithful observance of the Torah's commandments is careful attention to our speech. There is no better way to self-perfection than the earnest resolution, the silent promise before God, to allow one's mouth to utter nothing devious, to keep away from לזות, unbridled prattling, never permitting his lips to move arbitrarily. In fact, the mere glance of an eye can inflict deep distress; how much more so an unkind word!

If someone's heart, therefore, is inclined to achieve wisdom and obedience to the commandments, he has a ready way to train himself for that every moment of his life — through the wise use of his speech. But if someone does not exert control over his lips, does not accustom himself to careful speech — ילבט — he will stumble in his actions as well (לבט related to לפת, in ולפתו ארחות דרכים, Job 6, 18). Ultimately, his entire conduct will show lack of seriousness and conscientiousness.

In other words, the moral integrity of a person is reflected not only in his deeds, but also in his speech, whereas the unscrupulous person allows himself to prate at random.

כֶּסֶף נִבְחָר לְשׁוֹן צַדִּיק
לֵב רְשָׁעִים כִּמְעָט:

*The tongue of, the righteous is choice silver;*
*for the heart of the wicked, indiscrimination is sufficient. (10, 20)*

לֵב צַדִּיק יֶהְגֶּה לַעֲנוֹת
וּפִי רְשָׁעִים יַבִּיעַ רָעוֹת:

*The heart of the righteous reflects before answering,*
*while the mouth of the lawless utters evil. (15, 28)*

The same can be said for society as a whole: It can go to ruin not only as a result of evil acts but also, and mainly, because of the debasement

of its spoken words; that which was beneficially built up by a good man
can be destroyed by the talk of a bad one.

בְּבִרְכַּת יְשָׁרִים תָּרוּם קָרֶת
וּבְפִי רְשָׁעִים תֵּהָרֵס:

*By the blessing of the upright a city is exalted,*
*and by the mouth of the wicked it is destroyed.* (11, 11)

For an evil man, words will serve mendacity — even at the risk of being
refuted in the next moment.

שְׂפַת־אֱמֶת תִּכּוֹן לָעַד
וְעַד־אַרְגִּיעָה לְשׁוֹן שָׁקֶר:

*The lips of truth will be established forever,*
*but a lying tongue only for a moment.* (12, 19)

Nothing so degrades a man as lying:

לֹא־נָאוָה לְנָבָל שְׂפַת־יֶתֶר
אַף כִּי־לְנָדִיב שְׂפַת־שָׁקֶר:

*Superfluous speech is not becoming even to the characterless;*
*Much less do lying lips suit a man of distinction.* (17, 7)

תּוֹעֲבַת ד' שִׂפְתֵי־שָׁקֶר
וְעֹשֵׂי אֱמוּנָה רְצוֹנוֹ:

*Lying lips are an abomination before God,*
*but those who act in faith have His approval.* (12, 22)

And if in the course of his business activities lying has become a man's
habitual vice, Mishlé warns us of the consequences:

רַע רַע יֹאמַר הַקּוֹנֶה
וְאֹזֵל לוֹ אָז יִתְהַלָּל:

*"It is bad, it is bad," says the buyer,*
*and after he goes away, he praises himself.* (20, 14)

פֹּעַל אוֹצָרוֹת בִּלְשׁוֹן שָׁקֶר
הֶבֶל נִדָּף מְבַקְשֵׁי־מָוֶת:

*The acquisition of treasures by a lying tongue,*
*like a vanishing breath, brings on ruin.* (21, 6)

Once the tongue is in the employment of falsehood, it is only one step
further for falsehood to become the servant of crime. Lying and crime
are soul-brothers, conspirators in league.

מֵרַע מַקְשִׁיב עַל־שְׂפַת־אָוֶן
שֶׁקֶר מֵזִין עַל־לְשׁוֹן הַוֹּת:

*He who looks for evil listens to the lips of injustice,*
*and lies listen to the tongue of corruption.* (17, 4)

Liars are welcome accomplices for the criminal, and lies are the first approach towards crime. No one commits a breach of law without planning to save himself, in case of discovery, by lying. If you are unable to
tell a lie, you will never listen to anyone who wishes to persuade you to
do a misdeed. Truthfulness is a protective armor against criminality.

דִּבְרֵי רְשָׁעִים אֱרָב־דָּם
וּפִי יְשָׁרִים יַצִּילֵם:

*The words of the wicked [incite to] a death-trap,*
*but the mouth of the righteous shall save him.* (12, 6)

The lips of the unscrupulous are so ready to lie that they are prepared to perpetrate the craftiest attempt at murder. Once a person gets used to lying, no crime is too heinous for him; the lie is accessory to crime. The mouth of the righteous, however, which is unable to utter an untruth, protects and saves him from all perverse alluring thoughts.

◉

Lying is fatal — not only in its guise as accomplice to crime, but also when it appears in the form of malevolence, instigation, hypocrisy, flattery, corruption, deception and fraud. In all these forms it becomes a crime in itself, undermining moral and social welfare. As a matter of fact, where conscience orders silence, even an honest word can become a serious offense.

בָּז־לְרֵעֵהוּ חֲסַר־לֵב
וְאִישׁ תְּבוּנוֹת יַחֲרִישׁ:
הוֹלֵךְ רָכִיל מְגַלֶּה־סוֹד
וְנֶאֱמַן־רוּחַ מְכַסֶּה דָבָר:

*He who despises his neighbor has no heart,*
*but an understanding man keeps silent.*
*The talebearer reveals what should be secret,*
*but a trustworthy spirit can conceal a matter.* (11, 12—13)

גּוֹלֶה סוֹד הוֹלֵךְ רָכִיל
וּלְפֹתֶה שְׂפָתָיו לֹא תִתְעָרָב:

*The one who reveals a secret is a slanderer;*
*and with one who opens wide his lips, do not be in league.* (20, 19)

מְכַסֶּה־פֶּשַׁע מְבַקֵּשׁ אַהֲבָה
וְשֹׁנֶה בְדָבָר מַפְרִיד אַלּוּף:

*He who covers up a transgression seeks love,*
*but he who repeats a word separates the most esteemed friend.* (17, 9)

דְּבַר־שֶׁקֶר יִשְׂנָא צַדִּיק
וְרָשָׁע יַבְאִישׁ וְיַחְפִּיר׃

A righteous man hates an untrue word,
but a wicked man makes everything more shameful and contemptible.
(13, 5)

רוּחַ צָפוֹן תְּחוֹלֵל גָּשֶׁם
וּפָנִים נִזְעָמִים לְשׁוֹן סָתֶר׃

The north wind brings rain,
and a secret whispering tongue, angry faces. (25, 23)

שֶׁשׁ־הֵנָּה שָׂנֵא ד׳
וְשֶׁבַע תּוֹעֲבַת נַפְשׁוֹ׃
עֵינַיִם רָמוֹת לְשׁוֹן שָׁקֶר
וְיָדַיִם שֹׁפְכוֹת דָּם־נָקִי׃
לֵב חֹרֵשׁ מַחְשְׁבוֹת אָוֶן
רַגְלַיִם מְמַהֲרוֹת לָרוּץ לָרָעָה׃
יָפִיחַ כְּזָבִים עֵד שָׁקֶר
וּמְשַׁלֵּחַ מְדָנִים בֵּין אַחִים׃

There are six things which the Lord hates,
but the seventh is an abomination to His Being:*
haughty eyes, a lying tongue,
and hands that shed innocent blood;
a heart which devises thoughts of injustice,
feet that are swift in running to evil,
a false witness spreading lies,
and he who causes discord between brethren. (6, 16—19)

The seventh includes and generates all the preceding. He who sows discord cannot even fathom the mischief and wrong that he instigates.

*Compare שבע. "seven" to שנת־שבע. Esther 2, 16

אָדָם בְּלִיַּעַל אִישׁ אָוֶן
הוֹלֵךְ עִקְּשׁוּת פֶּה:
קֹרֵץ בְּעֵינָו מֹלֵל בְּרַגְלָו
מֹרֶה בְּאֶצְבְּעֹתָיו:
תַּהְפֻּכוֹת בְּלִבּוֹ
חֹרֵשׁ רָע בְּכָל־עֵת
מִדְיָנִים יְשַׁלֵּחַ:
עַל־כֵּן פִּתְאֹם יָבוֹא אֵידוֹ
פֶּתַע יִשָּׁבֵר וְאֵין מַרְפֵּא:

*An unprincipled man, a man of iniquity*
*is he who goes about with a crooked mouth.*
*He winks his eyes, scrapes his feet,*
*points his fingers.*
*Upheaval is in his heart,*
*he continually devises evil,*
*sows discord.*
*Then his misfortune shall come suddenly;*
*unexpectedly, irremediably, he shall be broken.* (6, 12—15)

בְּאֶפֶס עֵצִים תִּכְבֶּה־אֵשׁ
וּבְאֵין נִרְגָּן יִשְׁתֹּק מָדוֹן:
פֶּחָם לְגֶחָלִים וְעֵצִים לְאֵשׁ
וְאִישׁ מִדְיָנִים לְחַרְחַר־רִיב:

*Without wood, the fire goes out,*
*and where there is no quarreler, contention ceases.*
*As a torch is to coals, wood to fire,*
*such is a contentious man, kindling and perpetuating strife.* (26, 20—21)

Peace and harmony are values to which we should be prepared to subordinate and sacrifice everything — except duty and conscience. Discord
and disharmony, on the other hand, bring calamity; they banish every
true joy from life. A person who is aware of this will always succeed,
whenever a quarrel arises — no matter what its external cause may

be — to gain self-control, forgiving inflicted injustice and, what is even
more difficult, admitting his own mistakes and asking forgiveness. Such
a person will do everything from the start in order not to let the fires of
discord be fanned.

In the text cited above, quarrels are compared to fire; Mishlé also compares it to the other destructive element, water:

פּוֹטֵר מַיִם רֵאשִׁית מָדוֹן
וְלִפְנֵי הִתְגַּלַּע הָרִיב נְטוֹשׁ:

*A breakthrough of water is the beginning of a quarrel:*
*then before it becomes more exposed, leave off contention.* (17, 14)

דִּבְרֵי נִרְגָּן כְּמִתְלַהֲמִים
וְהֵם יָרְדוּ חַדְרֵי־בָטֶן:

*The words of a contentious person are like self-justification,*
*and penetrate into the innermost recesses.* (18, 8)

The *nif'al* tense for the habitually irascible man, נרגן, designates him as
being possessed by a passion for quarrelling. His agitation carries him
away to irresponsible utterances. His words seem to be as מתלהמים
(from להם, related to לחם — warfare), they sound like self-justification,
like defense. However, instead of fending off the insult, instead of confin-
ing himself to refuting unjustified agression, he offends his adversary
with insults which penetrate into the depths of his being. Instead of
protecting himself, he destroys the other.

⊙

The most contemptible and destructive forms of lying, however, are
hypocrisy, flattery, and deceptive persuasion. Hypocrisy covers up true
convictions and intentions; flattery deceives about the real character of
a person; and deceptive persuasion distorts the genuine value of an action about to be carried out.

כֶּסֶף סִיגִים מְצֻפֶּה עַל־חָרֶשׂ
שְׂפָתַיִם דֹּלְקִים וְלֶב־רָע׃
בִּשְׂפָתָו יִנָּכֵר שׂוֹנֵא
וּבְקִרְבּוֹ יָשִׁית מִרְמָה׃
כִּי־יְחַנֵּן קוֹלוֹ אַל־תַּאֲמֶן־בּוֹ
כִּי שֶׁבַע תּוֹעֵבוֹת בְּלִבּוֹ׃
תִּכַּסֶּה שִׂנְאָה בְּמַשָּׁאוֹן
תִּגָּלֶה רָעָתוֹ בְקָהָל׃
כֹּרֶה שַּׁחַת בָּהּ יִפֹּל
וְגֹלֵל אֶבֶן אֵלָיו תָּשׁוּב׃
לְשׁוֹן־שֶׁקֶר יִשְׂנָא דַכָּיו
וּפֶה חָלָק יַעֲשֶׂה מִדְחֶה׃

*Like silver dross covering sherds*
*are lips which ensnare with a wicked heart.*
*With his lips the enemy dissembles,*
*and within himself he harbors deceit.*
*When he makes his voice sound agreeable, do not believe him:*
*for there are seven abominations in his heart;*
*though he covers his hatred with deceit,*
*his wickedness shall become exposed to all.*
*He who digs a pit shall fall into it;*
*he rolls a stone that will fall back on himself.*
*A lying tongue hates the ones who were defrauded by it,*
*and a smooth mouth makes for a slippery course.* (26, 23—28)

בְּפֶה חָנֵף יַשְׁחִת רֵעֵהוּ
וּבְדַעַת צַדִּיקִים יֵחָלֵצוּ׃

*With his mouth the flatterer destroys his neighbor,*
*but through self-knowledge the righteous will gain strength.* (11, 9)

אִישׁ חָמָס יְפַתֶּה רֵעֵהוּ
וְהוֹלִיכוֹ בְּדֶרֶךְ לֹא־טוֹב׃

*A man of iniquity shall persuade his neighbor,*
*and shall lead him in ways which are not good.*

עֹצֶה עֵינָיו לַחְשֹׁב תַּהְפֻּכוֹת
קֹרֵץ שְׂפָתָיו כִּלָּה רָעָה:

*He narrows his eyes to devise wrong actions,*
*crooks his lips and the evil is completed.* (16, 29—30)

כִּי נֹפֶת תִּטֹּפְנָה שִׂפְתֵי זָרָה
וְחָלָק מִשֶּׁמֶן חִכָּהּ:
וְאַחֲרִיתָהּ מָרָה כַלַּעֲנָה
חַדָּה כְּחֶרֶב פִּיּוֹת:

*From the lips of a perverted woman drips honey,*
*and her palate is smoother than oil;*
*but her end is more bitter than wormwood,*
*sharp as a two-edged sword.* (5, 3—4)

שׁוּחָה עֲמֻקָּה פִּי זָרוֹת
זְעוּם ד׳ יִפָּול־שָׁם:

*A deep pit is the mouth of perverse women;*
*he that causes God's anger shall fall into it.* (22, 14)

The deception does not even have to be intentional. One thoughtless or
frivolous word can cause our fellow-man to go astray; by treating a
serious matter lightly, we may help cause his downfall. What we meant
as a joke can be taken seriously by him; it can shake his conscientiousness and undermine his morality.

כְּמִתְלַהְלֵהַּ הַיֹּרֶה זִקִּים
חִצִּים וָמָוֶת:

*As one who for his recreation casts firebrands,*
*arrows and death,** *

---

*\*לאה, to tire out. in פיעל; hence the verb here would mean relieved of
tiredness.

כֵּן־אִישׁ רִמָּה אֶת־רֵעֵהוּ
וְאָמַר הֲלֹא־מְשַׂחֵק אָנִי

*thus is a man who deceives his neighbor*
*and says: I am only joking. (26, 18—19)*

אַל־תְּהִי עֵד־חִנָּם בְּרֵעֶךָ
וַהֲפִתִּיתָ בִּשְׂפָתֶיךָ׃

*Do not be an unintentionally harmful witness against your neighbor,*
*causing deceptive persuasion by your lips.*
Or:
*Do not be a witness against your neighbor about something unfounded,*
*and, by your lips, cause deceit. (24, 28)*

(The word 'éd means not only a witness in the judicial sense, but anyone
who guarantees for anything. See עד כזבים etc. in verse 21, 28: "He who
testifies to deception should disappear, while he who listens always
deserves to speak." חנם as in חנם מזרה הרשת in verse 1, 17; or in אל תרב
עם אדם חנם, verse 3, 30. והפתית is a combination of *hif'il* and *pi'él*: not
persuade deceitfully directly, but be the cause.)

Another warning that Mishlé wants to give us, if we understand it correctly, is that sometimes both sides in a dispute or disagreement are
wrong. In such a case, silence alone would be judicious. If you know of
anything hateful about your fellow, it would be just as unwise to express
approval which is not genuine as to spread malicious talk about him.
The only right thing to do is: keep quiet. What we speak should be true,
but we do not have to say everything that is true. This, we believe, is the
idea behind the verses:

מְכַסֶּה שִׂנְאָה שִׂפְתֵי־שָׁקֶר
וּמוֹצִא דִבָּה הוּא כְסִיל׃

*He who hides hatred is of lying lips,*
*and he who speaks slander is a fool.*

בְּרֹב דְּבָרִים לֹא יֶחְדַּל־פָּשַׁע
וְחוֹשֵׂךְ שְׂפָתָיו מַשְׂכִּיל:

*Where there are many words, evil will not be lacking,*
*but he who refrains from talking is wise. (10, 18—19)*

As we have learned, misuse of speech is destructive. On the proper use of the right word, on the other hand, blessing rests. The talent of eloquence is a special gift from the benevolent Almighty; and it requires particular help from heaven, when a speech is to be delivered, to have at one's disposal the right words for expressing his thoughts and feelings.

לְאָדָם מַעַרְכֵי־לֵב
וּמֵיְיָ מַעֲנֵה לָשׁוֹן:

*The preparations of the heart are man's,*
*but the discourse of the tongue is from God. (16, 1)*

It is interesting that *ma'aneh* means discourse, and *'anéh* denotes not only answering but, in general, to start speaking. This reflects the idea that the word must be preceded by thought: it must, so to speak, "answer" the thought — correspond to it and reflect it. But when, in addition to this quality, our speech is also pleasing and attractive to the audience, if our words combine truthfulness with מתק, נועם, חן — sweetness, beauty and pleasure — then indeed such speech attains its greatest effect.

לַחֲכַם־לֵב יִקָּרֵא נָבוֹן
וּמֶתֶק שְׂפָתַיִם יֹסִיף לֶקַח:

*The wise of heart shall become known as a man of discernment,*
*while the sweetness of lips increases learning (16, 21).*

To be sure, *chochmah* [wisdom] and *t'vunah* (understanding) must precede speech. The fundamental wisdom, *chochmah*, and the resulting conclusions for our lives, *tvunah,* should be the basis of our speech; and the man who gives expression to the dictates of wisdom and its inference by *t'vunah* is rightly called *navon* (a man of understanding). The final success of instruction, however, is achieved by מֶתֶק שְׂפָתִים, pleasantly appealing speech.

צוּף־דְּבַשׁ אִמְרֵי־נֹעַם

מָתוֹק לַנֶּפֶשׁ וּמַרְפֵּא לָעָצֶם:

*Pleasant words are as a honeycomb,*
*sweet to the soul and health to the bones.* (16, 24).

Such words are beneficial and invigorating to the spirit; but:

תּוֹעֲבַת ד׳ מַחְשְׁבוֹת רָע

וּטְהֹרִים אִמְרֵי־נֹעַם:

*The thoughts of the wicked are an abomination before the Lord,*
*as only pure words are pleasant words.* (15, 26)

Woe indeed if the most valuable gift to man, the faculty of speech, serves mean, impure and morally wrong purposes.

אֹהֵב טְהָור־לֵב

חֵן שְׂפָתָיו רֵעֵהוּ מֶלֶךְ:

*A friend who has a pure heart,*
*with grace in his lips, shall be companion to a king.* (22, 11)

Whoever is lucky enough to have a friend with a pure heart and kind lips has no need to change places with kings. He has a friend who will always convince him to act rightly, and this is a treasure of which kings cannot always boast.

תַּפּוּחֵי זָהָב בְּמַשְׂכִּיּוֹת כָּסֶף
דָּבָר דָּבֻר עַל־אָפְנָיו:

*Like golden apples in a silver sheath*
*is a word streamlined for its purpose.* (25, 11)

(The final Hebrew phrase means literally "on its wheels," i.e. so constructed as to conduct it smoothly towards its aim — the hearts and
minds of their listeners.)

The contents of such words are gold, the outer "garments" silver. While
the content of such a word is the most valuable part, and is compared to
solid gold, the attire is also important, compared to a silvery trans-
parent sheath, not obstructing the contents but letting them glow and
shine forth (מַשְׂכִּיּוֹת, from שׂכה, to look at).

The most apt word, however, can lose its value if it is spoken at an un-
suitable time:

שִׂמְחָה לָאִישׁ בְּמַעֲנֵה־פִיו
וְדָבָר בְּעִתּוֹ מַה־טּוֹב:

*A man has joy in the utterance of his mouth,*
*and a word at the right time, how good it is.* (15, 23)

A man who speaks finds pleasure in his words at any time, but in reality
they are good only when spoken at the right time.

⊙

Speech serves the most elevated human interests:

לְהָבִין מָשָׁל וּמְלִיצָה
דִּבְרֵי חֲכָמִים וְחִידֹתָם:

*to convey proverbs and poetry,*
*the words of the wise and their profound sayings.* (1, 6)

All these are carried by words.

But the indispensable prerequisite, even for wisdom and understanding, still remains moral probity:

פִּי־צַדִּיק יָנוּב חָכְמָה
וּלְשׁוֹן תַּהְפֻּכוֹת תִּכָּרֵת:
שִׂפְתֵי צַדִּיק יֵדְעוּן רָצוֹן
וּפִי רְשָׁעִים תַּהְפֻּכוֹת:

*The mouth of the righteous brings wisdom to maturity,*
*but the tongue of evil shall be destroyed.*
*The lips of the righteous are pleasing to God,*
*but the mouth of the wicked is evil. (10, 31—32)*

פִּיהָ פָּתְחָה בְחָכְמָה
וְתוֹרַת־חֶסֶד עַל־לְשׁוֹנָהּ:

*A woman of valour*
*opens her mouth with wisdom*
*and the teachings of lovingkindness are on her tongue. (31, 26)*

And thus wisdom speaks in the name of the blessed Almighty:

הֲלֹא כָתַבְתִּי לְךָ שָׁלִשִׁים
בְּמוֹעֵצוֹת וָדָעַת:
לְהוֹדִיעֲךָ קֹשְׁטְ אִמְרֵי אֱמֶת
לְהָשִׁיב אֲמָרִים אֱמֶת לְשֹׁלְחֶיךָ:

*See, I have written command-givers for you*
*with counsel and knowledge,*
*to let you know the moral truth demanded by words of truth,*
*that you may bring back truth in speaking to those who send you. (22,*
*20—21)*

The "second-in-command" after the king is משנה למלך, his co-adviser. The שליש is the third one, the executive, who transmits the king's order to the people, urging and supervising its implementation. The words of the Torah are compared to שלישים; they were not written merely for theoretical knowledge, but are the "command-bearers" of God, delivering to us the commandments given by the blessed Almighty; במועצות דעת in His wisdom He has "advised" us on our temporal and eternal welfare, by His profound "knowledge" of our nature and relationships, giving us a basis on which to shape our thoughts and feelings. The expression used here is not merely *emeth*, truth — the factual preciseness of things — but *koshét*, meaning a claim to the ethical integrity of our character, derived from and founded upon truth (see Psalms 60, 6). Once we have learned this, have absorbed within us these קושט אמרי אמת, and have let them become our שלישים, the ruling principles of our thinking and desires, only then can we carry out the mission of those who send us to reach understanding and teach it to them, speaking truth. Surely it is for this reason that the letters of the Torah are equipped with זיינים and *tagim* (tittles) — "weapons and crowns" — to give them the appearance of שלישים!

In order to be effective in advising and instructing, we are mainly dependent on words — words which have entered into the service of moral rectitude.

שִׂפְתֵי צַדִּיק יִרְעוּ רַבִּים
וֶאֱוִילִים בַּחֲסַר־לֵב יָמוּתוּ:

*The lips of the righteous feed many,*
*but the foolish perish for want of understanding. (10, 21)*

The Hebrew for "feed" literally means "pasture, provide grazing"; it is the way of the righteous to lead many on the right way and maintain them on it (as a shepherd leads a flock). The wrong which is done in the world is not always the result of bad will; it is often due to lack of understanding. (Those who do evil are like sheep without a shepherd.) Accordingly, the world is often a field where a morally instructive word can be profitable.

בְּשִׂפְתֵי נָבוֹן תִּמָּצֵא חָכְמָה
וְשֵׁבֶט לְגֵו חֲסַר־לֵב:

*On the lips of him who has discernment, wisdom is found,*
*but a rod is for the back of him who is devoid of understanding.* (10, 13)

The term *navon* denotes a man who not only acquires theoretical
knowledge, חכמה, but is also able to draw the right conclusions for life
and all its aspects. The words of such a *navon* are well suited to offer
teachings of wisdom, and his advice to the unperceiving can bring
improvement — something which otherwise (and even this is doubtful)
could be achieved only by chastisement.

הַכֵּר־פָּנִים בְּמִשְׁפָּט בַּל־טוֹב:
אֹמֵר לְרָשָׁע צַדִּיק אָתָּה
יִקְּבֻהוּ עַמִּים יִזְעָמוּהוּ לְאֻמִּים:
וְלַמּוֹכִיחִים יִנְעָם
וַעֲלֵיהֶם תָּבוֹא בִרְכַּת־טוֹב:
שְׂפָתַיִם יִשָּׁק
מֵשִׁיב דְּבָרִים נְכֹחִים:

*To let recognition of a person influence judgment is certainly not good;*
*but /even in other, non-judicial circumstances/ if one says to the wicked*
*"you are righteous,"*
communities shall brand him, nations shall condemn him.
*But to those who show the right way, there shall be good will,*
*and a good blessing shall come upon them.*
*Those lips should be kissed*
*that answer the right words.* (24, 23—26)

In legal verdicts, it is manifest duty of the conscience to weigh every
word as though on the balance. In social association, though, words and
opinions do not carry so much weight. Social formalities and politeness
can easily become flattery and, ultimately, the denial of every sincerity.

Should a morally depraved person be admired in society, no one, no matter how sincere his intentions are, can dare open his mouth on behalf of truth and justice without being branded a trouble maker. And so, through such falsehood and insincerity, the foundation of society is being undermined, and the cause of nations is seriously harmed.

⊙

An apt word can bring balm of consolation and healing to a sorrowing or injured spirit, as well as a calming peace to the agitated.

דְּאָגָה בְלֶב־אִישׁ יַשְׁחֶנָּה
וְדָבָר טוֹב יְשַׂמְּחֶנָּה:

*Care in the heart of a man — let him hold it down,*
*but a good word can transform it into cheerfulness.* (12, 25)

The word ישחנה from שחה means to bend, to hold down. A man should not let himself be conquered (overwhelmed) by his sorrow. A sympathetic word, however, can raise him up to cheerfulness.

יֵשׁ בּוֹטֶה כְּמַדְקְרוֹת חָרֶב
וּלְשׁוֹן חֲכָמִים מַרְפֵּא:

*Some speak as the piercing of a sword,*
*but the tongue of a wise man brings healing.* (12, 18)

מַרְפֵּא לָשׁוֹן עֵץ חַיִּים
וְסֶלֶף בָּהּ שֶׁבֶר בְּרוּחַ:

*A soothing tongue (can generate) a tree of life,*
*but vacillation, a break in the spirit.* (15, 4)

A thoughtless word can inflict deadening pain; the word of a wise person, however, brings only healing to the spirit, and may even plant the seed for a fruitbearing tree throughout a lifetime. One vacillating word, on the other hand (see Exodus 23, 8) can cause a lasting split in personality.

מַעֲנֶה־רַּךְ יָשִׁיב חֵמָה
וּדְבַר־עֶצֶב יַעֲלֶה־אָף׃

*A gentle answer appeases anger,*
*while a vexing word aggravates wrath.* (15, 1)

בְּאֹרֶךְ אַפַּיִם יְפֻתֶּה קָצִין
וְלָשׁוֹן רַכָּה תִּשְׁבָּר־גָּרֶם׃

*By forbearance is a superior persuaded,*
*and a soft tongue breaks a bone.* (25, 15)

A gentle word can disable an arm raised for hitting.

◉

The Book of Proverbs is full of descriptions of contrasts between wise men and fools. Obviously, these contrasts are apparent also in their speech. We have already endeavored to bring some of these proverbs; now let us cite some additional ones:

בְּפִי־אֱוִיל חֹטֶר גַּאֲוָה
וְשִׂפְתֵי חֲכָמִים תִּשְׁמוּרֵם׃

*Through the mouth of a fool his pride becomes his stick,*
**but the lips of the wise shall preserve them.** (14, 3)

We believe this means: the faculty of speech becomes a tool to the foolish person through which his pride grows. He likes to hear himself hold forth about his self-imagined greatness and superiority. Without words to utter this, his arrogance would remain only an inner feeling

without external significance. For the wise, on the other hand, his very
caution about speaking prevents him from becoming too proud. If
sometimes an expression of pride comes to his lips, he immediately
senses how ridiculous and undignified it would sound. Consequently he
locks his lips, and the fact that he does not let an overbearing word cross
their threshold, restrains his pride so that no haughtiness will emerge.

A wise man listens to this warning:

יְהַלֶּלְךָ זָר וְלֹא־פִיךָ
נָכְרִי וְאַל־שְׂפָתֶיךָ׃

*Let another man praise you and not your own mouth,*
*a stranger, but not your own lips. (27, 2)*

Even if the fame of your spiritual or ethical competence has reached the
ears of a wide circle and enjoys their appreciation, your own lips should
not find it possible to utter a word of self-praise.

חֲכָמִים יִצְפְּנוּ־דָעַת
וּפִי אֱוִיל מְחִתָּה קְרֹבָה׃

*Wise men conceal wisdom,*
*but the mouth of a fool is an imminent horror. (10, 14)*

Wise people know a great deal and foresee many things which they keep
to themselves, so as not to spread unnecessary panic. A fool, however,
knows no such discretion; he likes to speak of frightening and horrible
things, and spreads terror even where no cause for it exists.

פִּי־כְסִיל מְחִתָּה־לוֹ
וּשְׂפָתָיו מוֹקֵשׁ נַפְשׁוֹ׃

*A fool's mouth brings him horror,*
*and his lips are a snare for his soul. (18, 7)*

נֹצֵר פִּיו שֹׁמֵר נַפְשׁוֹ
פֹּשֵׂק שְׂפָתָיו מְחִתָּה־לוֹ:

*He who guards his mouth protects himself;*
*who speaks thoughtlessly, prepares his own fright. (13, 3)*

A fool speaks thoughtless words, without having calculated their consequences — and then is alarmed to see what he has wrought, and the responsibility he has brought upon himself.

⊙

בְּאָזְנֵי כְסִיל אַל־תְּדַבֵּר
כִּי־יָבוּז לְשֵׂכֶל מִלֶּיךָ:

*Do not speak in the ears of a fool,*
*for he will only despise the wisdom of your words. (23, 9)*

A *k'sil* is actually a conceited fool. He believes himself cleverer than the entire world, and is beyond accepting any reasonable words.

שׁוֹט לַסּוּס מֶתֶג לַחֲמוֹר
וְשֵׁבֶט לְגֵו כְּסִילִים:
אַל־תַּעַן כְּסִיל כְּאִוַּלְתּוֹ
פֶּן־תִּשְׁוֶה־לּוֹ גַם־אָתָּה:
עֲנֵה כְסִיל כְּאִוַּלְתּוֹ
פֶּן־יִהְיֶה חָכָם בְּעֵינָיו:

*A whip for the horse, a bridle for the donkey,*
*and a rod for the back of fools.*
*Do not answer a fool according to his folly,*
*lest you also should be like him;*
*but answer such a fool as his folly deserves,*
*lest he think himself wise. (26, 3–5)*

A conceited fool (*k'sil*) cannot be influenced by intelligent reasoning. Such people learn their lesson only by chastisement, inflicted upon them by man or destiny. Therefore do not answer such a person by involving him in a profound discussion. He would take this to mean that you evaluate his opinions as equal to your own; he has his belief, and you have yours, and so you are standing ostensibly upon equal ground. On the other hand, you are not to keep silent either; for then such a person would consider himself irrefutably right. Answer him briefly, to the effect that his opinions and utterances are false and too objectionable for discussion, and refer him to the basic truth which causes you to reject his opinions.

# IV

## PARENTS AND CHILDREN

Parents can enjoy a great deal of happiness from their children during their lifetime — provided the children have been brought up well. But a child who turns out badly is bound to cause such anguish to his parents as to banish almost every other joy from their lives.

In the Book of Proverbs this fact is stressed time and again, as it urges parents to do their utmost to secure happiness, and not sorrow, from their children:

בֵּן חָכָם יְשַׂמַּח־אָב
וּבֵן כְּסִיל תּוּגַת אִמּוֹ:

*A wise son gladdens a father,*
*but a foolish son is the grief of his mother.* (10, 1)

It is interesting that joy from a successful son is foretold here to the father, while sorrow from an unsuccessful son is linked with the mother. We believe this may be based on the following consideration: No matter how much a father does for his child, it cannot be compared to the sacrifices and privations of a mother. For her, months and years of suffering and renunciation set in from the very beginning of her child's existence. By the time the father directs his personal attention to the child's development, the mother has already devoted years of constant care to his physical, spiritual, and moral growth. It follows that if the child turns out to be well-brought-up, and the parents are fortunate enough to find joy in a wise and successful son, the father has won a big prize — in return for a comparatively low stake. If, on the other hand, the child becomes a *k'sil,* an inept, foolish person, then who can fathom the grief of his mother? She is forced to admit that she has wasted years of anxious days and sleepless nights, that she has spent the best part of her physical strength and mental energy, and all this for what result? — a *k'sil*!

יֹלֵד כְּסִיל לְתוּגָה לוֹ
וְלֹא יִשְׂמַח אֲבִי נָבָל:

*He who begets an unwise son will have sorrow,*
*and the father of a depraved son has no joy.* (17, 21)

כַּעַס לְאָבִיו בֵּן כְּסִיל
וּמֶמֶר לְיוֹלַדְתּוֹ:

*A foolish son is a vexation to his father,*
*and bitterness to her who bore him.* (17, 25)

The term *ka'as* (vexation, anger, annoyance) specifically means a recurrent agitation caused by particular incidents. The word *memer* (bitterness), from מרר or מרה (as in מורת רוח), is in an emotion which constantly dominates the spirit. A man is diverted by outside interests and by his professional activities. A woman, even while attending to most of her work, can give free play to her thoughts. Accordingly, the gloom of a woman's soul is far deeper and more lasting.

גִּיל יָגִיל אֲבִי צַדִּיק
וְיוֹלֵד חָכָם יִשְׂמַח בּוֹ:

*The father of a righteous son has great happiness,*
*and he who begets a wise son has joy of him.* (23, 24)

The greatest joy to a father, the joy which may be voiced loudly (as indicated by the word *gil*, related to *kol*) is a son who knows where his duties lie and accomplishes them faithfully. Once the son proves this by his conduct in life, his spiritual and moral worth is established. The right conduct in life is the only proof of true wisdom. But the father of a wise son may also be happy, for he has reason to hope that the life of his son will remain in harmony with his wisdom, and that his conduct will be in keeping with the sterling worth and truth of this wisdom, if he but acknowledges and follows it.

Yet if parents wish to enjoy the happiness of righteous and wise children, they have to earn it! They will have to begin by influencing their child at an early age; they will have to be firm in their resolution to make his spiritual and moral development their prime concern. It is no coincidence that after the verse at the beginning of this chapter ("A wise son gladdens a father, but a foolish son is the grief of his mother") the next sentence in Mishlé reads:

לֹא יוֹעִילוּ אֹיצְרוֹת רֶשַׁע
וּצְדָקָה תַּצִּיל מִמָּוֶת׃

*Treasures acquired by lawlessness shall be of no avail,*
*but righteousness will save from fatal ruin.* (10, 2)

This conveys to parents: if you wish to see joy from your children, do not let their material wealth be your primary concern. First of all, make sure that they become upright, God-fearing, Torah-observing men and women; for this is the basis of their future well-being and their protection from ruin. "Fear of the Lord is the beginning of wisdom; fools despise both wisdom and discipline." This we read among the opening proverbs in the Book of Mishlé (1, 7).

מְשַׁדֶּד־אָב יַבְרִיחַ אֵם
בֵּן מֵבִישׁ וּמַחְפִּיר׃

*A robber of his father's property and his mother's domesticity*
*is a son who brings shame and disgrace.* (19, 26)

This expression is even stronger than the previous one: *m'shaddéd*, plunders; *yavri-ach*, drives away. This, we believe, is its meaning: The shame and disgrace that a misbehaving son causes his parents, make his father's possessions as well as his mother's domestic life worthless. Because of him, his father feels destitute and his mother homeless. The terms *mévish* and *machpir* actually denote that he frustrates the expectations of his parents and causes them to realize the futility, perhaps even the inadequacy, of their efforts at education. In general, בוש applies to the future, חפר to the past.

מַה־בְּרִי וּמַה־בַּר־בִּטְנִי
וּמֶה בַּר־נְדָרָי:

*What, my son? and what, son of my womb?*
*and what, son of my vows?* (31, 2)

Thus begins a mother's admonition to her son, the king. A true mother has been preparing her thoughts for the spiritual future of her child while he was yet in her womb; her solemn vows accompany his entrance into the world. He is the son of her womb and the son of her vows. A mother's thoughts and emotions during the time that she bears and suckles her child are not without effect. The saying "to imbibe something with one's mother's milk" is no empty phrase. That is the time when the seed is planted for the child's qualities of character, for gentleness or violence, for modesty or sensuality, for a conduct of nobility or vulgarity. This seed is planted within her child by his mother's thoughts while he is still physically connected with her. After that it is his mother's example which shows his awakening soul the ideas that he should follow — truth, decency, purity, or their opposites! Showing her child the right way takes intelligence and firm resolve on the part of a mother, for the success of his future behavior depends upon her teaching him the first requirement: to control his own will.

And so, when this son of a mother's womb and his mother's vows has become a king, wishing to transmit wisdom to his people, he looks back upon the period of his earliest childhood, saying:

כִּי־בֵן הָיִיתִי לְאָבִי
רַךְ וְיָחִיד לִפְנֵי אִמִּי:
וַיֹּרֵנִי וַיֹּאמֶר לִי
יִתְמָךְ־דְּבָרַי לִבֶּךְ
שְׁמֹר מִצְוֹתַי וֶחְיֵה:
קְנֵה חָכְמָה קְנֵה בִינָה

*Yet was I a son to my father,*
*tender and alone before my mother.*
*Then he taught me and said to me:*
*Let your heart hold fast my words,*
*keep my commandments, and live;*
*acquire wisdom, acquire understanding. . .(4, 3—5)*

⊙

חֲנֹךְ לַנַּעַר עַל־פִּי דַרְכּוֹ
גַּם כִּי־יַזְקִין לֹא־יָסוּר מִמֶּנָּה:

*Train a youth according to his way;*
*even when he grows old, he will not depart from it. (22, 6)*

The word חנך (train) actually means to dedicate, to initiate into one's
vocation. The next word is לנער (not את הנער) — literally, to the youth;
i.e. guide, train, dedicate whatever is "to" the youth, whatever he has
brought with him in the way of talents and capabilities for the life which
lies before him. The phrase על פי דרכו can mean either the way he will
have to follow in the future, or the way in which he acts already in his
early years.

גַּם בְּמַעֲלָלָיו יִתְנַכֶּר־נָעַר
אִם־זַךְ וְאִם־יָשָׁר פָּעֳלוֹ:

*Even by his childish doings a youth is known,*
*whether his actions are pure and honest. (20, 11)*

(מעלליו — his actions [while in the stage] of development, from עלל; a
young human being who is still in the process of development is עול.)

Here is the whole principle of education in a nutshell! Our task of educating is חנוך, initiation into a sacred calling; we are to conceive of it as *consecration*. However, just as our Sanctuary and our sacred objects were not consecrated by mere words but by being put initially to their predetermined use, so too our children are to be introduced and accustomed to their destined task in life not mainly by words, but by practical actions.

Eventually, having reached responsibility and maturity before God, they will have to know by themselves which duties to fulfill and what to avoid. These duties should be practiced already in childhood, under our guidance and supervision, so that when left to his own judgment in the future, our child will walk by nature only in good ways, pleasing to God, as we have shown him. Shown to whom? — *la-na'ar* — taking into account all his talents and aptitudes, his way of thinking, his sensibilities and his feelings, his wishes and his motivations, his talk and his actions. Every faculty should go into the service of the good, should be made ready for the good and deflected from evil. There is no tendency which, taken by itself, is innately either good or evil. Everything depends on the way in which it is used. By entrusting to us that which is most sacred to Him, a child's soul, God expects us to win *all* of our child's faculties *exclusively* for the good.

In working for this end, we should always have a twofold aim in mind: we are to teach the child על פי דרכו. It is not sufficient to consider his education as a general objective. We are enjoined to observe the young person individually and to study how his various faculties, abilities and tendencies relate to the various aspects of this task. In itself the duty of truthfulness, virtue, fairness and doing what is pleasing in God's sight is one and the same for everybody: the one duty revealed to us by God in His Torah. However, its fulfillment takes a different form with each person, according to his individual characteristics. Some things which are difficult for one person may be easy for another, and vice-versa. Some things which may be attractive to one person leave the next one indifferent. And so, each child has to be guided and trained either to restrain himself or to urge himself on, according to his own individual traits. Every child develops his education into an individual task.

There are, however, two traits of conduct which the Book of Proverbs particularly emphasizes. These characteristics may make the difference between a negative and a positive human character, and they reveal themselves already in childhood. If parents wish to have their children start out in the right direction, these characteristics should command their full attention: *im zach v'im yashar: moral purity* and *straightforward honesty*. They can be observed *b'ma'alalav*, when the child is acting in free, uncontrolled behavior, at such times when his inherent inclinations come to expression. Parents should ask themselves about each one of their children separately, whether he tends to greediness, or if he has a dominant trait of pleasure in sensual enjoyment. For these are inclinations which threaten to become obstacles to a child's future moral behavior. The same holds for insincerity and lack of veracity, which endanger his future conduct of integrity. Greediness (an undue demand for sweets) and lack of veracity are vices which a wise education should counteract most vigorously of all.

אִוֶּלֶת קְשׁוּרָה בְלֶב־נָעַר
שֵׁבֶט מוּסָר יַרְחִיקֶנָּה מִמֶּנּוּ:

*Foolishness is bound up in the heart of a youth,*
*but the rod of correction shall drive it far from him.* (22, 15)

Let us not speak of a "bad" child; there is no such thing as a bad child. A person can be branded "bad" only if he transgresses with a fully nature mind. The mind of a youth, however, has not come to full maturity; it has yet to reach maturity through your guidance and teaching. Your educating influence is called upon to combat not badness, but want of judgment.

Regarding the manner of educating, two terms recur in our proverbs which may easily be given a one-sided and therefore incorrect interpretation. These are words from the root יסר (derived from this: מוסר) and שבט. The term יסר includes every influence upon character-formation, whether by words, presentation, admonition, reproach or

reprimand, or by any other procedure that causes painful awareness —
for instance, non-fulfillment of wishes, refusal, deprivation, and even the
infliction of physical pain by beating. All of these means may be applied
according to necessity, but beating — and let this be said right now — as
a very last expedient. Only when speech is no longer — or not yet — effective, can striking a child be excused.

תֵּחַת גְּעָרָה בְמֵבִין
מֵהַכּוֹת כְּסִיל מֵאָה:

*More penetrating is a rebuke to one who understands*
*than a hundred blows given a fool.* (17, 10)

גַּם עֲנוֹשׁ לַצַּדִּיק לֹא־טוֹב
לְהַכּוֹת נְדִיבִים עַל־יֹשֶׁר:

*To the righteous, too, punishment does no good;*
*striking a noble-minded person goes beyond what is right.* (17, 26)

בִּדְבָרִים לֹא־יִוָּסֶר עָבֶד
כִּי־יָבִין וְאֵין מַעֲנֶה:

*A slave will not be corrected by words,*
*even though he understands and makes no reply.* (29, 19)

שׁוֹט לַסּוּס מֶתֶג לַחֲמוֹר
וְשֵׁבֶט לְגֵו כְּסִילִים:

*A whip for the horse, a bridle for the donkey,*
*and a rod for the back of fools.* (26, 3)

From all of these sayings, it follows that hitting (physical punishment)
should occur only as a rare and unfortunate exception, and that parents
whose ordinary means of discipline is beating will undoubtedly have
cause for alarm at the results of their education. A beating is degrading
to noble natures and, according to our Book of Proverbs, is unavoidable

only where an animal or a slave is concerned; in other words, where animal-like characteristics and a base nature dominate in the person.

Now, the word יסר does not necessarily mean punishment, and least of all physical chastisement. It is related to יצר, to form, to create—i.e. circumscription of spiritual and ethical energy, reducing it to its proper, predetermined boundaries and measurements; in other words, formation of a way of moral behavior. The admonitions and warnings of the king's mother to her son about the conduct expected of him and the duties he is to fulfill are characterized by forms of the word יסר.

While in the context of בן סורר ומורה and מוציא שם רע, the term יסר certainly denotes corporal punishment, it just as certainly means (in Deut. 21, 18 and 22, 18) the instruction by trial and privation which was meted out in the wilderness. The direct revelation of God on Mt. Sinai is also termed יסר (in Deut. 4, 36; see also Deut. 11, 2). In our Book of Proverbs, the word מוסר is always found alongside חכמה, connoting the practical lessons of morality that reinforce theoretic wisdom (thus 1, 2 and 7, and 23, 23).

Likewise, the word שבט does not always have to remind us literally of a rod. It designates equally any chastisement which is aimed at betterment through suffering, privation, etc., in other words, such dispensation from God as inflicts suffering for the sake of teaching (as evident from II Samuel 7, 14; Ps. 89, 33 and 23, 4, etc.). Accordingly, in Proverbs, too, we are to understand from the word *shévet* any influence which makes the child painfully aware of his incorrect behavior. We are not to shirk our duty and avoid exerting of such an influence, for its omission, especially during the years of early childhood, will not fail to take its toll.

Yet, it does not mean that for this purpose either a rod or a whip is needed. Anything which makes the child painfully realize his misbehavior, such as the denial of a pleasure, or even the denial of a mother's friendly look, her show of sorrow about the child's naughtiness —all these should be enough of a *shévet* in the right education, על פי דרכו, with particular attention to the individual traits of the child.

Basically, this requires calmness and a seriousness of purpose. Violence should be avoided, as well as excessive indulgence—and this is where mothers mainly go wrong. And so the Proverbs admonish us:

שֵׁבֶט וְתוֹכַחַת יִתֵּן חָכְמָה
וְנַעַר מְשֻׁלָּח מֵבִישׁ אִמּוֹ:

*Discipline and reprimand give wisdom,*
*while a child left to himself causes shame to his mother. (29, 15)*

חוֹשֵׂךְ שִׁבְטוֹ שׂוֹנֵא בְנוֹ
וְאֹהֲבוֹ שִׁחֲרוֹ מוּסָר:

*He who abstains from chastisement hates his child,*
*but he who loves him disciplines him diligently. (13, 24)*

אַל־תִּמְנַע מִנַּעַר מוּסָר
כִּי־תַכֶּנּוּ בַשֵּׁבֶט לֹא יָמוּת:
אַתָּה בַּשֵּׁבֶט תַּכֶּנּוּ
וְנַפְשׁוֹ מִשְּׁאוֹל תַּצִּיל:

*Do not withhold discipline from the child,*
*for even if you beat him with a rod, he will not die.*
*You beat him with a rod,*
*and save his soul from ruin. (23, 13—14)*

(In the phrases חושך שבטו and אל תמנע מנער both חשך and מנע mean the omission of something which is required — in this context, the omission of a corrective influence where it is needed for the education of the child.)

⊙

יַסֵּר בִּנְךָ וִינִיחֶךָ
וְיִתֵּן מַעֲדַנִּים לְנַפְשֶׁךָ:

*Be serious in the education of your child,*
*and it will give you satisfaction*
*and grant great joy to your soul. (29, 17)*

יַסֵּר בִּנְךָ כִּי־יֵשׁ תִּקְוָה
וְאֶל־הֲמִיתוֹ אַל־תִּשָּׂא נַפְשֶׁךָ:

*Influence your child by education, for there is always hope;*
*and do not pay attention to his crying.* (19, 18)

Educating a child is not an easy task, and often a great deal of patience
and constant serious application is needed in order to succeed. The success, however — this the Proverbs assure us — will not fail to come; and
if the task was hard, the knowledge that one has given his child a sound
upbringing is even more gratifying.

Our Proverbs give us two counsels: Never give up hope, never stop the
task of educating, thinking that in any case it won't help any more; and
never let your child obtain anything by sobbing.

Whatever you can permit your child, allow him to have it, and don't say
"no" too quickly when it is not necessary. However, once you have said
"no," don't let yourself be persuaded by his tearful crying to change
your mind. The first skill to be mastered by a mother who means to
bring up her children properly is to be able to bear a child's screaming.

בֵּן חָכָם מוּסַר אָב
וְלֵץ לֹא־שָׁמַע גְּעָרָה:

*A wise son /shows/ the education of his father,*
*but the sacrilegious has never heard a reprimand.* (13, 1)

(The word *létz* mostly means a person who mocks whatever is sacred.)

People rightly consider a well-behaved son the product of a good education, and the approval bestowed on him reflects upon the father too. On
the other hand, when people see someone who makes light of everything
sacred, they conclude that this is the result of some neglect in his upbringing and that he was not corrected at the right time in his youth.

שְׁמַע בְּנִי מוּסַר אָבִיךָ
וְאַל־תִּטֹּשׁ תּוֹרַת אִמֶּךָ:
כִּי לִוְיַת חֵן הֵם לְרֹאשֶׁךָ
וַעֲנָקִים לְגַרְגְּרֹתֶיךָ:

*Hear, my son, the educating word of your father,*
*and do not forsake the teaching of your mother;*
*for they shall be a charm of grace for your head*
*and gems about your throat. (1, 8—9)*

While educating and instructing a child are the tasks of parents on the
one hand, on the other hand obedience is the first and foremost duty of
the child. "Honor your father and mother" means primarily: Obey
your father and mother. All other demonstrations of filial love are mere
trimmings, if obedience is lacking.

In this passage we have מוסר אב and תורת אם; *torath ém,* a mother's lessons, are taught mainly before the child comes consciously to absorb
education, at an early age. When he grows older, he may easily think
himself more intelligent than his mother and rebel against the
educational demands of his father. For those reasons we are advised
here: Always accept your father's education and do not abandon your
mother's lessons. You may already have become an adult, whose head,
ראשך, rests maturely on your neck, גרגורתיך (the head resting on the
neck indicates the seat of mental ability and the controlling factor of
your entire creative and active being); yet even after you have become
an adult, a man of independent judgment — even then the lessons which
you have learned from your father in the past (and may be fortunate
enough to receive in the present too) — let them be your most precious
ornament, complementing your own intellectual ability. This לוית חן will
be the badge of nobility in your life and earn for you the goodwill of
both God and men. For the course of our thoughts and wishes, our
work and actions, will always remain based upon the influence exercised
by our parents; and their influence on our ethical and spiritual life
should remain our guide and our guard throughout life. Therefore:

נְצֹר בְּנִי מִצְוַת אָבִיךָ
וְאַל־תִּטֹּשׁ תּוֹרַת אִמֶּךָ:
קָשְׁרֵם עַל־לִבְּךָ תָמִיד
עָנְדֵם עַל־גַּרְגְּרֹתֶיךָ:
בְּהִתְהַלֶּכְךָ תַּנְחֶה אֹתָךְ
בְּשָׁכְבְּךָ תִּשְׁמֹר עָלֶיךָ
וַהֲקִיצוֹתָ הִיא תְשִׂיחֶךָ:
כִּי נֵר מִצְוָה וְתוֹרָה אוֹר
וְדֶרֶךְ חַיִּים תּוֹכְחוֹת מוּסָר:

*My son, preserve the commandments of your father,*
*and do not forsake the teaching of your mother.*
*Bind them continually on your heart,*
*tie them around your throat.*
*When you are walking, it shall lead you,*
*when you lie down, it shall watch over you;*
*and when you awake, it shall be first to address you.*
*For the commandment is a shining lamp,*
*and teaching is a beam of light,*
*and the course of life lies within the admonitions of education.* (6, 20—23)

Another proverb enjoins us to live in such a way that:

יִשְׂמַח־אָבִיךָ וְאִמֶּךָ
וְתָגֵל יוֹלַדְתֶּךָ:

*Your father and your mother shall be glad,*
*and she who bore you shall rejoice.* (23, 25)

The most powerful motive for leading a valiant and blameless life is to give happiness to one's parents. Again, the mother's share in her child's education, and consequently in its success, is particularly emphasized. And so, when she has gone the way of all flesh,

קָמוּ בָנֶיהָ וַיְאַשְּׁרוּהָ
בַּעְלָהּ וַיְהַלְלָהּ׃

*Her sons rise up and laud her,*
*her husband, and he praises her.* (31, 28)

⊙

The most dangerous symptom for a threatening era of decline is, according to the Book of Mishlé, the absence of filial respect. Once obedience, esteem and respect of parents have gone from the hearts of men, once the strong, all-knowing son looks down in disparagement on his aged mother, once disdain for the older generation becomes the main characteristic of the present one, as it arrogantly holds fathers and mothers in contempt, then a period of depravity is sure to set in, as it deteriorates toward everything which is base, brutal and evil.

שְׁמַע לְאָבִיךָ זֶה יְלָדֶךָ
וְאַל־תָּבוּז כִּי־זָקְנָה אִמֶּךָ׃

*Remain obedient to the father who begot you,*
*and do not despise when your mother has grown old.* (23, 22)

בֵּן חָכָם יְשַׂמַּח־אָב
וּכְסִיל אָדָם בּוֹזֶה אִמּוֹ׃

*A wise son endeavors to gladden his father,*
*but the most unwise among men is one who despises his mother.* (15, 20)

עַיִן תִּלְעַג לְאָב
וְתָבֻז לִיקֲּהַת־אֵם
יִקְּרוּהָ עֹרְבֵי־נַחַל
וְיֹאכְלוּהָ בְנֵי־נָשֶׁר׃

*An eye that mocks his father*
*and despises the dullness of his mother,*
*the ravens of the valley must pick it out,*
*and the young eagles shall eat it.* (30, 17)

מְקַלֵּל אָבִיו וְאִמּוֹ
יִדְעַךְ נֵרוֹ בֶּאֱשׁוּן חֹשֶׁךְ:

Whoever curses his father and mother,
his lamp shall be extinguished in blackest darkness. (20, 20)

דּוֹר אָבִיו יְקַלֵּל
וְאֶת־אִמּוֹ לֹא יְבָרֵךְ:
דּוֹר טָהוֹר בְּעֵינָיו
וּמִצֹּאָתוֹ לֹא רֻחָץ:
דּוֹר מָה־רָמוּ עֵינָיו
וְעַפְעַפָּיו יִנָּשֵׂאוּ:
דּוֹר חֲרָבוֹת שִׁנָּיו
וּמַאֲכָלוֹת מְתַלְּעֹתָיו
לֶאֱכֹל עֲנִיִּים מֵאֶרֶץ
וְאֶבְיוֹנִים מֵאָדָם:

A generation which curses its father
and has no blessing for its mother,
a generation that is blameless in its own eyes,
yet has not been washed of its filth —
that generation, how high are its eyes
and how lifted its eyelids —
that generation, whose teeth are swords,
and their fangs as knives,
to devour the poor from the earth,
and from mankind those unable to protect themselves. (30, 11—14)

◉

עֲטֶרֶת זְקֵנִים בְּנֵי בָנִים
וְתִפְאֶרֶת בָּנִים אֲבוֹתָם:

The crown of the aged are children's children,
and the glory of children are their parents. (17, 6)

The greatest happiness of aged parents is to see their children's children being raised in their spirit. Has the education that they gave their children been sound or not? The answer will be found in the way in which their grandchildren are brought up. If this is indeed in accordance with their ideas, it forms the crowning achievement of their lives and ambitions. But when does such a fortunate situation arise? — only when children can be proud of their parents and, in truth, are proud of them. It arises when the children in turn find their greatest happiness in bringing up their own sons and daughters in the same spirit, in order to make them worthy grandchildren of their parents.

# V

## RICH AND POOR

עָשִׁיר וָרָשׁ נִפְגָּשׁוּ
עֹשֵׂה כֻלָּם ד':

*Rich and poor meet,*
*God is the Maker of them all. (22, 2)*

When two people meet, each is going in a direction toward the starting-point of the other. The rich goes downhill, and the poor goes upwards. An observer who contemplates this simultaneous occurrence will conclude that man's destiny lies exclusively neither in wealth nor in poverty. Both conditions are equally necessary in God's purposes for human society as a whole, and even for the fulfillment of our task as individuals. Only one who proves himself both on the ascending and on the descending path of fate can reach such perfection as is attainable upon earth. God is the Maker of both the fall and the rise of human society.

⊙

שְׁתַּיִם שָׁאַלְתִּי מֵאִתָּךְ
אַל־תִּמְנַע מִמֶּנִּי בְּטֶרֶם אָמוּת:
שָׁוְא וּדְבַר־כָּזָב הַרְחֵק מִמֶּנִּי
רֵאשׁ וָעֹשֶׁר אַל־תִּתֶּן־לִי
הַטְרִיפֵנִי לֶחֶם חֻקִּי:
פֶּן־אֶשְׂבַּע וְכִחַשְׁתִּי

*Two requests I have of You,*
*deny them not before I die:*
*Vanity and falsehood remove far from me,*
*give me neither poverty nor riches.*
*For nourishment let me find the bread allotted to me,*

וְאָמַרְתִּי מִי ד'
וּפֶן־אִוָּרֵשׁ וְגָנַבְתִּי
וְתָפַשְׂתִּי שֵׁם אֱלֹהָי:

*lest I become full and deny, and say: Who is God!*
*Or lest I become poor and a thief,*
*and yet hold on to the name of my God!* (30, 7—9)

At both extremes temptation threatens us. Our moral rectitude and
purity are imperiled both at the height and in the depths. At the top,
glaring brightness dazzles the clarity of our view, while in the depths
darkness obscures it, and we run the risk of substituting useless baubles
for the gold of truth, and lies of deception for the confidence of conviction. When at the top, one thinks he can easily do without God, and he
says, "Why, who is God?" At the other extreme, menaced by impoverishment, one believes he may permit himself dishonesty, and still
be allowed to call the Deity *his* God. In other words, riches easily lead
to the denial of God, and poverty to חלול השם, the desecration of God's
name.

Therefore, the sage asks God to let him be neither wealthy nor poor, but
to merely let him find his daily bread. He realizes that his spiritual and
moral health remain out of danger only under moderate circumstances,
and he desires nothing else until the close of his life. He knows that the
molding of his being ends only with the end of his existence on earth,
and that no wise man can trust or assume that his own moral fortitude is
impervious to harm or corruption as long as he still breathes the air of
temporal life.

◉

רָשׁ וְאִישׁ תְּכָכִים נִפְגָּשׁוּ
מֵאִיר עֵינֵי שְׁנֵיהֶם ד'

*If a poor man and an artful man meet,*
*God gives the eyes of both illumination.* (29, 13)

If a poor man, on his way up, and a crafty, cunning man, going
downhill, meet on the way, God removes the scales from their eyes. The
poor man, who witnesses the descent of the artful one, is warned to hold

on to honesty, simplicity and probity, because he sees that it is the lack
of these qualities which caused the downfall of the cunning operator.
The latter, on the other hand, can learn from the ascent of the poor man
that it will be useless to redouble his crafty tricks in order to climb up
again. On the contrary, he would do better to shed his bad habits, which
could not even help him at the top when he was there already. How
much less can they enable him to make a truly lasting ascent! He can
see for himself that the man of small means is on his way up without
craft or cunning. Then let him learn from this that honesty, simplicity
and integrity are the best "climbing poles".

◉

כַּבֵּד אֶת־ד' מֵהוֹנֶךָ
וּמֵרֵאשִׁית כָּל־תְּבוּאָתֶךָ:
וְיִמָּלְאוּ אֲסָמֶיךָ שָׂבָע
וְתִירוֹשׁ יְקָבֶיךָ יִפְרֹצוּ:
מוּסַר ד' בְּנִי אַל־תִּמְאָס
וְאַל־תָּקֹץ בְּתוֹכַחְתּוֹ:
כִּי אֶת אֲשֶׁר יֶאֱהַב ד' יוֹכִיחַ
וּכְאָב אֶת־בֵּן יִרְצֶה:
אַשְׁרֵי אָדָם מָצָא חָכְמָה
וְאָדָם יָפִיק תְּבוּנָה:
כִּי טוֹב סַחְרָהּ מִסְּחַר־כָּסֶף
וּמֵחָרוּץ תְּבוּאָתָהּ:

*Honor God with your wealth,*
*and with the first fruits of all your produce.*
*Then your provisions will be filled with [the aura of] satisfaction,*
*and your vats shall overflow with new wine.*
*But, my son, do not despise God's chastening education,*
*and be not unwilling to accept His admonition;*
*For whom God loves, He corrects*
*even as a father [corrects] a son in whom he wants to delight.*
*For only such a man strides towards happiness, who has found Wisdom*
*and has gained Understanding from it.*
*For her trade is better than silver trade,*
*her gain better than the finest gold.*

יְקָרָה הִיא מִפְּנִינִים
וְכָל־חֲפָצֶיךָ לֹא יִשְׁווּ־בָהּ:
אֹרֶךְ יָמִים בִּימִינָהּ
בִּשְׂמֹאולָהּ עֹשֶׁר וְכָבוֹד:
דְּרָכֶיהָ דַרְכֵי־נֹעַם
וְכָל־נְתִיבֹתֶיהָ שָׁלוֹם:
עֵץ־חַיִּים הִיא לַמַּחֲזִיקִים בָּהּ
וְתֹמְכֶיהָ מְאֻשָּׁר:

*It is more precious than pearls,*
*and all the things you desire are not to be compared to her.*
*Length of days is in her right hand,*
*and in her left, riches and honor.*
*Her ways are the ways of bliss,*
*and all her paths are peace.*
*She is a tree of life to those who hold on to her,*
*and those who follow her find a blissful union* (3, 9-18)

The importance of material possessions should not be underestimated. Essentially they make it possible for us to fulfill our task in life and to advance the aims which God has entrusted to human care. If the material possessions which God has given into our care are faithfully put to such use as He has shown us, we may confidently look forward to receiving His lasting blessing. Make sure that God considers you a trustworthy administrator of His gifts; give priority to God's honor and His purpose, putting your own honor and calculations last. Then God will gladly appoint you as His custodian of charity and the treasurer of His goods, and He will increase your wealth.

But while material possessions do have importance, they are neither the *most* important nor the most desirable, nor even the most beneficial things a man might strive for. There are other, superior goals, far more promising to our happiness. These are seldom to be found, however, on the path of undisturbed well-being. On the contrary, flourishing material welfare makes us oblivious of these goals; and only at times when our material well-being has been thoroughly shaken do we become fully aware of the importance, eternal and inviolable, of these other values which give us inspiration and can never be impaired.

Let us therefore not underestimate God's salutary goodness, when His ever-educating hand endeavors to lead us to greater perfection, and when, by his *mussar*, His lesson in chastisement, He makes our prosperity — even if it was put to proper use — vanish. It means that we are being led into the school of renunciation and privation, so that we should not remain one-sided, but should prove ourselves on the reverse side of fortune's coin as well, and should acquire such perfection as can be found and practiced mainly in the school of suffering. Above all, let us willingly accept His chastisement of adversity when this change in our luck is meant as a warning to us, rousing us to investigate our way of life and, without self-deception, to ask ourselves before God and our conscience whether, when we walked in the ways of good fortune, we also walked in the ways of God. For God's admonition is a sign of His love; it means that we have not become totally unworthy of this love, and that, as a father educates his son, He wants to raise us to a higher level of perfection.

In times of הון, of wealth and material welfare, the qualities which are at the greatest disadvantage are *chochmah* (wisdom) and *t'vunah* (understanding), because their true, shining light is put in the shadow by the glitter of the luxury which surrounds us. Only God's *mussar* (His ethical lesson) and *tochachah* (His chastisement and admonition) can, by His grace, awaken us to deeper appreciation and better application of the precious possessions of *chochmah* and *t'vunah* which embrace and condition all others. *Chochmah*, the wisdom learned from God's word, and *t'vunah*, the resulting understanding of the precise relationships and duties in the world, stamp us with the ultimate imprint of humanity. To occupy ourselves with the Torah, which gives us this wisdom, is far more profitable than the pursuit of any other promising venture; it is more valuable than pearls: the entire inventory of all our other acquisitions cannot be compared to it in worth.

Her "right hand" grants eternal life. The knowledge of God's Word enriches our immortal soul with such spiritual perfection as accompanies us into the next world. And when we act on this knowledge and fulfill God's commandments, it imparts everlasting meaning to the most infinitesimal particle of our time passed in temporal life, supplementing the spiritual adornment of our immortal soul with unfadingly sublime moral perfection.

Riches and honor, too, for the duration of our sojourn on earth, are granted us thereby. All the tasks which the Torah sets, provided they are faithfully and completely fulfilled, are intended to bring into our temporal life the blessing of satisfaction and happiness. But these (wealth and esteem) the Torah grants only with her "left hand": i.e., they should be considered an additional beneficial gift. Whoever expects to receive riches and honors from her "right hand" as the main gifts, or whoever believes that the wisdom of the Torah is primarily a means to acquire wealth and honor from her right hand, forfeits the *orech yamin*, the long life, which this hand actually offers. Such wealth and honor as he obtains lack the genuinely beneficial qualities which are bestowed on her true friends. But he who accepts the gift of long life from her right hand benefits also from the wealth and honor of her left, even if his neighbors do not assess the possessions allotted to him as constituting wealth, nor his modest station in life as a rank of honor.

Wisdom and understanding, drawn from the teachings of the Torah, show us tʰ ways in which we are to walk, and all of these ways are bliss. For all her aims, and the actions which lead to the fulfillment of these aims, are designed to harmonize with the requirements and destiny of our God-given, spiritual-physical existence, which He has created and prepared for these very aims. Even the paths of our own individual endeavors are shaped and guided by the spirit of the God-given Torah towards fulfillment, without causing offense or danger to others, and with the preservation of both our outer and inner peace.

The tree of life in the middle of Paradise is no longer accessible. We have forfeited it because the tree of knowledge, while standing next to it, was yet separate, and we wanted to pluck the fruits of its knowledge against God's will. By giving us His Torah, granting wisdom and understanding, God has, however, given into our hands the tree of knowledge *and* the tree of life, united into one. Wherever we tend it, lovingly and faithfully, we may earn both the fruits of knowledge and the fruits of eternal life. And when a community gathers around this tree of life, becoming תומכיה, its supporters and followers, the plurality is transformed into unity. All are truly united in God, as God's community With the spiritual and moral support granted by God, reposing with Him, such a community becomes *me'ushar,* one harmonious unit. Should, however, this single beam of support, the Torah, be lacking, then every society, union, or community becomes mere pretense, held together only outwardly, but inwardly divided by the diverging interests of separate pluralities.

And so, even if God's education through suffering shakes the foundations of our hitherto existing prosperity, or even causes its total loss — if it but leads us toward regaining the tree of eternal life, then let us gratefully see in this מוסר ותוכחת ד' (His lesson of morality and chastisement), which is nothing else but God's love and His fatherly kindness towards us.

◉

כָּל־יְמֵי עָנִי רָעִים
וְטוֹב־לֵב מִשְׁתֶּה תָמִיד:
טוֹב־מְעַט בְּיִרְאַת ד'
מֵאוֹצָר רָב וּמְהוּמָה בוֹ:
טוֹב אֲרֻחַת יָרָק וְאַהֲבָה־שָׁם
מִשּׁוֹר אָבוּס וְשִׂנְאָה־בוֹ:

*All the days of the poor are wretched,*
*but if he has a good heart, his meal is a festive one always.*
*Better is a little with the fear of God*
*than great treasures and restlessness therewith.*
*Better a dish of vegetables where there is love*
*than a fattened ox where there is hatred.* (15, 15—17)

טוֹב מְעַט בִּצְדָקָה

*Better is a little with compliance to the law*

מֵרֹב תְּבוּאוֹת בְּלֹא מִשְׁפָּט:

*than great revenues with injustice* (16, 8).

טוֹב פַּת חֲרֵבָה וְשַׁלְוָה־בָהּ
מִבַּיִת מָלֵא זִבְחֵי־רִיב:

*Better dry bread and peacefulness with it*
*than a house full of meals eaten in strife.* (17, 1)

Far too often do we judge human happiness according to outward appearances. And far too often we accustom ourselves and our children to
overestimate the value of material acquisitions. Human happiness is by
no means determined by this kind of wealth. In fact, as such acquisitions
become everyday needs, they lose their value. On the other hand, if they
must, one day, be relinquished, our senses, which have become used to
those superficialities, feel sorely deprived. No man should be rated according to the quantity of his material acquisitions or his status in
society. We can rate him as "happy" or "unhappy" only by looking into
his heart and his domestic life.

True, "all the days of the poor are wretched" — in the eyes of the
world — in the sense that the poor person has to wage a day-to-day
struggle for his means of subsistence; no day gives him security for the
next one. How then, in the words of the Proverb, is "his meal a festive
one always"? — Because, while his outward position in life may deny
him certain "benefits," in his heart there is the certainty that he is the
constant beneficiary of God's bounty. His confidence in the blessed
Almighty allows him to start his day with serene trust, and, at the end of
the day's work, he can thank God with the blessing of *baruch ha-shem
yom yom,* "Blessed be the Lord day by day."

He is truly grateful for his measure of sustenance, even if it be that his
endeavors were successful, with the aid of the blessed Almighty, only
through the voluntary assistance of a brotherly helping hand. To him
every piece of bread that he can offer his family testifies to the nearness
of God, to his own honest effort and aspirations, and to the friendship

and love of his brothers. It is this consciousness which turns the simplest meal into an ever-festive one.

The wealthy man may be able to spread for himself an opulent repast — as a result of one single ray of heavenly grace bestowed on him, or on his ancestors from whose inheritance he now benefits. A poor man, on the other hand, who is "good-hearted," is God's personal guest each and every day. His table is prepared daily by God's benevolence, and at all times he can raise his eyes to God with a pure heart. The fear of God, a good conscience, the fulfillment of one's duties, domestic peace and harmony — those are the guardian angels which transform the poorest hovel into a paradise. Recriminations, unfairness, domestic discord and hatred can make the richest meal worthless and the choicest foods taste bitter.

If this was true at a time when "silver was valued for nothing" and "everyone dwelled under his own vine and under his own fig-tree" (I Kings 10, 21; 5, 5), surely today, when the ways to gain one's subsistence are so hard, the foundations of prosperity so shaky, and the rage for luxury and superfluous possessions so enormous, these words gain an even more serious significance. This teaching should accustom us to a simple way of life, and should teach us to accept every material gain and pleasure with such thankful appreciation that even the simplest status in life will be blessed with constant happiness. If we but follow this advice of the Proverbs in our lives, we and our children will be fortunate indeed.

⊙

בִּרְכַּת ד' הִיא תַעֲשִׁיר
וְלֹא־יוֹסִף עֶצֶב עִמָּהּ:

*The blessing of the* Lord, *that enriches,*
*and with it there is no deprivation.* (10, 22)

This proverb contains the essence of all that has been said in the paragraphs above. What makes us wealthy is not our success, but the One who grants it to us. *God's* blessing — that is what makes us feel rich and free from want. Be it much or little, if we have earned it by law-abiding work, sanctioned by God's commandments, if no moral blame or human curse blemishes it — then it is God's gift to us and we can be sure that we have earned our success in the ways of the Almighty, within His sight and with His assistance. The success bestowed by God not only brings happiness; it *is* the blessing of happiness. It is this blessing which gives us satisfaction and indeed lets us find the only real wealth, accepting gratefully what is granted and never feeling deprived — because the same loving Divine hand ever bestows or withholds.

A similar thought is expressed by our Sages in relation to Jeremiah 9, 22 (see *Yalkut Shim'oni* there): "Three good gifts can be attained upon earth: wisdom, valor, and riches. Should a man attain one of these, he has reached whatever is valuable on earth. But when? — when they are granted by God and sanctioned by the Torah. Wisdom, valor, and riches attained without God are worthless. In both the Jewish and non-Jewish worlds — Achitofel, Bileam, Korach, Haman, and Goliath, in spite of their cleverness, wealth, and strength — all of them failed in the end, because the use they made of their talents was not sanctioned by God. Even Samson failed in spite of his immense strength, indeed because of his strength, the moment he forfeited the condition which made his strength a "God-given" one.

⊙

When wealth does not rest entirely upon honest foundations approved by the Almighty, not only does it bring no blessing, but, sooner or later, a curse enters the home with it.

עָרֵב לָאִישׁ לֶחֶם שָׁקֶר
וְאַחַר יִמָּלֵא־פִיהוּ חָצָץ:

*However good the bread of deceit may taste,*
*in the end it fills the mouth with gravel.* (20, 17)

נַחֲלָה מְבֹהֶלֶת בָּרִאשׁוֹנָה
וְאַחֲרִיתָהּ לֹא תְבֹרָךְ:

*Property acquired at its source with restlessness*
*remains not blessed in the end.* (20,21)

If wealth was acquired with a bad conscience, even if its owner keeps it till his death, it can, in the end, bring no good to his heirs.

◉

לֹא־יוֹעִיל הוֹן בְּיוֹם עֶבְרָה
וּצְדָקָה תַּצִּיל מִמָּוֶת:

*Riches profit nothing on the day when God passes in judgment, but righteousness delivers even from death.* (11, 4)

לֹא־יוֹעִילוּ אוֹצְרוֹת רֶשַׁע
וּצְדָקָה תַּצִּיל מִמָּוֶת:

*The treasures of lawlessness are of no profit, but righteousness can deliver from death.* (10,2)

בֵּית צַדִּיק חֹסֶן רָב
וּבִתְבוּאַת רָשָׁע נֶעְכָּרֶת:

*In the home of the righteous, acquired goods gain value, but ill-gotten gains bring trouble.* (15,6)

מְאֵרַת ד׳ בְּבֵית רָשָׁע
וּנְוֵה צַדִּיקִים יְבָרֵךְ:

*The curse of the Lord comes to the home of the lawless, whereas He blesses the habitation of the righteous.* (3, 33)

מַרְבֶּה הוֹנוֹ בְּנֶשֶׁךְ וְתַרְבִּית
לְחוֹנֵן דַּלִּים יִקְבְּצֶנּוּ:

*Whoever accumulates wealth by interest and usury, gathers it for another who will be generous to the poor.* (28, 8)

Sometimes, when we witness a verdict by a human judge, the thought may arise that crime pays: the criminal merely has to amass a large enough fortune so that part of it can pay for his punishment. On the *yom evrah,* however, the day when the Almighty "passes in judgment," the greatest wealth, no matter how immense, will be of no avail. On that day there is only one appeal: sincere regret and return to obedience of the law. Such repentance, with a return to *tz'dakah,* charity, can expiate the sins of a lifetime of lawlessness; it can even rescue from ruin a life-spirit that has already been doomed.

And not only on such a fateful day, but in general, true happiness can never stem from dishonestly gathered wealth. On the other hand, even at the moment when a man's existence is already threatened, an effort to conduct his life in loyalty to his duty can lend new value to his being in the sight of God, and may well result in a new and fresh lease on life.

In a home governed by faithful observance of the Torah's command-ments, that which was gathered on the field, חוסן, acquires its real value; it becomes *rav* — gains added worth, because not only was it earned in the spirit of God's commandments, but it now also finds its end-use within the framework of these commandments. In this way, the means and the end fuse in a single aspiration to accomplish God's will. However, when a lawless man brings home the harvest of his transgres-sions, he believes — and many a shortsighted onlooker may believe it with him — that now he has brought happiness and rejoicing to his home, never realizing that בתבואת רשע נעכרת — his home will now be "troubled," as no pure and serene happiness can dwell where the fruits of lawlessness are eaten.

Wealth gathered by interest and usury will, in the end, not benefit its owner. What a man has assembled by the selfish exploitation of his brother's embarrassment, will be transferred by a higher destiny into the hands of others who are חונן דלים — who come to the help of the poor. Or, in the view of the Midrash *Tanchuma,* it will find its way into the public treasury for the use of projects from which the community will freely benefit.

# VI

# THE SOCIAL CLASSES

הוֹן עָשִׁיר קִרְיַת עֻזּוֹ
מְחִתַּת דַּלִּים רֵישָׁם:
פְּעֻלַּת צַדִּיק לְחַיִּים
תְּבוּאַת רָשָׁע לְחַטָּאת:

*The rich man's wealth is his citadel,*
*poor people's terror — their poverty.*
*And yet, only the gains of the righteous are towards life,*
*the winnings of the wicked — towards sin. (10, 15—16)*

נִבְחָר שֵׁם מֵעֹשֶׁר רָב
מִכֶּסֶף וּמִזָּהָב חֵן טוֹב:

*A good name is preferable to great wealth,*
*benevolence to silver and gold. (22, 1)*

הוֹן עָשִׁיר קִרְיַת עֻזּוֹ
וּכְחוֹמָה נִשְׂגָּבָה בְּמַשְׂכִּתוֹ:
לִפְנֵי־שֶׁבֶר יִגְבַּהּ לֵב־אִישׁ
וְלִפְנֵי כָבוֹד עֲנָוָה:

*The rich man's wealth is his citadel,*
*and like a high wall in his imagination.*
*Before the crisis, a man's heart is haughtiest,*
*but humility goes before honor. (18, 11—12)*

תַּחֲנוּנִים יְדַבֶּר־רָשׁ
וְעָשִׁיר יַעֲנֶה עַזּוֹת:

*The poor man speaks entreatingly,*
*while the rich man's answer always sounds harsh.* (18, 23)

עָשִׁיר בְּרָשִׁים יִמְשׁוֹל
וְעֶבֶד לֹוֶה לְאִישׁ מַלְוֶה:

*The rich rules over the poor,*
*and the borrower becomes a servant to the lender.* (22, 7)

הוֹן יֹסִיף רֵעִים רַבִּים
וְדָל מֵרֵעֵהוּ יִפָּרֵד:

*Wealth makes for many friends,*
*but the poor man becomes separated from his friend.* (19, 4)

גַּם־לְרֵעֵהוּ יִשָּׂנֵא רָשׁ
וְאֹהֲבֵי עָשִׁיר רַבִּים:

*Even to his friend, a poor man becomes detestable,*
*while the rich man has many friends* (14, 20)

רַבִּים יְחַלּוּ פְנֵי־נָדִיב
וְכָל־הָרֵעַ לְאִישׁ מַתָּן:
כָּל אֲחֵי־רָשׁ שְׂנֵאֻהוּ

*Many seek favor with a generous man,*
*and every friendship goes to the man of gifts.*
*All relations of the impoverished man hate that they are his [kin];*

אַף כִּי מְרֵעֵהוּ רָחֲקוּ מִמֶּנּוּ
מְרַדֵּף אֲמָרִים לוֹ־הֵמָּה:

*so much the more do his friends draw away from him,*
*though he pursues words [with them] that they are his [friends].*
(19, 6—7)

תַּאֲוַת אָדָם חַסְדּוֹ
וְטוֹב רָשׁ מֵאִישׁ כָּזָב:

*A man's longing is for the kindness promised to him,*
*but a poor man is better than a deceptive one.* (19, 22)

טוֹב רָשׁ הוֹלֵךְ בְּתֻמּוֹ
מֵעִקֵּשׁ דְּרָכַיִם וְהוּא עָשִׁיר:

*Better a poor man who walks on in his innocence*
*than one who walks on a crooked double path, though he be*
*wealthy.* (28, 6)

טוֹב רָשׁ הוֹלֵךְ בְּתֻמּוֹ
מֵעִקֵּשׁ שְׂפָתָיו וְהוּא כְסִיל:

*Better a poor man who goes on in his innocence*
*than one whose lips seek crookedness, and he is the fool!* (19, 1)

The wealthy and the poor, the social classes into which our society is
divided, are both equally inhibited by a fallacy of judgment. Both are
equally to blame for each other's misconceptions. Both rich and poor,
when assessing someone's worth, vastly overestimate the importance of
material possessions. The rich as well as the poor forget that one's real
value is determined by different factors entirely.

The rich man sees his wealth as a citadel of unmatchable height and
might. The poor man sees it in exactly the same way — and the fact

that he has no part in this "citadel" fills his whole being with a rending fright. Neither of them takes into consideration that one's true value lies not in the *sum* of his possessions, but in the *way* in which they were acquired. Did he attain them complying with the Torah's commandments, or in defiance of them? A man often forgets that far more valuable than riches, gold and silver, are the good name and kind nature of a person, attainable only by leading a good life.

Moreover, both the rich and the poor disregard the consequence of this misconception: The very delusion that possessions are a tower of strength and a protective wall lulls their owner into such pride and haughtiness as to endanger the continuance of his wealth. He is bound to become dangerously unscrupulous and thus causes the collapse of his "citadel" and his "wall."

Overrating material wealth in disregard of its true value precludes any mutual understanding between the social classes, which should be based on an ethical relationship. The poor man loses faith in his inherent dignity as a human being, which in truth no measure of poverty can impair. He thinks that he cannot hold his head high; his speech sounds like *tachanunim,* supplication. To the rich man, in turn, it never occurs that this pauper who is facing him may well surpass him by far, morally and spiritually, even though he has no material means. Consequently, his every word expresses insolence and overbearing pride. Thus, the wealthy deludes the poor, and the poor, in turn, the wealthy. The self-humiliation of the poor increases the haughtiness of the rich, and the pridefulness of the rich lowers the self-respect of the poor. Because תחנונים ידבר רש therefore ועשיר יענה עזות and vice-versa. Is it not true that the wealth of a rich man is often the very evidence of his moral weakness — while the lack of means of a poor person may well attest to his moral strength, which has restrained him from seizing indiscriminately upon a doubtful venture into money-making?

All this is overlooked, more often than not, by our entire society. How frequently does wealth, and only wealth, constitute the decisive factor on occasions when character and spiritual worth should count most? As from a master, the poor recoils before the wish and desire of the rich man and, should he owe him anything, even more so. Everybody seeks to ingratiate himself with the wealthy. Impoverishment, on the other hand, breaks the bonds even of kinship and previous friendships. Old promises, given an impoverished man in better times, vanish like shadows never to be caught (or, according to the oral form of the text, friends who assured him that they were on his side vanish). He looks for the promised sympathy which is not forthcoming . . . and yet, is not the deceived poor man far better than the one who lied to him (who let his promises turn to lies) because of his poverty?

How much better it would be if integrity — no matter how outwardly insignificant — counted for more than crafty cunning, though that is crowned by chance. A blameless man, though he be poor, is worth more than a wealthy man, ever treading on double paths (*d'rachayim*). For a person who has left the single straight road is always ready to step either way: to act virtuously where virtue counts, and frivolously where levity is in order.

Such an *ish d'rachayim* (man of double paths) is often called — in times when integrity is discredited — "the man of the middle-of-the-road." If he is wealthy, he is praised by all; everyone courts his favor. Every group proudly counts him as its member. Nevertheless, he is not worth the dust under the feet of a poor man who walks along the straight road. The one who holds on to honesty and integrity, although he remains poor in the process, is worth infinitely more than *ikkésh s'fathayim*, a man who, with a nimble tongue, succeeds in searching and finding crookedness.

Yet the text continues, *v'hu k'sil,* "he is a fool." Society regards as a fool the man who refuses to utter a dishonest word, even for his own advantage. (Or, if this refers to *ikkésh s'fathayim*, no matter how clever he seems to be to the world, in reality he is a fool, because he does not know the right way and believes that the wrong means will lead him to his aim.)

# VII

## INDUSTRY AND INDOLENCE

עֹכֵר בֵּיתוֹ בּוֹצֵעַ בָּצַע
וְשׂוֹנֵא מַתָּנֹת יִחְיֶה:

*The man greedy for gain troubles his house,*
*but he who dislikes [even] gifts attains life. (15, 27)*

הוֹן מֵהֶבֶל יִמְעָט
וְקֹבֵץ עַל־יָד יַרְבֶּה:

*The wealth that results from vanity will dwindle,*
*but he who gathers by his hand shall increase. (13, 11)*

אַל־תִּיגַע לְהַעֲשִׁיר
מִבִּינָתְךָ חֲדָל:
הֲתָעִיף עֵינֶיךָ בּוֹ וְאֵינֶנּוּ
כִּי עָשֹׂה יַעֲשֶׂה־לּוֹ כְנָפַיִם
כְּנֶשֶׁר יָעוּף הַשָּׁמָיִם:

*Do not exert yourself to gather riches,*
*desist from your understanding.*
*Once you let your eyelids close over it, it no longer exists.*
*For quite often it grows wings*
*like an eagle and bird of heaven. (23, 4-5)*

מַחְשְׁבוֹת חָרוּץ אַךְ־לְמוֹתָר
וְכָל־אָץ אַךְ־לְמַחְסוֹר:

*The deliberations of the industrious always lead to advantage,*
*but overhaste causes damage. (21, 5)*

154

אִישׁ אֱמוּנוֹת רַב־בְּרָכוֹת
וְאָץ לְהַעֲשִׁיר לֹא יִנָּקֶה:

*The conscientious is richly blessed,*
*but he who hastens to gather wealth cannot keep clean hands.* (28, 20)

עֹבֵד אַדְמָתוֹ יִשְׂבַּע־לָחֶם
וּמְרַדֵּף רֵיקִים חֲסַר־לֵב:

*The tiller of his land shall satisfy his hunger with bread,*
*but he who chases phantoms is bereft of his senses.* (12, 11)

עֹבֵד אַדְמָתוֹ יִשְׂבַּע־לָחֶם
וּמְרַדֵּף רֵיקִים יִשְׂבַּע־רִישׁ:

*The tiller of his land shall satisfy his hunger with bread*
*but he who chases phantoms will get his fill of poverty.* (28, 19)

רָב־אֹכֶל נִיר רָאשִׁים
וְיֵשׁ נִסְפֶּה בְּלֹא מִשְׁפָּט:

*Even the field of the poor yields plenty of food,*
*though some are ruined by disorder and injustice.* (13, 23)

נֶפֶשׁ עָמֵל עָמְלָה לּוֹ
כִּי־אָכַף עָלָיו פִּיהוּ:

*The worker toils for his own body,*
*because his mouth compels him.* (16, 26)

טוֹב נִקְלֶה וְעֶבֶד לוֹ
מִמִּתְכַּבֵּד וַחֲסַר־לָחֶם:

*Better to be lowly esteemed, but one's own servant,*
*than to have haughtiness with lack of bread.* (12, 9)

הָכֵן בַּחוּץ מְלַאכְתֶּךָ
וְעַתְּדָהּ בַּשָּׂדֶה לָךְ
אַחַר וּבָנִיתָ בֵיתֶךָ:

*Prepare your work on the outside,*
*and make it ready in the fields for your future;*
afterwards, *build your house.* (24, 27)

יָדֹעַ תֵּדַע פְּנֵי צֹאנֶךָ
שִׁית לִבְּךָ לַעֲדָרִים:
כִּי לֹא לְעוֹלָם חֹסֶן
וְאִם־נֵזֶר לְדוֹר וָדוֹר:
גָּלָה חָצִיר וְנִרְאָה־דֶשֶׁא
וְנֶאֶסְפוּ עִשְּׂבוֹת הָרִים:
כְּבָשִׂים לִלְבוּשֶׁךָ
וּמְחִיר שָׂדֶה עַתּוּדִים:
וְדֵי חֲלֵב עִזִּים לְלַחְמְךָ
לְלֶחֶם בֵּיתֶךָ
וְחַיִּים לְנַעֲרוֹתֶיךָ:

*Be personally concerned with the appearance of your sheep,*
*direct your attention to your herds.*
*For gathered wealth does not endure forever,*
*nor princeliness for generations.*
*When the hay is mown and the grass becomes visible*
*and the herbs of the mountains are gathered in,*
*you will have sheep for your clothing,*
*and bucks for the purchase of a field,*
*and there will be goats' milk enough for your nourishment*
*and the food of your household*
*and maintenance for your maidens.* (27, 23-27)

In the proverbs of Mishlé, an independent livelihood acquired by honest effort is very highly regarded. Mere profiteering, without consideration whether it is lawful or not, does not bring happiness into the home: sooner or later such profit makes for sorrow. Nor should subsistence by charity satisfy us, even if it is bestowed in a way which honors its donor and does not humiliate the one who receives it.

The *so-ney mattanoth*, the man who hates gifts reaches a truly independent position in life; *yichyeh*, "he will live" — only if he himself finds ways and means to become self-supporting by honest and diligent work — disliking even gifts.

Two qualities should characterize his wealth; it should testify to moral dignity, *yakar* (the opposite of *zolel*, baseness, meanness), and חרוץ, it should be a product of diligence. Certainly the teachings of Mishlé do not advocate acquiring wealth by speculation or a stroke of luck; in any case that would not last. Only the *kovétz al yad*, what is gathered by a working hand, will gradually increase. However, *hon mé-hevel*, a sudden windfall, *mé-hevel yim'at*, will vanish with the same speed. Such possession has no footing, no roots to regenerate it and make it grow; it has nothing to rest upon, and so it is bound to vanish again, with the same facility as it was come by. A parvenu, who has effortlessly enriched himself, soon becomes wasteful. He loves extravagance and his money goes as easily as it came, because he believes that he will always be able to win it back again and his luck will hold forever. He forgets, though, that the big prize in the lottery is rarely drawn a second time.

The *kovétz al yad*, on the other hand, knows how hard-won his every penny is. He well knows that special *hashgachah p'ratith*, Heaven's own providential help, is needed to earn an honest living in a lawful way. Hence he prizes his earnings as a sacred charge entrusted to him for safekeeping — and spending — for purposes pleasing in God's sight; and to that, with a light heart, he gladly consecrates it. His earnings will always prosper because they are rooted in firm ground — in the industrious work of their owner.

But even for the thrifty, Mishlé has some advice which should be taken to heart: First of all, *al ti-ga l'ha'ashir*, do not exert yourself to become rich; do not let it be your main aim in life to be wealthy. Not the collection of riches is the true destination of man. Moreover, to preserve it is just as difficult, perhaps even more so, than to acquire it. You may acquire it thanks to a momentary opportunity which you were lucky enough, perhaps judicious enough, to utilize. Retaining it, however, needs unceasing supervision. For your day-to-day requirements, you are entitled always to count on heavenly assistance, and you may confidently pray to the blessed Almighty, "Provide me with my daily needs." For the profitable safekeeping of fortunes, luxuries and riches, on the other hand, you are — according to Mishlé — dependent entirely on your own "understanding." Who ever heard anybody pray, "Dear God, make me a wealthy man! Let me remain a wealthy man!"?

Do not believe for a moment that through your own intelligence you can protect your possessions without assistance from the blessed Almighty. You can never foretell and calculate, merely by your own intelligence, all circumstances and situations, existing or future, which may affect your wealth. מבינתך חדל. You cannot possibly keep your eyes open rigidly; you must close your eyes occasionally, whether you want to or not. In the same way, you cannot uninterruptedly watch your fortune. Before you notice it, your wealth has vanished, because the superfluous has wings like an eagle in the clouds and birds in the sky. It flies away; you cannot hold it back. Therefore: do not exert yourself for something so volatile as money; *al ti-ga l'ha'ashir.* Many become rich, but how many remain rich?

A second lesson for the diligent is: be thoughtful! Consider carefully on what and for what purpose you are staking your efforts. Do not think that preliminary deliberation is time lost, because you may pass up an opportunity. The deliberations of a thrifty man, מחשבות חרוץ, are always to his advantage. Even the possibility that he might have been spared a hazardous enterprise is a gain.

On the other hand, וכל אץ, every thoughtless rashness, leads to damage — and perhaps mostly so when it succeeds. Once an impetuous act succeeds, it easily leads to foolhardiness, a policy of staking all and losing all. Deliberate consideration is necessary, and not only so that thrift may be crowned with success. At every step of his efforts to earn his livelihood, one needs the most earnest deliberation in order to remain an *ish emunim*, to retain the probity in which alone blessing is solidly present. An *atz l'ha'ashir*, who is tempted by every opportunity to make money and is swept on to thoughtless acts, will not be able to keep his integrity.

A third admonition to the industrious: beware of specters — empty projects! The primordial objective for mankind was to work the land, and this should be the prototype of our work for sustenance. When a farmer invests his strength in tilling his land, when he entrusts the seed to the carefully plowed soil, then he does not have to rely on unrealistic expectations or imagination. He is entitled to hope that his efforts will be crowned with success and his field will yield bread, through God's help in providing sunshine and rain. Your own efforts should be based on a similarly rational foundation. Then beware of *rékim*, phantasmagoria, unrealistic projects, promising returns for which any reasonable prerequisite is nonexistent. The one who chases phantoms, מרדף רקים, is devoid of sense — חסר לב.

Finally, Mishlé tells us to consider that earning a living does not depend on capital — at least not principally on capital. The best and most valuable investment is work, combined with contentment and honesty. If an impecunious man possesses even the smallest piece of land which he can work, it will yield sufficient food. If a farmer becomes ruined, it is because he neglects either the right way of agriculture or the right way of life (both are called *mishpat*).

The true laborer is a free man. He works for himself; his toil and efforts have been imposed on him by himself, his own necessities (אכף, from *ukaf*, saddle). Even if he must do everything himself and cannot keep a servant, even if everyone considers him a servant and not a master — he is well off! Better that he be his own servant, not considering work demeaning, than believe that he is too good for work and go hungry.

In conclusion: a tableau, in which Mishlé pictures a simple country life of serene and sensible cheerfulness. First, the admonition not to start with marriage, but to begin by preparing one's land for the future, and only afterward to think of starting a household. The advice is further, to the best of our understanding, to concentrate initially on sheep breeding and ultimately to gain land-property from it. In the mountains and plains, pasture for goats and sheep is easily found. The livestock, in turn, can provide their owner with whatever is necessary, clothing and nutrition for himself and his household (characteristically maids, whose place the master cannot take — not servants). By the sale of less profitable male goats he can gradually get the means for acquiring land.

Again, however, we have the admonition to participate personally in the work, to be personally responsible and personally attentive, even if we enjoy inherited prosperity or even princely prosperity.

For property and prosperity are passing, and not always transferred to descendants. The best inheritance for the following generation is the example of industrious, attentive and careful activities.

Where have the days gone, and when will they return, for us to go back to the simple, happy, ancestral way of life? Yet even if we are very far away from such conditions and must find our own livelihood in entirely different areas, we can well learn a lesson for our own lives from the spirit which speaks out of this tableau in Mishlé, the spirit of a simple and contented life, the spirit of industry and activity, the spirit of careful attention and love of work, the spirit of refusing to give oneself airs. It would be well if this were our own and our children's heritage, and that the saying in Koheleth 7, 29, would not hold so true for ourselves: אלקים עשה את האדם ישר והמה בקשו חשבונות רבים God has created man straightforward — but they invented many calculations. The "many calculations" are the enemies of our happiness.

⊙

לֵךְ־אֶל־נְמָלָה עָצֵל
רְאֵה דְרָכֶיהָ וַחֲכָם:

*Go to the ant, sluggard,*
*consider her ways and become wise.*

אֲשֶׁר אֵין־לָהּ קָצִין שֹׁטֵר וּמֹשֵׁל׃
תָּכִין בַּקַּיִץ לַחְמָהּ
אָגְרָה בַקָּצִיר מַאֲכָלָהּ׃
עַד־מָתַי עָצֵל תִּשְׁכָּב
מָתַי תָּקוּם מִשְּׁנָתֶךָ׃
מְעַט שֵׁנוֹת מְעַט תְּנוּמוֹת
מְעַט חִבֻּק יָדַיִם לִשְׁכָּב׃
וּבָא־כִמְהַלֵּךְ רֵאשֶׁךָ
וּמַחְסֹרְךָ כְּאִישׁ מָגֵן׃

*She has no overseer, superior, or ruler.*
*She prepares her bread in the summer,*
*and gathers her food in the harvest.*
*And you, sluggard, how long will you lie?*
*When will you arise from your sleep?*
*Yet a little sleep, a little slumber,*
*a little folding of the hands to rest,*
*and, like a wanderer, your poverty will come,*
*and your want, as an armed man.* (6, 6-11)

עַל־שְׂדֵה אִישׁ־עָצֵל עָבַרְתִּי
וְעַל־כֶּרֶם אָדָם חֲסַר־לֵב׃
וְהִנֵּה עָלָה כֻלּוֹ קִמְּשֹׂנִים
כָּסּוּ פָנָיו חֲרֻלִּים
וְגֶדֶר אֲבָנָיו נֶהֱרָסָה׃
וָאֶחֱזֶה אָנֹכִי אָשִׁית לִבִּי
רָאִיתִי לָקַחְתִּי מוּסָר׃

*I passed by the field of a lazy man,*
*and by the vineyard of a man devoid of understanding,*
*and I saw everything come up in thistles;*
*the surface was covered with thorns,*
*and the stone wall was torn down.*
*This I saw and set my heart to it,*
*I saw it and learnt the lesson:*

מְעַט שֵׁנוֹת מְעַט תְּנוּמוֹת
מְעַט חִבֻּק יָדַיִם לִשְׁכָּב:
וּבָא־מִתְהַלֵּךְ רֵישֶׁךָ
וּמַחְסֹרֶיךָ כְּאִישׁ מָגֵן:

*Yet a little sleep, a little slumber,*
*a little folding of the hands to rest,*
*and your poverty will stalk you;*
*your want will come as an armed man. (24, 30—34)*

אַל־תֶּאֱהַב שֵׁנָה פֶּן־תִּוָּרֵשׁ
פְּקַח עֵינֶיךָ שְׂבַע־לָחֶם:

*Love not sleep, lest you come to poverty.*
*Have your eyes open, and you shall have bread aplenty. (20, 13)*

עַצְלָה תַּפִּיל תַּרְדֵּמָה
וְנֶפֶשׁ רְמִיָּה תִרְעָב:

*Laziness brings on deep sleep,*
*but the idle soul will go hungry. (19, 15)*

מֵחֹרֶף עָצֵל לֹא יַחֲרֹשׁ
וְשָׁאַל בַּקָּצִיר וָאָיִן:

*Because of the winter's cold, the lazy one will not plow.*
*Therefore he shall search in harvest time and find nothing. (20, 4)*

מִתְאַוָּה וָאַיִן נַפְשׁוֹ עָצֵל
וְנֶפֶשׁ חָרֻצִים תְּדֻשָּׁן:

*The soul of the lazy one longs, but finds nothing,*
*while the soul of the diligent shall be satisfied with plenty. (13, 4)*

תַּאֲוַת עָצֵל תְּמִיתֶנּוּ
כִּי־מֵאֲנוּ יָדָיו לַעֲשׂוֹת:
כָּל־הַיּוֹם הִתְאַוָּה תַאֲוָה
וְצַדִּיק יִתֵּן וְלֹא יַחְשֹׂךְ:

*The yearning of the lazy one will destroy him,*
*for his hand refuses to work;*
*all his days he indulges in longing.*
*The righteous, however, even spends and does not hold back.* (21,
25—26)

רָאשׁ עֹשֶׂה כַף־רְמִיָּה
וְיַד חָרוּצִים תַּעֲשִׁיר:

*The hand which does not do its duty will cause poverty,*
*while the working hand of a diligent man brings wealth.* (10, 4)

יַד־חָרוּצִים תִּמְשׁוֹל
וּרְמִיָּה תִּהְיֶה לָמַס:

*The hand of the diligent will reach mastery,*
*while negligent laxity will cause dependence.* (12, 24)

לֹא־יַחֲרֹךְ רְמִיָּה צֵידוֹ
וְהוֹן־אָדָם יָקָר חָרוּץ:

*Laxity will not bring its prey to roast;*
*a man's wealth becomes worthy only by diligence.* (12, 27)

אֹגֵר בַּקַּיִץ בֵּן מַשְׂכִּיל
נִרְדָּם בַּקָּצִיר בֵּן מֵבִישׁ:

*[Even] in summer, the wise son gathers in,*
*but a disappointing son sleeps in harvest time.* (10, 5)

אָמַר עָצֵל אֲרִי בַחוּץ
בְּתוֹךְ רְחֹבוֹת אֵרָצֵחַ:

*The lazy man says: There is a lion outside,*
*I shall be murdered in the streets. (22, 13)*

אָמַר עָצֵל שַׁחַל בַּדָּרֶךְ
אֲרִי בֵּין הָרְחֹבוֹת:
הַדֶּלֶת תִּסּוֹב עַל־צִירָהּ
וְעָצֵל עַל־מִטָּתוֹ:
טָמַן עָצֵל יָדוֹ בַּצַּלָּחַת
נִלְאָה לַהֲשִׁיבָהּ אֶל־פִּיו:
חָכָם עָצֵל בְּעֵינָיו
מִשִּׁבְעָה מְשִׁיבֵי טָעַם:

*The lazy man says: There is a jackal in the way,*
*a lion in the streets.*
*The door is already turning on its hinges,*
*and the sluggard is still on his bed.*
*The sluggard already puts his hand on the plate,*
*but is too lazy to bring it to his mouth.*
*The lazy man is wiser in his own eyes*
*than seven sensible counselors. (26, 13—16)*

In the teachings of Mishlé there is great emphasis on opposing the vice of sloth and idleness, and on rousing us to energetic and industrious activity. They never cease to portray to the lazy person the ridiculous and absurd as well as the unfortunate consequences of his behavior.

Particularly interesting is the term *r'miyah*, repeatedly used in Mishlé to signify the opposite of industry. This expression, which is usually found in an ethical connotation — meaning deceit — is here used in an economic context as the opposite of industry, thus meaning sloth, idleness, negligence, etc. And in truth the person who does not spend his life and the spiritual and physical powers which were bestowed upon him for their manifest purpose does commit deceit. He betrays the sacred charge and opportunity entrusted to him; he betrays his Maker, who grants him his strength, by failing in the duty which is expected from him in return; and he betrays the world which his actions should benefit. Consequently, the very air that a lazy person breathes can be considered theft.

The meaning of *r'miyah* is also found in the expression *kesheth r'miyah,* signifying a projectile which deceives the one who releases it by not going off, or even turning back upon him instead of hurtling in the intended direction.

Let us suppose, though, that someone does not possess this sense of duty; yet necessity and the natural instinct for self-preservation should urge him on to use his time in diligent work like an ant. Riches have to be searched out, but poverty approaches by itself; it finds its way to whoever dreams his time away, leaving his hands folded in his lap. Furthermore, once want has arrived, it is like an "armed man" — difficult to fight. One needs only a little bit of observation in order to learn the value of industry and diligence from the fate of the lazy!

◉

Even wealth which is already in existence can be lost by laziness. The consequences of negligent indolence are poverty, hunger, unrequited longing for elementary necessities, and humiliating subordination. Even if a lazy person has a stroke of luck, his laziness prevents him from making proper use of it — because of *r'miyah*. Not being used to disciplined work, לא יחרך צידו — he eats raw whatever fell to his share even without his volition. Or: it gets away again, leaving him unable to prepare it for consumption.

הון אדם יקר A man's wealth acquires dignity only by being הון חרוץ, the wealth of an industrious person. Or: *hon adam*, human wealth, should have two characteristics: it should be *yakar*, ethically sound (the opposite of *zolel*, base, mean) and *charutz*, it must bear the mark of industry.

Indolence also amounts to culpable negligence where the acquisition of knowledge and education is concerned. There too, laziness means betraying the Creator who has given us our strength and capabilities.

בֵּן מַשְׂכִּיל, the son who diligently uses his mind, differs, by his industry, already in his youth from בֵּן מֵבִישׁ, the one who betrays justified expectations by his indolence. The diligent son already "gathers in summer," is already rich in knowledge and education before the actual harvest-time has begun; while the lazy son wastes even the time of spiritual harvest in deep slumber.

The mirror that Mishlé holds up to the lazy person shows him two things: his laughable faculty for inventing excuses to shirk a required activity, and the ridiculously sorry light in which he appears. He is still turning over in his bed, while the door of the diligent already turns on its hinges; he sits with open mouth and cannot make up his mind to bring a bite to his mouth!

Indolence, however, constitutes a fatal hindrance not only in earning a living and acquiring an education. No matter what the area where one wishes to do anything, either for himself or for others, to fulfill any task at all, laziness is always in the way. Therefore, as a general rule, Mishlé says:

דֶּרֶךְ עָצֵל כִּמְשֻׂכַת חָדֶק
וְאֹרַח יְשָׁרִים סְלֻלָה:

*"The way of the sluggard is as a hedge of thorns,*
*but the path of the upright is paved." (15, 19)*

כַּחֹמֶץ לַשִּׁנַּיִם וְכֶעָשָׁן לָעֵינָיִם
כֵּן הֶעָצֵל לְשֹׁלְחָיו:

*"As vinegar to the teeth and as smoke to the eyes,*
*thus is the sluggard to them that send him." (10, 26)*

While the opposite of עָצֵל is usually רמיה, in this context the word ישרים is used as the antonym (in the plural) of עָצֵל. *Yashar* is a man whose thoughts and will are directed exclusively upon the aim which has been set for him by his sense of duty and destination. Such a person can easily overcome very real difficulties thanks to his straight way of life. His *orach,* his way, also in social relationships, is always even, goes ever straight upwards; for this is what *s'lulah* actually means. The sluggish person, however, never gets ahead; his name, *atzél* (related to אזל, but having the *tzadi* sound), designates a progression which is constantly battling obstacles.

The *atzél* shrinks back before real difficulties, and in his laziness he finds obstructions even where there are none. Even if he endeavors to pursue some objective in which he may be interested, his way is always like a hedge of thorns. Should he have to carry out an errand for someone else, he proves to be like vinegar to the thirsty, and smoke to one who is lighting a fire in order to see. Instead of having their purpose fulfilled, the former gets his teeth blunted, and the latter remains with smarting eyes. Instead of carrying out an order, the lazy one causes his employer only annoyance.

# VIII

## THE PROPER USE OF WEALTH

יֵשׁ מִתְעַשֵּׁר וְאֵין כֹּל
מִתְרוֹשֵׁשׁ וְהוֹן רָב:
כֹּפֶר נֶפֶשׁ־אִישׁ עָשְׁרוֹ
וְרָשׁ לֹא־שָׁמַע גְּעָרָה:

*There is one who considers himself rich and has nothing;*
*there is one who thinks himself poor and has great wealth.*
*The ransom of a man's soul are his riches,*
*and poor is he who has listened to no warning.* (13, 7—8)

יֵשׁ מְפַזֵּר וְנוֹסָף עוֹד
וְחוֹשֵׂךְ מִיֹּשֶׁר אַךְ־לְמַחְסוֹר:

*One man spends freely, and thereby obtains more,*
*while another withholds more than is right, only to suffer want.* (11, 24)

עֹשֵׁק דָּל לְהַרְבּוֹת לוֹ
נֹתֵן לְעָשִׁיר אַךְ־לְמַחְסוֹר:

*He who withholds from the poor to increase his own wealth*
*[believes he] adds to his own riches, but it will only lead to want.* (22, 16)

עֹשֵׁק דָּל חֵרֵף עֹשֵׂהוּ
וּמְכַבְּדוֹ חֹנֵן אֶבְיוֹן:

*He who withholds from the poor insults his Maker,*
*but he who is gracious to the needy honors Him.* (14, 31)

נִבְהָל לַהוֹן אִישׁ רַע עָיִן
וְלֹא־יֵדַע כִּי־חֶסֶר יְבֹאֶנּוּ:

*He who is greedy for wealth is envious,*
*and does not know that want shall come upon him.* (28, 22)

נוֹתֵן לָרָשׁ אֵין מַחְסוֹר
וּמַעְלִים עֵינָיו רַב־מְאֵרוֹת:

*He who gives to the poor shall not lack [because of it]*
*but he who averts his eyes will reap adversity.* (28, 27)

What is it that makes a man rich? Certainly not hoarded wealth, but rather that which is being spent on purposes pleasing in God's sight. How many people believe themselves to be rich and, in fact, own nothing of value! Others, again, may think themselves poor and possess valuable, imperishable fortunes.

God put man on this earth and spread the world at his feet. Now, what is man's *kofer nefesh,* atonement for his soul, ransom for his existence, if not the conversion of the world's transitory goods into spiritual, ethical, timeless treasures? Having been created in His image, man should implant on earth the values of truth, morality, justice and love, and cultivate them with everything in his power and means. What is it that justifies his existence? How can even the act of self-preservation become fulfillment of duty towards God? Certainly not by the accumulation of material possessions, but by the right and proper *use* of the means and abilities that he finds at his disposal. The part of his property which he gives to others sanctifies even that part which he keeps and uses for himself, provided he keeps and uses it to be able to apply his energies even more properly and beneficially.

This is what כופר נפש איש עשרו means: the justification to live in time and eternity is gained by dispensing charity. A man's real wealth, accordingly, is the money he has *used* for the benefit of his soul. Whatever you accumulate will be forfeited; whatever you use in accordance with the commandments will remain your property forever. (Compare Exodus 30, 12; Psalms 49, 7–9.)

And who is really property-less? — the man who may have money but is unable to interpret the warnings which reach him through God's instructions or through the fate which God sends him in order to teach him how to use his wealth in compliance with the commandments. Although, outwardly, he may be the owner of wealth, he remains [inwardly] poor. Our proverb warns us: His wealth will grow wings; and once this has happened, he has missed his opportunity to earn those possessions which will never "fly away."

That is what Mishlé means when it teaches that many a person believes himself rich and is in reality poor. Again, many another who has spent all his days doing good and trying to fulfill his obligations may well think himself poor, never realizing how many treasures he has collected for his eternal life. Such a person never remembers today what he has accomplished the day before, but merely welcomes with every new day his new task. Someone can therefore be *m'fazzér,* spend more than he is in duty bound, yet become richer with every such expenditure, provided the aims for which he gives his wealth are among those that provide *kofer nafsho,* ransom for his soul. To give less than is right, however, leaves him a pauper in the ethical dimension.

We call charity *tz'dakah;* not a free-will offering, but *tz'dakah,* with the connotation of *tzedek,* justice. Therefore, to withhold from the poor what is due him becomes literally עוֹשֵׁק, denial of justice. עוֹשֵׁק דָּל, whoever denies to the poor what he owes him, in the belief that as a result he himself will keep more, is seriously mistaken. Moreover, to deny a poor person the gift due him constitutes a veritable irreverence toward his Creator. In whose name, after all, does this impecunious man come to us? He approaches us in the name of his Creator and the Shaper of his fate! He presents to us a bill from the blessed Almighty, drawn upon ourselves. Certainly, if we want to treat him harshly, he must humbly submit, not having any recourse to a human court of justice. But whoever does not honor his claim, expresses his lack of respect for the One who has sent the poor man to us. To be merciful to an *evyon,* a man in need, on the other hand, means to honor the blessed Almighty.

◉

נֶפֶשׁ־בְּרָכָה תְדֻשָּׁן
וּמַרְוֶה גַּם־הוּא יוֹרֶא :

*The benevolent soul shall be gratified,*
*and he who refreshes shall be refreshed himself.* (11, 25)

טוֹב יַנְחִיל בְּנֵי־בָנִים
וְצָפוּן לַצַּדִּיק חֵיל חוֹטֵא :

*A kindly man leaves inheritance to his children's children,*
*but the wealth of the sinner is stored away for the righteous.* (13, 22)

This is the case where one's whole being is *happy* to dispense blessings, not only out of a sense of duty or reasoning. Such a soul knows no greater happiness than to be "God's almsgiver," His manager or dispenser of charity, spreading blessing all around him. Such a person *t'dushan,* gains incomparable bliss, far greater than the one who receives from him the help to alleviate his misfortunes. For no matter how large his gift may be, it always remains within human limits. However, ומורה גם הוא יורא — whoever heartens a languishing soul, as the rain moistens a parched field, feels in that moment an even greater freshness in himself, as if he himself were like rain. (The last word is spelled with an *alef,* though, to preclude — in this moment of supreme bliss — an overweening thought, which would undo the entire merit.)

Furthermore, according to these proverbs of our sacred Scripture, the good deeds of a man will benefit his children and grandchildren for generations, while ill-gotten and ill-administered money will not last. Instead, *tzafun,* in a concealed way, it will ultimately reach the hands of the benevolent.

בְּאֵין אֲלָפִים אֵבוּס בָּר
וְרָב־תְּבוּאוֹת בְּכֹחַ שׁוֹר:

*Where no cattle are, the manger remains clean;*
*much harvesting, however, lies in the strength of an ox.* (14, 4)

מֹנֵעַ בָּר יִקְּבֻהוּ לְאוֹם
וּבְרָכָה לְרֹאשׁ מַשְׁבִּיר:

*He who withholds grain, the people curse him,*
*but blessings shall abide upon him who sells it.* (11, 26)

In these two sentences, Mishlé wishes, if we understand it properly, to teach us two additional lessons. It is true that if these teachings are not observed, no injustice is involved; yet they should be observed from a purely rational point of view.

In the first place, Mishlé points out that economy may at times be untimely and irrational. For example, a man might not keep an ox for plowing, so as to save on feed and keep the stall or the manger clean! Such unwise parsimony brings a sad reckoning at harvest-time. A wise outlay at the proper time, however, will make for profit.

Another piece of advice which Mishlé gives us is that we would do well, in planning our business undertakings, to listen not only to the voice of justice and reason, but also to the voice of the people. Even if there is nothing wrong or unjust in our profit-making, still, if public opinion disapproves or objects, we should rather forego this particular way of gain. This is exactly the thought that our Sages find in the Torah's words, וִהְיִיתֶם נְקִיִּם מד' וּמִישְׂרָאֵל, "and you shall be free of obligation to the Lord and to Israel" (Numbers 32, 22). It is also included in the teachings of Pirké Avoth: Rabbi said: Which is the right course that a man should choose for himself? — That which is an honor for him who acts, but at the same time brings him honor from mankind.

Whatever we undertake should, first of all, be fair and honest in itself. In addition, however, we are to take into consideration the judgment of people and proceed with our enterprise only if public opinion does not object. In illustration of this maxim, the proverb brings as an example the grain trade. A grain merchant may keep back his stores, speculating on a rise in prices, a practice which in other lines of business might be quite acceptable. In his case, however, the public may curse him, while another trader who sells willingly may earn its blessing [since grain is an essential element in the food supply]. Basically, the one does not deserve more praise than the other, since both are merely interested in making a profit. Nevertheless, we should always take into account any prejudice involved in such and similar business ventures and not be tempted exclusively by the profit they offer.

# IX

## ACTS OF RIGHTEOUSNESS AND KINDLY JUSTICE

אַל־תִּמְנַע־טוֹב מִבְּעָלָיו
בִּהְיוֹת לְאֵל יָדֶיךָ לַעֲשׂוֹת׃

*Do not withhold good from one to whom it is due,*
*when it is in your power to do it. (3, 27)*

It is highly significant that the Jewish code of law demands of us, with every stringency of a legal obligation, to carry out actions which others could ask from us as an act of charity, but not claim as due them by right. As soon as we are in a position to do good to our neighbor, we are to consider him as בעליו, as someone entitled to demand it from us, and we are not to deny him any benefit that we are able to grant him. God has given legal title to any person who is in need of help or support, to claim from us by the word of His law what no man could demand by his own rights.

⊙

עשֶׁק דָּל לְהַרְבּוֹת לוֹ
נֹתֵן לְעָשִׁיר אַךְ־לְמַחְסוֹר׃

*Whoever withholds from the poor what is due him*
*in order to increase his own [gain]*
*gives it to the rich, only to diminish his property. (22, 16)*

אַל־תִּגְזָל־דָּל כִּי דַל־הוּא
וְאַל־תְּדַכֵּא עָנִי בַשָּׁעַר׃

*Do not rob the poor because he is poor,*
*and do not oppress one who depends upon society;*

כִּי־ד' יָרִיב רִיבָם
וְקָבַע אֶת־קֹבְעֵיהֶם נָפֶשׁ:

*for God fights for their cause*
*and strikes those who strike them, to their very life. (22, 22—23)*

אֹטֵם אָזְנוֹ מִזַּעֲקַת־דָּל
גַּם־הוּא יִקְרָא וְלֹא יֵעָנֶה:

*Whoever closes his ears to the cry of a poor man,*
*he too shall cry out and not be answered. (21, 13)*

נֹתֵן לָרָשׁ אֵין מַחְסוֹר
וּמַעְלִים עֵינָיו רַב־מְאֵרוֹת:

*Whoever gives to the poor will have no loss,*
*but one who averts his eyes shall have many curses. (28, 27)*

הַצֵּל לְקֻחִים לַמָּוֶת
וּמָטִים לַהֶרֶג אִם־תַּחְשׂוֹךְ:
כִּי־תֹאמַר הֵן לֹא־יָדַעְנוּ זֶה
הֲלֹא־תֹכֵן לִבּוֹת הוּא־יָבִין
וְנֹצֵר נַפְשְׁךָ הוּא יֵדָע
וְהֵשִׁיב לְאָדָם כְּפָעֳלוֹ:

*Rescue them who are in the grip of death*
*and are bound to be slain if you withdraw,*
*if you say, "Behold, we did not know this."*
*But He who gauges the hearts understands,*
*and He who guards your soul knows;*
*and He shall render to each man according to his action. (24, 11—12)*

Let no one believe that the charity or alms he gives to the poor are taken
from his own property. According to God's laws of duty, whatever is
due to the poor belongs to them already, and is no longer the property
of the well-to-do. If the wealthy man nevertheless keeps this property of

the poor man for himself, adding it to his own, he will not increase his wealth by such an act. Every penny due the poor man that is denied him causes loss of property, and instead of increase, it will bring the wealthy man want.

From a poor man who possesses nothing, nothing can be stolen. However, even if he has no possessions, for that very reason he has a claim on the obligation of the well-to-do. This claim is his property, and whoever takes no notice of it defrauds him. Let no one become guilty of such robbery. Let no community neglect these claims, granted by God to the destitute and dependent in its midst, just because in this world they cannot bring action against us. True, among men they cannot sue; and before a human judge they can make no appeal; but their lawyer is God! He is their Judge too, and He knows how to apprehend those who put the existence of the poor in jeopardy by ignoring their claim for the fulfillment of our duty.

Whoever turns a deaf ear to the anguish of the unfortunate cannot expect God to listen to his own cry for help; and a person who averts his eyes from the misery of his fellow-man should not believe for a minute that he will find shelter under God's protection and benefit from His blessing on his own ventures and possessions.

By God's will, we are in duty bound to help and rescue our brethren whenever poverty oppresses them, and whenever their life, health or welfare is endangered. Woe to us if we pretend ignorance about the danger that threatens our fellow-man. The omniscient God looks into our hearts and knows whether we are aware of our neighbor's plight or not. God, the Keeper of our souls, examines them, and He sees whether we are worthy of His protection; and He rewards everyone according to his actions.

⊙

טוֹב־עַיִן הוּא יְבֹרָךְ ·

*One who has a friendly eye shall be blessed,*

כִּי־נָתַן מִלַּחְמוֹ לַדָּל:

*for he gave from his bread to the poor.* (22, 9)

יוֹדֵעַ צַדִּיק נֶפֶשׁ בְּהֶמְתּוֹ
וְרַחֲמֵי רְשָׁעִים אַכְזָרִי:

*The righteous man knows the soul of his animal,*
*but the compassion of the wicked is cruelty.* (12, 10)

בָּז־לְרֵעֵהוּ חוֹטֵא
וּמְחוֹנֵן עֲנָוִים אַשְׁרָיו:

*He who despises his neighbor sins,*
*but one who is gracious to the humble strides towards happiness.*
(14, 21)

מַלְוֵה ד' חוֹנֵן דָּל
וּגְמֻלוֹ יְשַׁלֶּם־לוֹ:

*One who graciously gives to the poor lends to God,*
*and He pays him his reward.* (19, 17)

Blessings await a man who is glad about the blessings of his neighbor and looks kindly on his neighbor's prosperity. Such a person surely cannot enjoy his own food when next to him a poor man goes hungry. In fact, he will not eat before he gives some of his food to the poor, for he considers it his own only after he has shared it.

Our moral obligations, as taught to us by the Divine law, educate us toward a feeling of active duty in the face of suffering. A person who has been educated and guided toward such duty-fulfillment and righteous behavior by the principles of the Divine law will be mindful even of the needs of the animals which depend upon him, to spare their strength and provide for their wants, whenever the Law requires him to do so. By contrast, when someone's pity is not rooted in the Law but derives from his own inclination, he can just as easily become cruel as compassionate, depending upon his mood, momentary state of mind, or some presumptive notion of his own.

At times an unfortunate person presents an unattractive appearance, as a result of his misery and poverty. Woe to him who lets himself be induced to contempt by a man's run-down appearance; blessings upon him who is used to seeing through the often repellent exterior of such an unfortunate person, right through to his innermost yearning for compassion; and who, by a comforting act of duty, lifts up his spirit.

The poor man, who appeals to our obligatory sense of duty, presents us with a draft [a check or promissory note, as it were] drawn upon God. Fortunate is the person who duly honors his draft, for God considers that man His creditor, and He shall not fail to reimburse him.

◉

מַתָּן בַּסֵּתֶר יִכְפֶּה־אָף
וְשֹׁחַד בַּחֵק חֵמָה עַזָּה:

*A charitable gift made in secret can overcome anger,*
*and [like] a hidden bribe [can stay] strong wrath. (21, 14)*

בְּחֶסֶד וֶאֱמֶת יְכֻפַּר עָוֹן
וּבְיִרְאַת ד׳ סוּר מֵרָע:

*By charity and good faith, iniquity is expiated,*
*and by the fear of God, as [proven by] departure from evil. (16, 6)*

מוֹקֵשׁ אָדָם יָלַע קֹדֶשׁ
וְאַחַר נְדָרִים לְבַקֵּר:

*It is a snare to a man to set his hands on something holy,*
*and to look after it later by making vows. (20, 25)*

A charitable gift presented secretly, in particular if even the one who receives it does not know who the donor is, is in the nature of an atonement. Such an act of charity, which is completely free of any self-

interest, has the power of restraining God's anger, even if it has already
been deserved. It has an influence comparable to the effect of a secret
bribe on a human judge. In other words, an act of charity can atone for
a sinful past, provided it is prompted by true fear of God as proven by
the sincere decision to refrain from evil in the future. But if someone
violates God's sanctuary with the premeditation to redeem himself later
by vows and solemn promises, he acts under a serious misconception.
The charity that he later vows and gives, instead of being an atonement,
becomes part and parcel of his transgression.

אַל־תֹּאמַר לְרֵעֲךָ לֵךְ וָשׁוּב
וּמָחָר אֶתֵּן וְיֵשׁ אִתָּךְ:

*Do not say to your neighbor, "Go and come again,*
*and I will give you tomorrow," while it is now with you. (3, 28)*

This adage demands of us to attend punctually to the fulfillment of our
obligations. We are to meet those engagements demanded of us
without delay, and not postpone till tomorrow what we are able to do today.

⊙

אַל־תְּהִי בְתֹקְעֵי־כָף
בַּעֹרְבִים מַשָּׁאוֹת:
אִם־אֵין־לְךָ לְשַׁלֵּם
לָמָּה יִקַּח מִשְׁכָּבְךָ מִתַּחְתֶּיךָ:

*Do not be one of those who shake hands,*
*or of those who are guarantors for debts.*
*If you will not be able to pay,*
*why should he take your bed from underneath you? (22, 26—27)*

אָדָם חֲסַר־לֵב תֹּקֵעַ כָּף
עֹרֵב עֲרֻבָּה לִפְנֵי רֵעֵהוּ:

*A thoughtless man gives a handshake,*
*gives a guarantee for his neighbor. (17, 18)*

רַע־יֵרוֹעַ כִּי־עָרַב זָר
וְשֹׂנֵא תוֹקְעִים בּוֹטֵחַ:

*He who guarantees for a stranger shall suffer serious damage,*
*but he who hates handshake-transactions shall remain secure.* (11, 15)

קַח־בִּגְדוֹ כִּי־עָרַב זָר
וּבְעַד נָכְרִיָּה חַבְלֵהוּ:

*Take his garment, because he has given security for a stranger;*
*and for a strange woman, hold him in pledge.* (27, 13)

בְּנִי אִם־עָרַבְתָּ לְרֵעֶךָ
תָּקַעְתָּ לַזָּר כַּפֶּיךָ:
נוֹקַשְׁתָּ בְאִמְרֵי־פִיךָ
נִלְכַּדְתָּ בְּאִמְרֵי־פִיךָ:
עֲשֵׂה זֹאת אֵפוֹא בְּנִי וְהִנָּצֵל
כִּי בָאתָ בְכַף־רֵעֶךָ
לֵךְ הִתְרַפֵּס וּרְהַב רֵעֶיךָ:
אַל־תִּתֵּן שֵׁנָה לְעֵינֶיךָ
וּתְנוּמָה לְעַפְעַפֶּיךָ:
הִנָּצֵל כִּצְבִי מִיָּד
וּכְצִפּוֹר מִיַּד יָקוּשׁ:

*My son, if you have guaranteed for your neighbor,*
*if you have given your handshake for a stranger,*
*have become ensnared by the words of your mouth,*
*have been caught by the words of your mouth —*
*do this, in any way you can, my son, and save yourself;*
*for you have come into the hands of your neighbor:*
*Go, humble yourself to the dust,*
*and acknowledge the power of your neighbor.*
*Do not give sleep to your eyes*
*nor slumber to your eyelids.*
*Save yourself as a gazelle from the [hunter's] hand*
*and as a bird from the snare.* (6, 1—5)

All of these proverbs caution us primarily not to take it upon ourselves to guarantee the debts of others. In a wider sense, however, these adages, repeated with such striking frequency, warn us of taking upon ourselves any obligations within the broad concept of ערובה or ערבות, security for situations where we can exert no influence. Presumably, such situations will never arise, but their occurrence or non-occurrence is entirely beyond our control. For this, after all, is the characteristic of any guarantee: One gives it under the assumption that its beneficiary will himself live up to his obligations and the guarantor will never be troubled. These proverbs mean to show us the shaky foundations which are at the basis of such engagements, and to make sure we realize that we may be faced with the contrary of what we assume, in which case the consequences are likely to be most unfavorable. Once a promise has been made, it remains binding and may well prove to be a self-set trap.

The concept of giving security by a handshake that entangles us in obligation includes all actions that put us under an obligation for situations over whose happening we have no control; while we suppose they will never occur, it is still beyond our power to prevent their occurrence. We are warned, in particular, not to give security for any bets, games, or similar gambling-ventures.

It is noteworthy that in chapter 17, verse 18, the expression used is actually not "for" your neighbor, but לפני, "before" your neighbor. This may be on account of the following consideration: In general, it is much more difficult to refuse a request for a guarantee than to refuse a request for a loan. If a person will not give a guarantee, it can only be due to his lack of confidence (in the borrower), while the refusal to give a loan may after all be because a man lacks the means to give it. Thus it might be more difficult to refuse a guarantee to the lender לפני, in presence of, the one who requests the loan, than in his absence. However this may be, all these proverbs teach the danger of each and every guarantee, so that even in the presence of the person in question it would be mindlessness to be lulled into giving it.

Should we nevertheless have entered upon such an obligation, our proverbs advise us not to give our eyes sleep but to do everything possi-

ble, even by making sacrifices, to be released from it, rather than remain
saddled with it into the insecurity of an unfathomable future.

⊙

נְשִׂיאִים וְרוּחַ וְגֶשֶׁם אָיִן
אִישׁ מִתְהַלֵּל בְּמַתַּת־שָׁקֶר:

*Like clouds and wind, and no rain forthcoming,*
*so is a man who boasts with false gifts.* (25, 14)

שֵׁן רֹעָה וְרֶגֶל מוּעָדֶת
מִבְטָח בּוֹגֵד בְּיוֹם צָרָה:

*Like a loose tooth and a slipping foot*
*is the promise of a faithless man on a day of need.* (25, 19)

Here the talk of a man who promises plentiful gifts, but whose promises
prove to be so many lies, is compared to clouds and wind: To the expec-
tant farmer they look promising, but his hopes are shattered when the
expected rain is not forthcoming. Even more pernicious are promises of
assistance in times of need, which, when the need arises, prove to be
faithless. They are likened to a loose tooth and a slipping foot on which
we depend, yet which, at the time they are most needed, leave us in the
lurch.

# X

## FRIENDSHIP

בַּרְזֶל בְּבַרְזֶל יָחַד
וְאִישׁ יַחַד פְּנֵי־רֵעֵהוּ:

*Iron sharpens iron,*
*and a man sharpens the mind of his friend.* (27, 17)

כַּמַּיִם הַפָּנִים לַפָּנִים
כֵּן לֵב־הָאָדָם לָאָדָם:

*As water reflects face to face,*
*so the heart of man to man.* (27, 19)

לְתַאֲוָה יְבַקֵּשׁ נִפְרָד
בְּכָל־תּוּשִׁיָּה יִתְגַּלָּע:

*He who isolates himself looks to fulfill selfish desires;*
*this shows itself in each essential action.* (18, 1)

Nothing so influences the faculties of the mind as communication with friends who strive toward the same goal. Our thinking is shaped and corrected only through the exchange of thoughts with others. An intellect which depends entirely upon itself is prone to stagnation, or to fantasies and erroneous ideas.

Just as the communication of minds results in mutual improvement, so too the association of similarly attuned hearts. As a face is reflected in clear water, so kindred hearts find their sentiments, feelings and convictions reflected in one another; and at the same time they may recognize in this reflection such blemishes as should be removed. So we find enjoyment in the pure and good traits of our friend, and benefit from the strengthening and support of each other's characters.

Isolation, on the other hand, brings neither intellectual nor ethical gain; neither does it lead to תּוּשִׁיָה. This term תּוּשִׁיָה is a concept for which we lack the exact definition, but it refers to the energetic effectuation of any real purpose (the word is derived from יֵשׁ). Thus תּוּשִׁיָה definitely calls for the cooperation, and accordingly the joining, of as many like-minded friends as possible. When a man is נִפְרָד, when he withdraws from everyone and everything, when nobody is good enough to merit his association, when all communal matters are of no concern to him and he refuses to cooperate in anything — let him try to explain his seclusion by whatever excuse he wishes, if he honestly examines his heart he will find some egotistic motive for his isolation, even if only a selfish desire for renown.

אִישׁ רֵעִים לְהִתְרוֹעֵעַ
וְיֵשׁ אֹהֵב דָּבֵק מֵאָח:

*A man of many comrades is good for companionship,*
*but there is a friend who is more closely attached than a brother.* (18, 24)

The kind of harmony of mind and spirit that is at the basis of friendship exists only between few. We can have many companions, but only few friends. Someone who has succeeded in finding the lifelong treasure of a really true friend may be called fortunate indeed. However, a person who has many companions, being "a friend of all the world," may be suited for sociability, but as a rule he lacks the depth of feeling which makes for real friendship.

Friends become at times more deeply attached to one another than brothers. Mere blood-relationship as a rule, taken by itself, does not

have this effect of a strong bond. Common descent is an external factor;
and while belonging to the same family confers upon its members common mentality and tendencies, which should actually provide a ready
basis for a happy friendship, the very proximity and parallel course of
development in a family present many opportunities for friction and
misunderstandings which cause differences before there has been a
chance for true mutual appreciation and esteem. Friendship, on the
other hand, is founded on choice, and the very fact that it has developed
guarantees that the hearts and minds have come to know, appreciate
and esteem one another. Accordingly, many a friend is more closely
"related" than a brother. And yet, the peak of a community of souls is
found when brothers are also friends, and the bonds of the soul are
woven from strands of both family relation and friendship, as expressed
by David the Psalmist: שבת אחים גם יחד, "for brothers to dwell together
in unity" (Psalms 133, 1).

לֵב יוֹדֵעַ מָרַּת נַפְשׁוֹ
וּבְשִׂמְחָתוֹ לֹא־יִתְעָרַב זָר:

*The heart knows the bitterness of its soul,*
*and with its joy too no stranger can interfere.* (14, 10)

בְּכָל־עֵת אֹהֵב הָרֵעַ
וְאָח לְצָרָה יִוָּלֵד:

*A friend loves at all times,*
*and becomes as a brother in adversity.* (17, 17)

שֶׁמֶן וּקְטֹרֶת יְשַׂמַּח־לֵב
וּמֶתֶק רֵעֵהוּ מֵעֲצַת־נָפֶשׁ:

*Oil and incense gladden the heart,*
*and the sweetness of friends' relations more than self-counsel.*

רֵעֲךָ וְרֵעֵה אָבִיךָ אַל־תַּעֲזֹב
וּבֵית אָחִיךָ אַל־תָּבוֹא בְּיוֹם אֵידֶךָ
טוֹב שָׁכֵן קָרוֹב מֵאָח רָחוֹק׃

*Your own friend and the friend of your father do not forsake,*
*and on the day of your misfortune do not come to your relative's house;*
*better is a near neighbor than a far brother.* (27, 9–10)

No outsider can fathom the depth of a heart's sorrow, nor can he
measure its joy. A candid friend, however, proves his friendship in joy
and in sorrow, and through this faithful participation he becomes a
brother in need. What a mother's womb is to brothers, a community of
life experiences is to friends; and this shows itself most clearly in times
of distress. Friendship is beneficial in good and in bad days, but it is in
times of trouble that we can best appreciate the "brother" that 've have
gained by acquisition.

The enjoyment we find in communication with a true friend is comparable to the physical refreshment provided by ointment and perfume,
and such communication is far better than what we can gain if we have
only ourselves to consult.

You will do well to cultivate the companionship of a person who has
proven himself to be a faithful friend to you or to your parents' house.
His friendship may be more valuable than family relationships: in times
of trouble you can count on it more surely than on relatives. A neighbor
who has already proven himself sympathetic to you is better than a
brother who has remained at a distance.

רָב־אָדָם יִקְרָא אִישׁ חַסְדּוֹ
וְאִישׁ אֱמוּנִים מִי יִמְצָא׃

*Many call someone the man of their sympathy,*
*but who shall find a man of dependable faith?* (20, 6)

Do not be hasty to call someone your friend. and do not consider
everyone your companion who calls himself so. There are far more peo-

ple who reckon themselves our friends, or whom we call friends, than actually prove their friendship when the need arises.

דְּבַשׁ מָצָאתָ אֱכֹל דַּיֶּךָ
פֶּן־תִּשְׂבָּעֶנּוּ וַהֲקֵאתוֹ׃
הֹקַר רַגְלְךָ מִבֵּית רֵעֶךָ
פֶּן־יִשְׂבָּעֲךָ וּשְׂנֵאֶךָ׃

*Have you found honey? Eat as much as is enough for you,*
*lest you be filled with it and throw it up.*
*Make your foot dear by restraining it from the house of your neighbor,*
*lest he become fed up with you, and be antagonistic.* (25, 16—17)

If you are fortunate enough to have a friend, try not to make yourself burdensome by too many visits, even if you have cause to believe that your visits are welcome. One can become weary of too much of a good thing!

# XI

## STRIFE AND ANGER

אַל־תָּרִיב עִם־אָדָם חִנָּם
אִם־לֹא גְמָלְךָ רָעָה:

*Do not quarrel with a man without cause
if he has done you no harm.* (3, 30)

אֹהֵב פֶּשַׁע אֹהֵב מַצָּה
מַגְבִּיהַּ פִּתְחוֹ מְבַקֶּשׁ־שָׁבֶר:

*He who loves strife, loves crime;
whoever makes his threshhold high looks for an accident.* (17, 19)

כָּבוֹד לָאִישׁ שֶׁבֶת מֵרִיב
וְכָל־אֱוִיל יִתְגַּלָּע:

*It is an honor for a man to keep aloof from strife,
but a fool makes [his foolishness] obvious.* (20, 3)

שִׂנְאָה תְּעוֹרֵר מְדָנִים
וְעַל כָּל־פְּשָׁעִים תְּכַסֶּה אַהֲבָה:

*Hatred stirs up strife,
but love covers up all transgressions.* (10, 12)

Quarrelling can become a passion. No matter what the object may be, a
quarrelsome person enjoys making retorts. He likes to be right always,

and to have the last word; he quarrels for the sake of quarrelling. Be aware of such a tendency. If you are forced to have a dispute with someone, then it should be solely because by his misbehavior he has given you a very good reason for it.

Do not think that a quarrel is of no account. You can never foresee what it may lead to in the end. In the excitement of the dispute, you or your adversary may easily commit some wrong. Only a person who does not shirk from doing wrong likes to quarrel. Hence, whoever wishes to avoid wrongdoing, for himself and for others, let him keep away from dispute and avoid any occasion for friction. Whoever does not want others to stumble, let him not make his threshold too high.

It honors a man to remain calm and not let himself be drawn into a quarrel even if he has good cause for it. Only a fool does not avoid dispute, and thereby he makes his foolishness obvious.

Hatred is not the outcome of a quarrel; it is the cause of it. If two people have unfriendly feelings towards each other, they take offense at anything and everything between them. Love, however, is forgiving and pardons even serious wrongs.

⊙

מַחֲזִיק בְּאָזְנֵי־כָלֶב
עֹבֵר מִתְעַבֵּר עַל־רִיב לֹא־לוֹ:

*It is like grasping the ears of a dog*
*to become passionate over a quarrel which does not concern one.* (26, 17)

אַל־תֵּצֵא לָרִב מַהֵר
פֶּן מַה־תַּעֲשֶׂה בְּאַחֲרִיתָהּ
בְּהַכְלִים אֹתְךָ רֵעֶךָ:

*Do not go out hastily to quarrel;*
*think what you will have to do in the end,*
*when your neighbor covers you with shame.*

רִיבְךָ רִיב אֶת־רֵעֶךָ
וְסוֹד אַחֵר אַל־תְּגָל:
פֶּן־יְחַסֶּדְךָ שֹׁמֵעַ
וְדִבָּתְךָ לֹא תָשׁוּב:

*Have your quarrel out with your neighbor,*
*but the secret of another do not reveal;*
*your listener may favor you again,*
*but your aspersions will remain.* (25, 8—10)

Disputes are compared to biting animals. Do not meddle if a quarrel does not concern you. If you mix in, you are (as it were) grasping the ear of a biting animal: it will let go of its previous adversary and direct its attacks at you. So even if you have a good reason for dispute, consider carefully whether you should let yourself be involved. For even if you have firmly resolved to conclude the matter with calm composure, you can never foresee how far your opponent will let himself go. He might cover you with insults that you cannot leave unanswered.

If you nevertheless should become involved in a quarrel, keep to your own business and do not entangle someone else in it. This might bring you to utter לשון הרע (evil tale-bearing); and while you and your adversary may come to terms and become reconciled, the slander you have spoken, which has harmed a third party, cannot be "unsaid."

אָח נִפְשָׁע מִקִּרְיַת־עֹז
וּמִדְיָנִים כִּבְרִיחַ אַרְמוֹן:

*A brother who has been offended [becomes more inaccessible] than a*
*strong city,*
*and quarrels separate more than the bolt of a castle.* (18, 19)

If two members of a family have become estranged by insults or other grievances, their reconciliation is often very difficult to achieve. It is compared to "entry into a fortified city," and the discord between them is likened to the bolts of a castle, which are hard to move.

אִם־נָבַלְתָּ בְהִתְנַשֵּׂא
וְאִם־זַמּוֹתָ יָד לְפֶה:
כִּי מִיץ חָלָב יוֹצִיא חֶמְאָה
וּמִיץ־אַף יוֹצִיא דָם
וּמִיץ אַפַּיִם יוֹצִיא רִיב:

*If you have made a fool of yourself by being overbearing,*
*or [even] if you have [merely] thought it, [put] your hand to your mouth.*
*For churning milk brings forth butter,*
*and pressing the nose, blood,*
*and pressure on patience brings strife. (30, 32—33)*

If you have overreached yourself by boasting, or even if you have merely been taken by an overbearing thought, better keep still. Do not voice
the thought. If, to your shame, you have already given utterance to your
arrogant statement, then at least do not maintain it and insist on it.
Nothing so provokes contradiction as arrogant contentions. Like butter-
fat in milk and blood in the nose, the tendency to contradiction is present in every person. And just as the churning of milk causes the formation of butter and pressure on the nose brings on bleeding, so continuous
irritation can provoke even the most patient person to angry contradiction. (אפים occurs only once in the sense of anger — in Daniel 11, 20.
Otherwise it always denotes a "striving desire." Hence ארך אפים denotes
a person who gives his "striving desires" time, and is thus patient and
forbearing. The opposite is קצר אפים, an impatient, short-tempered
person; see Genesis 2, 7 and Exodus 15, 8. Other proverbs relating to
disputes have been explained above, in chapter 3.)

◉

אִישׁ־אַף יְגָרֶה מָדוֹן
וּבַעַל חֵמָה רַב־פָּשַׁע:

*An irascible man stirs up strife,*
*and a man of wrath [commits] much transgression. (29, 22)*

אִישׁ חֵמָה יְגָרֶה מָדוֹן
וְאֶרֶךְ אַפַּיִם יַשְׁקִיט רִיב:

*A wrathful man stirs up strife,*
*but a forbearing person calms conflict.* (15, 18)

אַל־תִּתְרַע אֶת־בַּעַל אָף
וְאֶת־אִישׁ חֵמוֹת לֹא תָבוֹא:
פֶּן־תֶּאֱלַף אֹרְחֹתָיו
וְלָקַחְתָּ מוֹקֵשׁ לְנַפְשֶׁךָ:

*Do not associate with a man of temper,*
*and do not approach a man of wrath,*
*lest you learn his ways*
*and bring on danger to your soul.* (22, 24—25)

אַכְזְרִיּוּת חֵמָה וְשֶׁטֶף אָף
וּמִי יַעֲמֹד לִפְנֵי קִנְאָה:

*Rage is cruel and anger is overwhelming,*
*and who can withstand jealous rage!* (27, 4)

טוֹב אֶרֶךְ אַפַּיִם מִגִּבּוֹר
וּמֹשֵׁל בְּרוּחוֹ מִלֹּכֵד עִיר:

*A man of forbearing excels over a hero,*
*and he who controls his emotions is better than the conqueror of a city.*
(16, 32)

These proverbs emphasize how destructive a vehement disposition,
which gives rise easily enough to rage and fury, can be, even in its less
violent forms. On the other hand, they illustrate how much blessing is inherent in patience and forbearing. In the vicinity of a short-tempered

person there is no tranquillity; his angry rages will rob him of his senses and of whatever gentleness he might have. He will talk and act in a way that he would avoid in times of calm consideration; and once his anger has been dispelled and calm has returned, he will deeply regret his words and remember them with shame.

It is interesting to note that, according to these proverbs, angry vehemence is contagious. In associating with a short-tempered person, one can easily adopt his bad qualities for oneself. Perhaps this is because, very often, short-tempered people are quite respected and have a good and kind character, so that one feels attracted to them and lets their example influence his own character.

We should counteract any inclination to anger from the start, from earliest youth. For if we let this tendency raise its head, self-control becomes progressively more difficult. Anger can become as uncontrollable as an inundating flood which can no longer be resisted. In fact the awareness of one's own short-temperedness should be its strongest deterrent, for surely one's anger, this unfortunate, destructive flaw in his character, is as disagreeable to him as it is to those around him. Surely he would like to rid himself of this vice — but he believes himself unable to do so, and therefore he expects everyone else to bear with him. Then why is he not as patient with the faults of those around him as he expects them to be with him? Why does he fly into a rage at those faults?

It follows that this task of self-control is an obvious one; and yet it is rated as being so difficult that a person who succeeds in it deserves far more praise and fame than the conquering hero of a city.

⊙

שֵׂכֶל אָדָם הֶאֱרִיךְ אַפּוֹ
וְתִפְאַרְתּוֹ עֲבֹר עַל־פָּשַׁע:

*A man who has shown patience has shown intelligence,*
*and it is his glory to overlook an offense inflicted on him. (19, 11)*

גְּדָל־חֵמָה נֹשֵׂא עֹנֶשׁ
כִּי אִם־תַּצִּיל וְעוֹד תּוֹסִף:

*He who is in great wrath shall suffer punishment;*
*if you come to his rescue, you merely add aggravation.* (19, 19)

אֶרֶךְ אַפַּיִם רַב־תְּבוּנָה
וּקְצַר־רוּחַ מֵרִים אִוֶּלֶת:

*He who is patient gains insight,*
*but one who is impatient acquires folly as his portion.* (14, 29)

Someone who tolerates a good deal from others is usually despised. People believe that he compromises his dignity by keeping silent if he has suffered an offense. In fact, however, the man who can control his anger, disregard an unfairness and forget it, is sensible. Forgiveness is the mark of nobility.

Once a person is caught in the throes of a towering rage, he can hardly be helped anymore; and he will have to bear the consequences, which may prove very unfortunate. A neighbor may try to save him and his victim by persuasion, but he will only succeed in incensing him more.

We have learned that patience is a valuable quality, and impatience a harmful one, as far as our behavior is concerned. But in our search for knowledge, too, patience is as advantageous as impatience (shortness of temper) is injurious. If we want to achieve real understanding of a subject, we need much patience. An impatient student does not check very thoroughly, and he accepts the first result that comes to his mind, no matter how unwise it might be.

# XII

## JUDGMENT AND PUBLIC OPINION

מַצְרֵף לַכֶּסֶף וְכוּר לַזָּהָב
וְאִישׁ לְפִי מַהֲלָלוֹ:

*The refining pot is for silver, and the crucible for gold,*
*and a man is tried according to what he praises.* (27, 21)

If you desire an immediate assessment of the character, way of thought,
and principles of a person, merely listen to the things he praises. Just as
a crucible shows up the purity in the contents of silver and gold, the
things a man praises and the actions he approves reveal his entire set of
values. By listening to his judgments, we can get to know whether he
rates ethical behavior highly or not so highly, whether his convictions
have magnanimity, whether his principles have integrity, and whether
his views reflect purity and truth — in short, all of a person's moral
values.

⊙

הַכֵּר־פָּנִים לֹא־טוֹב
וְעַל־פַּת־לֶחֶם יִפְשַׁע־גָּבֶר:

*Judging people according to appearances is not good;*
*else a man would transgress for a piece of bread.* (28, 21)

A double standard for right and wrong, depending on the person it concerns, is harmful not only in court but also in social communication and
conversation. To rate unethical or illegal behavior according to the
status of the person, whether he is rich or poor, whether he belongs to
the so-called higher echelons of society or to the lower classes, means to
distort public opinion and to mislead people's consciences. If the highly-
placed find excuses for indulging in unethical and illegal practices to

satisfy tendencies and penchants which belong to their life of luxury,
then why should the "common" man — as we so commonly call him —
not excuse himself, indeed justify himself, if he commits a crime to
satisfy *his* basic needs?

To such distortion of general public opinion, the following proverb is
applicable:

מַצְדִּיק רָשָׁע וּמַרְשִׁיעַ צַדִּיק
תּוֹעֲבַת ד' גַּם־שְׁנֵיהֶם:

*He who justifies the lawless man, and he who condemns a righteous
man,*
*both of them are an abomination to God.* (17, 15)

⊙

עֹזְבֵי תוֹרָה יְהַלְלוּ רָשָׁע
וְשֹׁמְרֵי תוֹרָה יִתְגָּרוּ בָם:

*They who forsake the Law praise the wicked,*
*but those who keep the Law rise up to contend with them.* (28, 4)

Our Proverbs extol peace and repeatedly warn us to avoid strife; but
they are far from agreement with those who proclaim "peace at any
price" as their slogan. Peace at any price should be upheld, even at the
cost of possessions, rights and honor, only if our personal interest,
property rights or recognition is at stake. In that case, we should avoid
even the most justified quarrel. But if values of the highest communal interest are concerned, if it involves sanctified moral values for humanity
in general and for our Jewish vocation in particular, then we may not remain silent. Then we must intercede, even if it means forfeiting the
highest good: peace. If a false love of peace or a lack of strength were to
silence those who know what is good and true, and who deplore in the
depth of their hearts the betrayal of the holiest values of mankind and
Judaism, then these values would indeed be lost.

Only those who do not observe God's Law in their own private life, or are not active on behalf of its maintenance within the community (both are called "abandoning the Law"), speed or even encourage the way of the lawless. However, he who conscientiously fulfills God's Law in his private life and is aware of his duty to uphold its observance within the community (both are called שמירת התורה, keeping the Law) will not keep silent. Wherever he sees betrayal of the Torah, he rises up to reprove, to oppose, to fight — and not only בו (with him) but בם (with them) — even if many commit this betrayal. For we are all appointed to be שומרי התורה; the Torah was given in sacred trust to each of us, and we are in duty bound to be its conscientious custodians. Just as a *shomer* (a sentry or guard) should never lose sight of his charge, has to protect it to the best of his ability and strength, and must defend it against any attack, to preserve it whole and undamaged for its owner, so too we have the duty always to vigilantly watch and vigorously defend the Torah, that was given to us in trust by God, as His holiest valuable treasure, to preserve it for Him in utter wholeness and unmitigated purity, and to transmit it whole and pure into the hands of our descendants, for the same conscientious care by them.

Where goods that we are entitled to call our own are concerned, which we have the right to dispose of, we may and should come to an agreement even at a sacrifice. But if values which are merely in our custody are concerned, we are not entitled to "negotiate a settlement." We may be forced to submit to violence, but never can we give violence the status of justice. We may never make concessions just for the sake of having peace, and never sign a compromise peace settlement. On such a document our signature would be null and void, because we lack the authorization.

⊙

בְּאֵין חָזוֹן יִפָּרַע עָם
וְשֹׁמֵר תּוֹרָה אַשְׁרֵהוּ:

*If vision, publicly proclaimed, is lacking, the people lose their restraint, but one who keeps the Law, happy is he.* (29, 18)

The term חזון, vision, publicly proclaimed, as we know from our
prophets, refers to statements that penetrate beyond the surface and the
present scene, right to the core. Such חזון can evaluate circumstances
and measure them by the eternally valid standard of the Divine law.
Such חזון can point to consequences which will unavoidably develop
from present circumstances unless they are changed. Such a חזון sets at
all times an incorruptible standard of inalienable truth; it calls upon men
to come to their senses and be thoughtful.

According to our Proverbs, such a חזון should never be lacking in any
period and in any community, lest men lose true perception about
themselves and their circumstances. In the absence of חזון, the truth
becomes distorted, and the perceptive insight which should constitute
the basis of Torah-fulfillment becomes obscured. Hence, without חזון the
bond and support which is to uphold us in unalterable faithfulness to
fulfill our God-given duty will be severed. But any man who by speaking
words of חזון proves himself a keeper of the Divine law is promised
every happiness, no matter how many conflicts and enmities his position
as such a custodian will entail.

# XIII

## HUMILITY AND PRIDE

עֵקֶב עֲנָוָה יִרְאַת ד'
עֹשֶׁר וְכָבוֹד וְחַיִּים:

*In the wake of humility comes fear of the Lord,*
*even riches, and honor, and life.* (22, 4)

Our holy Scriptures know of no higher, more ennobling virtue than ענוה, the mentality residing in the profoundness of the spirit which is totally unconscious of its own importance. Whatever the ענו may be, possess, desire, or accomplish is never of his own making; it is exclusively the product of a higher Being. Himself he considers a creature, created by the one and only God, as His child and servant. The word "I," emphatically spoken, is completely strange to his trend of thought and mentality.

According to our Proverbs, the immediate effect of ענוה is ירֵאת ד', the fear of God. In the sense of a person's inner conviction, ירֵאת ד' is actually synonymous with ענוה, not merely its consequence. In fact, ענוה without ירֵאת ד' is entirely inconceivable. On the contrary, ענוה is the purest expression of true ירֵאה. But in the sense of the stamp upon a life led in obedience to God, ירֵאת ד' is the direct consequence of ענוה, which automatically resolves itself into the fulfillment of God's will.

ירֵאת ד', however, is not the only consequence of ענוה. Our Proverbs also mention עושר וכבוד וחיים, riches, honor, and life—even though nothing is further from the direct intention and endeavors of the ענו than obtaining such goods. For if a person is called "rich" when he "reaches" what he desires, then עושר וכבוד וחיים are the natural consequence, the logical reward of ענוה. To quote from the ethical proverbs of the Fathers, איזהו

עשיר השמח בחלקו, he who is satisfied with that which is allotted to him is rich. It follows that the humblest person on earth is also the richest one. He always has what he needs. In fact, he has more than he might hope for, more than he thinks he merits קטונתי מכל החסדים (as Jacob the Patriarch said — Genesis 32, 11), "I am far too insignificant for all the love and faith which God has shown me", is no empty phrase in his mouth; it expresses the essence of his feelings and convictions.

Another saying in the ethical proverbs of our Fathers reads, איזהו מכובד המכבד את הבריות — he who honors others shall be honored. Such an ענו never begrudges anyone the deference due him, he respects every person and allows him every courtesy. All these qualities are inherent in the character and nature of an ענו, who himself is far from any search for appreciation. In fact, it would never occur to him that he merits any appreciation.

Yet such a completely selfless way of conduct is so rare and outstanding an occurrence that, in spite of his unassuming attitude, people cannot but accord the full measure of their homage to a person who makes the least pretense to it.

Most of all, however, humility makes for חיים, life. The ענו to whom our Proverbs refer is poles removed from the false modesty by which a person backs away from any action or activity for the welfare, rescue, or advancement of others by affecting total insignificance and inadequacy, not venturing to say a loud word or take a step forward. That kind of modesty can be excused at the most as impotence, but never can it be considered a virtue.

The ענוה which our Scriptures praise goes hand in hand with the most vigorous energy. Was not Moshe, the greatest man of action, at the same time the greatest ענו, the most selfless man on earth? In the highest selflessness lies the greatest power. Ultimately, neglect of duty is due to selfishness. Because of selfishness we omit the good and commit the bad. Selfishness makes us shrink from the fulfillment of our life-task. But the ענו with integrity has no trace of selfishness; his self-sacrifice is not obstructed by egotism. He is always ready to use the last spark of his energy and the last fibre of his being in the service of the good. He feels that he has been granted life only  for this purpose, to use every breath for the energetic fulfillment of the good, but never for his own good. His entire sojourn on earth, regardless of the length of its duration, is true חַיִּים, true living. When he has departed from this world, one may say of him: He was alive.

◉

תּוֹעֲבַת ה׳ כָּל־גְּבַהּ־לֵב
יָד לְיָד לֹא יִנָּקֶה:

*An abomination to God is a haughty man,*
*hand to hand, he shall not remain pure.* (16, 5)

The extreme opposite of humility is haughtiness, which should be avoided as assiduously as humility should be pursued. One who looks down disdainfully upon all other people and their dealings, while at the same time he holds the highest opinion of himself and his own concerns, will inevitably become filled with such egotism as to make him completely self-centered, raising his own demands and expectations beyond all bounds. Because of this self-centered attitude, he is unable to evaluate in a true light the correct relationship of himself and his duties towards God and towards those around him. Consequently, he cannot remain innocent of mistakes and wrongdoing.

(The expression יד ליד occurs only here and in 11, 21. Its meaning is not quite clear. It may mean "from hand to hand," i.e., immediately, at once, similar to the rabbinic term מִיד. Or it may mean "upon my hand," certainly, for sure, you can shake hands on it, as תנו יד לד׳, II Chron. 30, 8, and מי הוא לידי יתקע, Job 17, 3.)

◉

גַּאֲוַת אָדָם תַּשְׁפִּילֶנּוּ
וּשְׁפַל־רוּחַ יִתְמֹךְ כָּבוֹד:

*A man's pride shall bring him low,*
*But the humble in spirit shall attain honor.* (29, 23)

Vainglorious pride, in itself, is debasing. It deprives one's character of dignity and strips every action of value, however praiseworthy such action may have been in itself. Moreover, it makes for painful humiliation, since those who associate with a prideful person will refuse to cater to his immoderate demands. The humility of the humble, on the other hand, will earn him respectful esteem; and since he does not look for honors, he remains shielded from insults.

לִפְנֵי־שֶׁבֶר גָּאוֹן
וְלִפְנֵי כִשָּׁלוֹן גֹּבַהּ רוּחַ:

*Pride goes before destruction,*
*and haughtiness before stumbling.* (16, 18)

לִפְנֵי־שֶׁבֶר יִגְבַּהּ לֵב־אִישׁ
וְלִפְנֵי כָבוֹד עֲנָוָה:

*Before destruction the heart of a man is haughty;*
*but before honor comes humility.* (18, 12)

בֵּית גֵּאִים יִסַּח ה׳
וְיַצֵּב גְּבוּל אַלְמָנָה:

*God will demolish the house of the proud,*
*but will firmly establish the boundaries of the widow.* (15, 25)

טוֹב שְׁפַל־רוּחַ אֶת־עֲנָוִים
מֵחַלֵּק שָׁלָל אֶת־גֵּאִים:

*Better to be humble with the modest*
*than to divide the spoil with the prideful.* (16, 19)

Haughtiness itself often causes the collapse of its own prideful structure of fortune. On the one hand, there is the hostile reaction of those who are made to suffer by a man's pride; and on the other hand, there is the lack of circumspection which is characteristic of those who stand on the pinnacle of their good fortune, which leads them to overlook circumstances and considerations which with any prudence they might well have perceived. These factors bring about his collapse. Pride at its most inflated, therefore, announces to the practiced observer an imminent downfall.

In any case, Divine providence strides towards its goal over the ruins of the constructions of haughtiness. It levels the edifices of those whose proud fortunes, instead of leading them to an ever more grateful obedience to God and an ever more generous furthering of the well-being of their fellow-men, have misled them to mere self-idolizing pridefulness. But the humble, forsaken widow is taken into His care, and He establishes her in a position of self-sufficient independence.

Therefore have no admiration for those who count themselves among the high-and-mighty and participate proudly in their much-coveted attainments. Better to praise those who, in a spirit of modesty, share the modest fortunes of the humble.

אָכֹל דְּבַשׁ הַרְבּוֹת לֹא־טוֹב
וְחֵקֶר כְּבֹדָם כָּבוֹד:

*It is not good to eat too much honey,*
*and to strive for honor is their honor!* (25, 27)

Sweets are agreeable and beneficial when eaten in moderation. When consumed in excess or as the main course, they become harmful. The same can be said of honor. To be respectfully esteemed is pleasant, and it is also conducive to thriving efficacy. But to pursue it as a target in itself and as one's main purpose, to enjoy an honor only because it may lead to more, and to use it only as a stepping stone to reach for additional adulation and glory — such an insatiable passion for honor will ultimately lead to ruin.

# XIV

## GOD'S OMNISCIENCE AND
## DIVINE PROVIDENCE

בְּכָל־מָקוֹם עֵינֵי ד׳
צֹפוֹת רָעִים וְטוֹבִים:

*The eyes of God are in every place,*
*observing both the evil and the good. (15, 3)*

שְׁאוֹל וַאֲבַדּוֹן נֶגֶד ד׳
אַף כִּי־לִבּוֹת בְּנֵי־אָדָם:

*The grave and decay are manifest to God;*
*how much more the hearts of mankind. (15, 11)*

אֹזֶן שֹׁמַעַת וְעַיִן רֹאָה
ד׳ עָשָׂה גַּם־שְׁנֵיהֶם:

*The hearing ear and the seeing eye,*
*God has made indeed both of them. (20, 12)*

נֵר ד׳ נִשְׁמַת אָדָם
חֹפֵשׂ כָּל־חַדְרֵי־בָטֶן:

*A lamp of God is man's soul,*
*probing all inner chambers. (20, 27)*

God's eyes [so to speak] are everywhere and see everything. No circumstance and no situation escapes God's view. He observes both the wicked and the just. Unthinkingly you might say, "God never notices the evil on earth, nor the wicked who perpetrate it — or else He would not tolerate it." Yet, this too fits into God's well-considered world-plan, that it is possible for bad things to happen, that man can also be bad. Were it not for this possibility, the good would not be good; people would not be "good" if they did not have the choice to be bad. As we have learned previously, in 26, 10 and 16, 4, even the bad stands in the service of the Master of the Universe; in His hand, it furthers the good and benefits the just.

Even the grave and decay, which men consider the end of existence, where human vision can go no further—these too are still objects of God's care. From the grave He awakens new life, and from decay, resurrection. Surely then, living, pulsing hearts, whether they are near or far from moral goodness, are also the object of God's care. They can also be revived from moral decay to moral health, and from the grave of immorality to a life of moral purity.

God has created the eye as an instrument for seeing and the ear as a tool for hearing. He has bestowed on your soul the power to see with the eye and to hear with the ear. Surely it is not conceivable that He should lack power to see and hear! Surely your own seeing and hearing are merely a feeble reflection of His all-penetrating vision and His all-perceiving hearing!

The very soul you harbor within you proclaims God's seeing and hearing. Can you not feel that, with this soul, God has implanted His lamp within you, that it fills every crevice of your inner being with its light, and that it listens to you? Can you not sense that it censures all your mistakes, warns you before you commit a wrong, gives you no peace after you have done it, and does not let you enjoy life until you have admitted your wrong before God and promised atonement and betterment? This divine light, which we call conscience, is also a seeing of God's eyes and a hearing of God's ear.

⊙

מֶלֶךְ יוֹשֵׁב עַל־כִּסֵּא־דִין
מְזָרֶה בְעֵינָיו כָּל־רָע:

*A king sits on the throne of justice,*
*sifts with his eyes all evil.*

מִי־יֹאמַר זִכִּיתִי לְבִּי
טָהַרְתִּי מֵחַטָּאתִי:

*Who can say: I have kept my heart clear,*
*have remained pure from sin!* (20, 8—9)

מַצְרֵף לַכֶּסֶף וְכוּר לַזָּהָב
וּבֹחֵן לִבּוֹת ד':

*The refining pot is for silver and the crucible for gold,*
*but God examines the hearts.* (17, 3)

To sift the bad (זרה as in Isaiah 30, 24), thrust it out more and more
from the minds of individuals, from society, and from human circumstances — so that man should become ever better, society ever more
just, and circumstances ever more salutary — this is the object of divine
providence. For this purpose God sits on the throne of justice, and
whatever a wink of His eye decrees over the world is intended to achieve
such sifting. And if such a decree should come to us and sentence us to
suffering for the sake of purification and improvement — who can reject
it with the claim that he does not need such purifying and betterment,
that he has succeeded in keeping his heart clear and unsullied, and his
conduct free from fault?

Yet as a crucible purges precious metals from dross and establishes their
value-contents, so too the sentences of divine providence purify and
evaluate the hearts of men, and establish the value of *their* contents.

רַבּוֹת מַחֲשָׁבוֹת בְּלֶב־אִישׁ
וַעֲצַת ד' הִיא תָקוּם:

*Many are the thoughts in a man's heart,*
*but only what God decides, shall stand.* (19, 21)

אֵין חָכְמָה וְאֵין תְּבוּנָה
וְאֵין עֵצָה לְנֶגֶד ד':
סוּס מוּכָן לְיוֹם מִלְחָמָה
וְלַד' הַתְּשׁוּעָה:

*Neither wisdom nor understanding*
*nor counsel avails against God.*
*The horse is prepared for the day of battle,*
*but victory is only from God.* (21, 30—31)

לֵב אָדָם יְחַשֵּׁב דַּרְכּוֹ
וַד' יָכִין צַעֲדוֹ:

*A man's heart considers his way,*
*But [only] God lets his step reach the aim.* (16, 9)

גֹּל אֶל־ד' מַעֲשֶׂיךָ
וְיִכֹּנוּ מַחְשְׁבֹתֶיךָ:

*Direct your actions toward God,*
*and your thoughts shall become the right ones.* (16, 3)

Certainly we should use the intelligence we have and the advice of judicious people that is accessible to us, to attain what is best. We are, however, always to remain aware of the fact that all our considerations, intelligence, advice and preparations are of no avail if God does not approve of our undertaking and does not grant its success. Hence, before we deliberate and take counsel with others, before we think of preparing the means towards an end, let us first take counsel with God. Let us ask ourselves whether the means which lead to this aim are agreeable to Him, in accordance with His Laws revealed in the Torah. Only then are we entitled to wish and hope for success, and to utilize such means as are at our disposal in order to reach a desirable goal.

⊙

שֹׁחֵר טוֹב יְבַקֵּשׁ רָצוֹן
וְדֹרֵשׁ רָעָה תְבוֹאֶנּוּ:

*He who tries for the good, seeks favor;*
*but if one looks for evil, it will come to him. (11, 27)*

טוֹב יָפִיק רָצוֹן מֵד׳
וְאִישׁ מְזִמּוֹת יַרְשִׁיעַ:

*A good man seeks to obtain favor from God,*
*but a man of self-sufficient thoughts will act wrongly. (12, 2)*

אַךְ־מְרִי יְבַקֶּשׁ־רָע
וּמַלְאָךְ אַכְזָרִי יְשֻׁלַּח־בּוֹ:

*The wicked man seeks only disobedience;*
*then as a merciless messenger he will be sent against himself. (17, 11)*

הֲלוֹא־יִתְעוּ חֹרְשֵׁי רָע
וְחֶסֶד וֶאֱמֶת חֹרְשֵׁי טוֹב:

*Those who plow evil, have error in their minds,*
*but those who plow goodness, plow love and truth. (14, 22)*

מִרְמָה בְּלֶב־חֹרְשֵׁי רָע
וּלְיֹעֲצֵי שָׁלוֹם שִׂמְחָה:

*Deceit is in the heart of those who plow evil,*
*but to the counsellors of peace comes joy. (12, 20)*

If we desire the good, let us try exclusively for the good; whoever desires
evil shall reap it. This is the basic thought of these sentences. Only what

is agreeable to God is good in the absolute sense, and relative to ourselves. Then only an איש מזימות, a person who overestimates cleverness in general and his own cleverness in particular, who thinks that the results of his own intelligence are sufficient — only such a person dares act against God's Law. He believes that thereby he merely offends or spites God; but in fact, he prepares the greatest vexation for himself. For God makes him become the most merciless cause of ill-fate to himself.

Consequently, all those who sow and plow evil into the field of their future are victims of a deceptive error. Love and truth and happiness from God thrive only for those who in all their actions cultivate the good.

אִם־לַלֵּצִים הוּא־יָלִיץ
ולעניים [וְלַעֲנָוִים] יִתֶּן־חֵן:

*While He prepares scorn for the scorners,*
*He extends gracious appreciation to the humble. (3, 34)*

For those who, in frivolous conceit, degrade any God-willed sanctity and seek to make a mockery of it in the minds of men, God's providence has ruin in store. They themselves and their ideas, so highly praised in their opposition to Godly sanctity, shall ultimately be exposed as such futile nonsense that they cannot escape the laughter of the world.

As for those people, on the other hand, who subordinate themselves in humble modesty to the Divine will and His sacred values, and whose entire existence resolves itself into obedience to Him, by the nobility and integrity of their conduct, they shall gain חֵן, gracious favor, not only in God's eyes, but also in the views of men.

◉

יִרְאַת ד' לְחַיִּים

*The fear of God grants life,*

וְשָׂבֵעַ יָלִין בַּל־יִפָּקֶד רָע:

*And he who has it shall rest satisfied,*
*without fear that evil shall be visited on him.* (19, 23)

The awareness of standing under God's providential protection is, to the
God-fearing, a source of constant life. Whether the day has brought him
loss or gain, he always concludes it "satisfied." Even if a wish was
denied him, he considers the denial as having been effected through
God's loving attention, and it presents an opportunity to prove his
faithfulness in duty, even in the face of such a denial. He accepts the
night without fear that he shall be visited by evil. The same satisfaction
and peacefulness fills him even when he sees the sun setting over his
temporal days, and he enters into the final night, which transforms the
death of the God-fearing into eternal light.

⊙

אַנְשֵׁי־רָע לֹא־יָבִינוּ מִשְׁפָּט
וּמְבַקְשֵׁי ד׳ יָבִינוּ כֹל:

*Men committed to evil do not understand the justice of Providence,*
*but they who seek God understand all things.* (28, 5)

People who are committed to the wrong, to whom there is nothing more
important than the assertion of their egotism and the satisfaction of their
sensual desires, characteristically judge joy and unhappiness, and the
distribution of fates by God's ordinance, according to their point of
view. But this view prevents them from gaining even the slightest inkling
of insight into the ways of Divine providence. In fact, they completely
negate such a providence, and its rule remains an enigma to them.
Others, however, do understand the ways of God, which educate and
purify man, elevating him to the highest destiny and to the height of happiness. These are people who stake their total physical and spiritual existence and endeavors upon gaining closeness to God, and who consider
the highest human happiness to be the awareness of Divine favor, acquired by faithful fulfillment of duty. For such as those, the ways of
Divine providence are no mystery.

צַנִּים פַּחִים בְּדֶרֶךְ עִקֵּשׁ
שׁוֹמֵר נַפְשׁוֹ יִרְחַק מֵהֶם:

*Thorns and snares are in the way of the crooked;*
*He who watches his soul should remain far from them.* (22, 5)

As surely as our entire way in life is under the guard and guidance of
Divine providence, just as surely are we not allowed to close our eyes
and walk blindly, relying on God's protection. God has not given men
eyes and intelligence for nothing. We have to use them conscientiously,
to recognize hindrances and dangers which might stand in our way,
whether through nature (צנים, thorns) or through human hand (פחים,
snares), to circumvent them and remove them. Only after we have used
the intelligence which has been granted us for our preservation may we
count on God's help. A blind attitude of "let us rely on God", instead of
using our eyes, would be עקשות, a wrongheadedness which can by no
means be excused.

# XV

## INTEGRITY AND CONSCIENTIOUSNESS

אַל־תַּסֵּג גְּבוּל עוֹלָם
אֲשֶׁר עָשׂוּ אֲבוֹתֶיךָ:

*Do not remove boundaries drawn for eternity,*
*which your fathers made.* (22, 28)

אַל־תַּסֵּג גְּבוּל עוֹלָם
וּבִשְׂדֵי יְתוֹמִים אַל־תָּבֹא:
כִּי־גֹאֲלָם חָזָק
הוּא־יָרִיב אֶת־רִיבָם אִתָּךְ:

*Do not remove boundaries drawn for eternity,*
*and do not trespass into the fields of orphans;*
*for their Redeemer is strong,*
*He shall fight their cause against you.* (23, 10—11)

Our fathers made restricting regulations, limiting our authority to act. These גזרות, מנהגים and תקנות, enacted to remain valid for all times, are compared by our Proverbs to שדי יתומים, possessions of fatherless orphans. Like children without a parent, the decrees of the national fathers who have departed are left without a representative on earth. They remain, therefore, a sacred legacy of the past, entrusted to the living present as a pledge to our sense of honor and duty. Our Proverbs warn us: do not infringe upon them! The departed may not be able to rise from their graves and defend their decrees against the arbitrariness of the present times, but their vigorous Divine Defender lives and wages the fight against those who demolish boundaries set down by the ancients, just as He defends the cause of orphans against those who violate their possessions.

212

פֶּלֶס וּמֹאזְנֵי מִשְׁפָּט לַד׳
מַעֲשֵׂהוּ כָּל־אַבְנֵי־כִיס:

*Just balances and scales are God's;*
*all the weights in one's pockets are made in His name.* (16, 11)

מֹאזְנֵי מִרְמָה תּוֹעֲבַת ד׳
וְאֶבֶן שְׁלֵמָה רְצוֹנוֹ:

*A false balance-scale is an abomination to God,*
*but a perfect weight is his desire.* (11, 1)

תּוֹעֲבַת ד׳ אֶבֶן וָאָבֶן
וּמֹאזְנֵי מִרְמָה לֹא־טוֹב:

*A stone and a stone are abomination to God,*
*and a misleading balance-scale is not good.* (20, 23)

אֶבֶן וָאֶבֶן אֵיפָה וְאֵיפָה
תּוֹעֲבַת ד׳ גַּם־שְׁנֵיהֶם:

*A stone and a stone, a weight and a weight,*
*both of them are an abomination to God.* (20, 10)

Not only the act of deceiving someone by false measuring and weighing, but even the presence, the making or possession of inaccurate measures and weights is repugnant to God. Making a means of measurement or weight is an act of the greatest responsibility, and the act of a man who makes those weights correspond to a certain volume or contents is of far-reaching importance. Correct weights are made in the name of God and in the name of justice, which God has established as the immovable basis of human communication; false weights are a blasphemy of God, because they defy justice. Only a full measure, neither too big nor too small, is in accord with His will.

Even if you were to keep two sets of weights or measurements out of scrupulousness, to buy with the small ones and to sell with the large ones (so as to "bend over backwards" in favor of others) — this too would be לֹא טוֹב, not good. You yourself may use them in this way, as a matter of conscientiousness; but if they should come into the hands of others, they could be misused for cheating, and for such deceitful misuse, you should not provide the means or the opportunity.

⊙

בָּז לְדָבָר יֵחָבֶל לוֹ
וִירֵא מִצְוָה הוּא יְשֻׁלָּם:

*Whoever disdains anything will be pledged because of it,*
*but he who respects the commandments shall be rewarded. (13, 13)*

Even a pin should not be disdained; some day you might miss it. Neither should you consider any duty too insignificant for you to fulfill. Whoever neglects his duty in the smallest detail will be answerable for it. Just as you should be God-fearing, so too you should be "mitzva-fearing." To fear God is to respect His mitzvoth, for it means the fear of violating any one of His laws. To one who respects God's laws, nothing is insignificant; he attends to the law, not to its object, and whatever God makes the object of His law gains importance, no matter how insubstantial it may be in itself. The God-fearing person pays attention to the smallest detail of Divinely-directed law, and for this attention his conscientiousness is richly rewarded.

הוֹלֵךְ בְּיָשְׁרוֹ יְרֵא ד'
וּנְלוֹז דְּרָכָיו בּוֹזֵהוּ:

*In uprightness walks the one who fears God,*
*but he who disregards Him is unsteady. (14, 2)*

הוֹלֵךְ תָּמִים יִוָּשֵׁעַ
וְנֶעְקַשׁ דְּרָכַיִם יִפּוֹל בְּאֶחָת:

*He who walks in integrity shall be helped,*
*but he who looks for double, crooked ways shall collapse. (28, 18)*

Fear of God is the only guiding star of conduct which does not leave us in doubt about what we should do. It shows us the exact course of duty and allows for no deviations. But whoever disdains this guiding star, the נלוז, remains without any support. The most varied interests and enticements, both inner and external, pull him in different directions and gain alternating influence over him.

The second proverb refers to a person of moral duplicity. He tries to walk simultaneously in דרכיים, two opposite directions, and, since one of them must be wrong, he will inevitably fall in that path. On the other hand, someone who does not leave his actions subject to external influences and follows only the voice of duty is תמים, a man of simple integrity, fully committed to his obligations. He shall benefit by unexpected help from above.

⊙

הֲפַכְפַּךְ דֶּרֶךְ אִישׁ וָזָר
וְזַךְ יָשָׁר פָּעֳלוֹ:

*If the conduct of a man is in constant change, he is a stranger to the right way;*
*but one of inner purity, his doings are straightfoward.* (21, 8)

If you observe someone whose behavior is subject to constant moody changes, so that you cannot predict today how you will find him tomorrow, you can be sure that he is not on the right way. But someone whose inner life is consistently pure proceeds in the right direction, like a straight line which knows no deviation.

# XVI

## CONDUCT TOWARDS ENEMIES

אַל־תֹּאמַר כַּאֲשֶׁר עָשָׂה־לִי
כֵּן אֶעֱשֶׂה־לּוֹ
אָשִׁיב לָאִישׁ כְּפָעֳלוֹ׃

*Do not say, "As he has done to me, so I shall do to him;*
*so will I render to the man according to his work." (24, 29)*

אַל־תֹּאמַר אֲשַׁלְּמָה־רָע
קַוֵּה לַד׳ וְיֹשַׁע לָךְ׃

*Do not say "I will requite evil";*
*hope unto God, and He will help you. (20, 22)*

בִּנְפֹל אוֹיִבְךָ אַל־תִּשְׂמָח
וּבִכָּשְׁלוֹ אַל־יָגֵל לִבֶּךָ׃
פֶּן־יִרְאֶה ד׳ וְרַע בְּעֵינָיו
וְהֵשִׁיב מֵעָלָיו אַפּוֹ׃

*When your enemy falls, do not rejoice,*
*and when he stumbles, do not let your heart be glad,*
*lest God see it and it displease Him,*
*and He take away His anger from him. (24, 17—18)*

אִם־רָעֵב שֹׂנַאֲךָ הַאֲכִילֵהוּ לָחֶם
וְאִם־צָמֵא הַשְׁקֵהוּ מָיִם

*If your enemy is hungry, give him bread to eat,*
*and if he is thirsty, give him water to drink,*

כִּי גֶחָלִים אַתָּה חֹתֶה עַל־רֹאשׁוֹ
וַד' יְשַׁלֶּם־לָךְ:

*for you will heap coals on his head,*
*and God will reward you.* (25, 21—22)

בִּרְצוֹת יְהוָה דַּרְכֵי־אִישׁ
גַּם־אוֹיְבָיו יַשְׁלִם אִתּוֹ:

*When a man's ways please God,*
*He shall make even his enemies be at peace with him.* (16, 7)

Nothing is more natural than the wish to take revenge, and seemingly nothing corresponds to justice as much as a "just" revenge. And yet Divine law warns us: You are not to take revenge! Still, the desire for revenge is so strong in us, it is aroused so powerfully by the wrong inflicted on us, and is so difficult to subdue in compliance to the Law, that the Proverbs add some reflections which come to our aid in obeying this difficult precept.

You may think that you are allowed to defend yourself by countering such evils as may threaten you, by equally evil actions — for instance, defamation by defamation. Do not believe it! Evil does not become good because you use it in the fight against bad. Even at the time of fighting your enemies, you are to remain free from moral defilement, worthy of God and of yourself. Do not try to help yourself by unworthy weapons. "Hope unto God," because He helps those who remain pure for His sake.

Even when God helps and the enemy who pursues you comes to grief and suffers a fall which is not of your making, do not be glad of his downfall. Do not rejoice over his moral degradation because all the world can now see how evil he is! Such a malicious vengeful joy is also a sin. After all, even the evil that people inflict upon us cannot happen without God's permission, and it may well be that the animosity you encountered is a trial which God has imposed on you in order to test your own moral stamina. Hence if your rejoicing, which is displeasing to God, now gives proof of your persisting moral immaturity, it might well lead to renewed activity by your enemy, whose downfall you have thus prematurely celebrated.

Only one kind of "revenge" is permissible: to do a kindness to your enemy! If you are good to your enemy, without stressing his animosity against you ("See, I am not like you"), if you quietly do him a favor, he will look back with burning shame upon his behavior to you, and God will reward you.

On the whole, if you have enemies and antagonists, rather than scheming on ways to fight them, it were better that you concentrate on perfecting your own life and intensifying your duty-observance. In this way, instead of enmity on earth, you will acquire God's amity; and if your conduct is agreeable to Him, God will make your moral valor appreciated by your peers as well, and will change their animosity into esteem.

Now, if even the revenge of evil by evil is so seriously censured, how much worse is ingratitude, which repays good with evil:

מֵשִׁיב רָעָה תַּחַת טוֹבָה
לֹא־תָמוּשׁ רָעָה מִבֵּיתוֹ:

*Whoever rewards evil for good,*
*evil shall not depart from his house. (17, 13)*

# XVII

## CHEERFULNESS

תּוֹחֶלֶת מְמֻשָּׁכָה מַחֲלָה־לֵב
וְעֵץ חַיִּים תַּאֲוָה בָאָה:

*Deferred hope makes the heart sick,*
*but a wish which has come is a tree of life.* (13, 12)

מְאוֹר־עֵינַיִם יְשַׂמַּח־לֵב
שְׁמוּעָה טוֹבָה תְּדַשֶּׁן־עָצֶם:

*The light of the eyes rejoices the heart;*
*good news gives marrow to the bones.* (15, 30)

מַיִם קָרִים עַל־נֶפֶשׁ עֲיֵפָה
וּשְׁמוּעָה טוֹבָה מֵאֶרֶץ מֶרְחָק:

*As cold water to a tired soul*
*so is good news from a far land.* (25, 25)

חַיֵּי בְשָׂרִים לֵב מַרְפֵּא
וּרְקַב עֲצָמוֹת קִנְאָה:

*The life of the flesh trains the heart,*
*but envy rots the bones.* (14, 30)

לֵב שָׂמֵחַ יֵיטִב פָּנִים
וּבְעַצְּבַת־לֵב רוּחַ נְכֵאָה:

*A joyful heart makes for a cheerful countenance,*
*but by a sorrowful heart the spirit is depressed.* (15, 13)

לֵב שָׂמֵחַ יֵיטִב גֵּהָה
וְרוּחַ נְכֵאָה תְּיַבֶּשׁ־גָּרֶם:

*A merry heart keeps the spirit up,*
*but a depressed spirit dessicates the limbs.* (17, 22)

רוּחַ־אִישׁ יְכַלְכֵּל מַחֲלֵהוּ
וְרוּחַ נְכֵאָה מִי יִשָּׂאֶנָּה:

*A man's spirit sustains him in sickness,*
*but if the spirit is broken, who shall uplift it?* (18, 14)

A cheerful disposition is an inestimable treasure. It preserves health, promotes convalescence, and helps us cope with adversity. Anyone who has experienced the debilitating effect of a drawn-out longing knows how profoundly the body can be affected by our state of mind. On the other hand, fulfillment of a desire, or good news, has an invigorating effect on us.

Our Proverbs make it clear that nothing is so detrimental to our health as envy. An envious person has constant opportunity for dissatisfaction, since most people are bound to posses something he is lacking, which seems desirable to him. If any one of his wishes is denied to him, everything else appears valueless to him. Hence, our Proverbs express great praise for the opposite of envy: a gentle, generous heart, which grudges nothing to others.

A discontented, dissatisfied heart weakens the limbs and paralyzes activity, but good cheer brightens the outlook and straightens the body. The worst illness, according to our Proverbs, is an affliction of the mind and spirit. If the body needs healing, the mind can contribute a great deal — it acts as a nurse to the sick body. But if the mind is affected, who can raise up the mind again?! It is not the body which sustains the spirit; the spirit supports the body.

אַל־תִּתְהַלֵּל בְּיוֹם מָחָר
כִּי לֹא־תֵדַע מַה־יֵּלֶד יוֹם:

*Do not boast of the coming day,*
*for you do not know what it may bring forth.* (27, 1)

מְכַסֶּה פְשָׁעָיו לֹא יַצְלִיחַ
וּמוֹדֶה וְעֹזֵב יְרֻחָם:
אַשְׁרֵי אָדָם מְפַחֵד תָּמִיד
וּמַקְשֶׁה לִבּוֹ יִפּוֹל בְּרָעָה:

*He who covers up his transgressions shall not succeed,*
*but one who confesses and atones shall obtain mercy.*
*Fortunate is one who always fears,*
*but he who hardens his heart shall fall into misfortune.* (28, 13—14)

חֶרְדַּת אָדָם יִתֵּן מוֹקֵשׁ
וּבוֹטֵחַ בַּד' יְשֻׂגָּב:

*A man's terror brings ruin,*
*but he who trusts in God shall have a conqueror's strength.* (29, 25)

הִתְרַפִּיתָ בְּיוֹם צָרָה
צַר כֹּחֶכָה:

*Have you shown weakness on the day of adversity?*
*Then your real adversity was your lack of strength.* (24, 10)

While true cheerfulness is a precious treasure, it must be distinguished from lighthearted nonchalance which takes life easy in general, for which seriousness does not exist. That attitude lives only for the present moment, and thinks neither of the future nor of the consequences of actions. The cheerfulness that our Proverbs call a precious possession is rooted not in frivolity but in inner serenity, attuned to God. It is a positive attitude, glad of life, including its seriousness and the difficult challenges assigned by God. A serenely cheerful person knows that on earth nothing is more enduring than change, and that nobody can predict what the morrow has in store for him. Yet the future's uncertainty does not trouble his good humor. One thing he knows for sure: it will bring him new tasks as well as new assistance from above to solve them.

Even the most depressing awareness — of having committed some wrong — does not irredeemably rob him of his good spirits. Once he has recognized his wrong deed, he tries not to cover it up and let it gnaw at him in the dark recesses of his subconscious. He knows that such self-deception will get him nowhere. He rather views his act undisguisedly, in a clear light, admits it to himself and before God, and tries to make up for it as best as possible. Before God he earnestly promises to avoid such guilty acts in the future; and from this serious determination he regains the serenity that is essential to the fulfillment of our duty.

A person blessed with such cheerful serenity has only one concern: not to fall short of accomplishing his duty. But this is the very concern which is meant to accompany us throughout life — and it is the only one that relieves us of all other worries! In this one concern, moreover, we are strengthened by our trust in God, which steels us to joyfully overcome all difficulties. Moreover, in times of danger it keeps us from losing our head and giving way to panicky unclear view of matters, and from there to thoughtless actions, which instead of warding off the threat merely precipitate it.

If we have shown weakness on a day of danger, it means that the danger was more within us than without. The real danger was our own weakness. Had we remained strong, we would have overcome the danger and come out of the struggle victorious. In situations of distress, it is the limitation in our strength which constitutes the most regrettable factor.

(The word כחכה, "your lack of — or weakened — strength," is like ידכה, "your weaker hand," in Exodus 13, 16.)

# XVIII

## PLEASURE—INDULGENCE AND GREED

מְפַנֵּק מִנֹּעַר עַבְדּוֹ
וְאַחֲרִיתוֹ יִהְיֶה מָנוֹן:

*He who spoils his slave from youth,*
*his end will be dependency. (29, 21)*

As long as a craving or an appetite is still young, we can easily subdue it
by granting it only what is admissible, and thus keep it under control for
the rest of our life. But if we allow it more than its due from the beginning, and spoil it by over-indulgence, it will soon cease to be submissive
and will make ever-growing demands upon us. From a servant, it
becomes as a child to whom we are finally unable to deny anything and
who demands maintenance, care, and satisfaction of all his habits. More
than that — the one servant becomes not only a child, but מנון (connoting נין, great-grandchild; in general, descendants; and מנון, a whole
progeny of children). *One* craving that has been humored acquires many
companions and engenders many appetites. Once these dominate a
person, he will find his ruin in a debauched way of life.

⊙

נֶפֶשׁ שְׂבֵעָה תָּבוּס נֹפֶת
וְנֶפֶשׁ רְעֵבָה כָּל־מַר מָתוֹק:

*He who is satiated disdains a honeycomb;*
*but to the hungry, even the bitter is sweet. (27, 7)*

Were we to eat only when hungry, we would not miss delicacies. We like
such unnecessary stimuli to our appetite only because we eat beyond
our actual need; and this may easily lead to harmful pampering.

אִישׁ מַחְסוֹר אֹהֵב שִׂמְחָה
אֹהֵב יַיִן־וָשֶׁמֶן לֹא יַעֲשִׁיר:

*He who loves entertainment is a man of want;*
*he who loves wine and oil shall not become rich.* (21, 17)

לֵץ הַיַּיִן הֹמֶה שֵׁכָר
וְכָל־שֹׁגֶה בּוֹ לֹא יֶחְכָּם:

*Wine is a mocker, strong drink a rioter;*
*whoever reels in them shall not become wise.* (20, 1)

Entertainment, wine and oil, may not be objectionable in themselves, but
we are not to become their *companions*. The *love* of enjoyments and the
pleasures of luxury ultimately leads to impoverishment. What is worse,
the character of our thinking and behavior toward our peers is
dangerously affected by indulgence in wine. It arouses sensual desires,
and it causes us to ridicule and degrade values which in our sober
periods are of the highest importance and sanctity to us. And in-
temperance is also an enemy of peaceful conduct toward our fellow-
men. Whoever indulges in immoderate wine-drinking will not become
wise and will not remain wise.

⊙

אַל־תְּהִי בְסֹבְאֵי־יָיִן
בְּזֹלְלֵי בָשָׂר לָמוֹ:
כִּי־סֹבֵא וְזוֹלֵל יִוָּרֵשׁ
וּקְרָעִים תַּלְבִּישׁ נוּמָה:

*Do not be among wine-bibbers*
*or those who degrade themselves by gluttony of meat;*
*for drinkers and gluttons shall become poor,*
*and their sleepiness shall clothe them in rags.* (23, 20–21)

People who become dehumanized by excessive eating and drinking
finally waste whatever they possess and become unable to reacquire
what they need. Do not join them and do not be of their party!

לְמִי אוֹי לְמִי אֲבוֹי לְמִי מִדְיָנִים
לְמִי־שִׂיחַ לְמִי פְּצָעִים חִנָּם
לְמִי חַכְלִלוּת עֵינָיִם:
לַמְאַחֲרִים עַל־הַיָּיִן
לַבָּאִים לַחְקוֹר מִמְסָךְ:
אַל־תֵּרֶא יַיִן כִּי יִתְאַדָּם
כִּי־יִתֵּן בכיס [בַּכּוֹס] עֵינוֹ
יִתְהַלֵּךְ בְּמֵישָׁרִים:
אַחֲרִיתוֹ כְּנָחָשׁ יִשָּׁךְ
וּכְצִפְעֹנִי יַפְרִשׁ:
עֵינֶיךָ יִרְאוּ זָרוֹת
וְלִבְּךָ יְדַבֵּר תַּהְפֻּכוֹת:
וְהָיִיתָ כְּשֹׁכֵב בְּלֶב־יָם
וּכְשֹׁכֵב בְּרֹאשׁ חִבֵּל:
הִכּוּנִי בַל־חָלִיתִי
הֲלָמוּנִי בַּל־יָדָעְתִּי
מָתַי אָקִיץ אוֹסִיף אֲבַקְשֶׁנּוּ עוֹד:

Who has woe, and who alas?
who has strife, who complaints, and who needless injuries?
who has redness of eyes? —
those who tarry long at the wine,
those who come to try out new drinks!
Do not look upon the wine, how it reddens,
how it lends color to the glass,
how smoothly it glides down.
For in the end it shall bite like a snake,
and sting like a basilisk.
Your eyes shall see strange things,
and your heart shall utter nonsense;
and you shall be as one afloat in the middle of the sea,
or who lies on top of a mast.
"They struck me and I felt nothing,
they beat me and I knew nothing;
when I awaken, I will continue and seek it anew." (23, 29—35)

Thus our Proverbs picture the condition of an incorrigible drunkard, as a vivid warning and deterrent!

⊙

עִיר פְּרוּצָה אֵין חוֹמָה
אִישׁ אֲשֶׁר אֵין מַעְצָר לְרוּחוֹ:

*Like an open, unwalled city*
*is a man who cannot restrain his desire.* (25, 28)

שְׁאוֹל וַאֲבַדּ֑וֹ לֹא תִשְׂבַּעְנָה
וְעֵינֵי הָאָדָם לֹא תִשְׂבַּעְנָה:

*Tomb and decay are never sated,*
*And the eyes of a man remain unsatisfied.* (27, 20)

רְחַב־נֶפֶשׁ יְגָרֶה מָדוֹן
וּבֹטֵחַ עַל־ד' יְדֻשָּׁן:

*The greedy in spirit stirs up strife*
*but he who trusts in God shall be abundantly satisfied.* (28, 25)

Greed is even more ruinous than pleasure-seeking. While pleasure has a saturation point, and an excess of indulgence finally makes it impossible to tolerate more, greed is insatiable. To a man who has been unable to check it, it becomes a passion against which he remains totally defenseless. Like the grave and decay, which devour and decompose everything without making use of it, so too the insatiable desire of the greedy seeks constantly more possessions without ever being content.

There is only one limit to greed: the self-inflicted one of arousing opposition on the part of competitors. As for cure, however, greed has only one remedy: faith in God. Only someone who thinks that his and his family's destiny is dependent entirely upon himself and his own abilities can become a victim of unlimited greediness. He believes that every new acquisition will afford him security against penury, and once he has finished providing for his own needs, he amasses for his children and grandchildren into the infinite future. But whoever trusts in God, confident that it is only God's favor which insures his future and the future of his family, is easily contented. He merely endeavors to fulfill his duty, even in his search for material possessions, and whatever God lets him find, within the framework of the Divine commandments, satisfies him.

# XIX

## CONDUCT TOWARD THE GREAT

מַתָּן אָדָם יַרְחִיב לוֹ
וְלִפְנֵי גְדֹלִים יַנְחֶנּוּ:

*A man's liberality opens ways for him*
*and brings him before great men. (18, 16)*

חָזִיתָ אִישׁ מָהִיר בִּמְלַאכְתּוֹ
לִפְנֵי־מְלָכִים יִתְיַצָּב
בַּל־יִתְיַצֵּב לִפְנֵי חֲשֻׁכִּים:

*If you see a man diligent in his work,*
*he shall stand before kings.*
*He need not present himself before those who stand in the shadow. (22, 29)*

אַל־תִּתְהַדַּר לִפְנֵי־מֶלֶךְ
וּבִמְקוֹם גְּדֹלִים אַל־תַּעֲמֹד:
כִּי טוֹב אֲמָר־לְךָ עֲלֵה הֵנָּה
מֵהַשְׁפִּילְךָ לִפְנֵי נָדִיב
אֲשֶׁר רָאוּ עֵינֶיךָ:

*Do not glorify yourself before a king,*
*and where great men stand, do not set yourself up.*
*For it is better to be told, "Come up here"*
*than to be lowered in the presence of the nobleman*
*whom your eyes have already seen. (25, 6—7)*

רַבִּים מְבַקְשִׁים פְּנֵי־מוֹשֵׁל
וּמֵד' מִשְׁפַּט־אִישׁ:

*Many seek the face of a ruler,*
*And yet a man's fate comes from God.* (29, 26)

כִּי־תֵשֵׁב לִלְחוֹם אֶת־מוֹשֵׁל
בִּין תָּבִין אֶת־אֲשֶׁר לְפָנֶיךָ:
וְשַׂמְתָּ שַׂכִּין בְּלֹעֶךָ
אִם־בַּעַל נֶפֶשׁ אָתָּה:
אַל־תִּתְאָו לְמַטְעַמּוֹתָיו
וְהוּא לֶחֶם כְּזָבִים:

*If you sit down to eat with a ruler,*
*understand well what is before you,*
*and put the knife to your mouth*
*if you are a man of appetite.*
*Do not lust for his delicacies,*
*as his meal is not meant sincerely.* (23, 1–3)

The relationship that most people have with those on a socially higher level, commonly called "the Great" (or people of importance or distinction), is not viewed by our Proverbs in a very favorable light. According to Mishlé, it does not always require personal dignity, but often merely some liberality (munificence) toward the entourage of such great people, in order to gain access to them. However, if someone is an expert in his field, his personal ability will pave the way to the highly-placed, and he does not need the intervention of the lower echelons. In general, though, our Proverbs advise us not to seek out the environment of princes and the highly-placed, and certainly not to insinuate ourselves into their surroundings. Far better to modestly remain in the background and to be asked why you are staying behind and not coming up front, than to be given to understand, upon finally having succeeded in approaching the great person, that you really do not belong there.

Many people consider it a worthwhile pursuit to ingratiate themselves with a highly-placed person, and disregard the fact that their real fate lies in the hands of God!

Now, curiously, our Proverbs indicate clearly that even if you are fortunate enough to have been invited to the table of the great, you would be wise to taste little or nothing. Instead of putting your knife to the roast, rather keep your mouth closed and let your appetite pass. If you are the guest of a friend, he considers your presence an honor. But if an important personality invites you, he believes no doubt that he is extending some extraordinary honor to you and that the delicacies which he is offering you would not otherwise be within your reach. These are his thoughts, even if he is polite enough not to express them. But you should understand it, consider the implications, and act accordingly.

# XX

## THE STATE

יְרָא־אֶת־ד׳ בְּנִי וָמֶלֶךְ
עִם־שׁוֹנִים אַל־תִּתְעָרָב:
כִּי־פִתְאֹם יָקוּם אֵידָם
וּפִיד שְׁנֵיהֶם מִי יוֹדֵעַ:

*Fear God, my son, and the king,*
*and do not meddle with dissenters;*
*for their calamity shall rise suddenly,*
*and who can know the ruin of both? (24, 21–22)*

Respect and attention should be paid to the Divine order, valid forever and everywhere, as well as to the human order which the society in whose midst you live has established as the basis and directive for conducting its affairs. Keep away from dissenters who by their opinions, principles, speech and actions take a hostile stand against both the Divine and human order. Keep away from them even if you think that you will certainly not become a partner in their aims or activities, else both—you and they—will not end well. Their downfall comes of a sudden, so that you will be unable to say, "I shall disassociate myself from them before their ruin comes"; and neither you nor they can tell how great a devastation it will bring.

בְּרָב־עָם הַדְרַת־מֶלֶךְ
וּבְאֶפֶס לְאֹם מְחִתַּת רָזוֹן:

*In the multitude of people is the king's glory;*
*but in decrease of population, the dread of want. (14, 28)*

According to one opinion in the world, which looks with fear upon over-population and is apprehensive of increasing numbers of people, the

State should aim to decrease the population. Our Proverbs are clearly
opposed to this, asserting that it should be a point of pride to the State to
administer, superintend and direct the territories under its mandate in
such a way that the greatest possible number of inhabitants can find
satisfaction of their needs. Moreover, a reduction in population by no
means guarantees greater prosperity to the remaining inhabitants. On
the contrary, the situation which caused the reduction may well persist
until it threatens them with scarcity.

צְדָקָה תְרוֹמֵם־גּוֹי
וְחֶסֶד לְאֻמִּים חַטָּאת:

*Dutiful justice exalts a nation,*
*but the mercy of states is sin.* (14, 34)

The term צדקה means justice, denoting that justice under which *everybody* is guaranteed his rights, according to what he is entitled to
legally, or because of the social obligation which the community owes
him in view of special circumstances. This principle, provided it is upheld fully and unreservedly, is what promotes the national commonweal.
It is the principle under which every individual member of a nation is
held equal, both in rights and obligations, and under which the full
benefit of justice is extended to everyone.

The term חסד, on the other hand, means favor, loving-kindness. By its
nature it can be practiced properly only by individuals, for the benefit of
individuals. For a state it would be preferential treatment, favoritism: for
example, making grants or allowing dispensations; accordingly, it
should not be practiced by a state. An individual has means and
privileges belonging exclusively to him, and he can therefore utilize them
according to his private judgment or inclination, without thereby depriving others. But the state, as such, has no private means at its disposal; it
merely has means and rights which belong to the population collectively.
Accordingly, it cannot give individual dispensations or grant special
privileges to anyone, without at the same time doing an injustice to
others. In short, the state cannot practice חסד without at the same time
perpetrating a חטאת.

חֶסֶד וֶאֱמֶת יִצְּרוּ־מֶלֶךְ
וְסָעַד בַּחֶסֶד כִּסְאוֹ:

*Mercy and truth protect the king,*
*and by mercy he upholds his throne. (20, 28)*

מֶלֶךְ שׁוֹפֵט בֶּאֱמֶת דַּלִּים
כִּסְאוֹ לָעַד יִכּוֹן:

*A king who truly enacts the rights of the poor —*
*his throne shall be established forever. (29, 14)*

In the Book of Mishlé a king is represented as the most highly placed
person in society, with a wealth of means and rights put at his disposal
by the population to use according to his best judgment to benefit individuals and the community. The word for sovereign in our holy
language is נשיא, a person lifted high as a "cloud" above the earth,
gathering from it life-promoting moisture, in order to re-bestow it upon
the earth as a gift for its fecundity and life. A king may indeed practice
mercy; in fact חסד is his most beneficial prerogative, provided it is based
on wise consideration of the meritoriousness, deserving or especially
needy circumstances of those who look to him. In that way, he practices
mercy in truth, and this חסד and truth constitute the mightiest lifeguards
of a sovereign. If the powerless and unprotected levels of his people feel
personally sheltered by their king — then his throne is securely established, and even a change in times cannot shake it.

קֶסֶם עַל־שִׂפְתֵי־מֶלֶךְ
בְּמִשְׁפָּט לֹא יִמְעַל־פִּיו:
פֶּלֶס וּמֹאזְנֵי מִשְׁפָּט לַד׳
מַעֲשֵׂהוּ כָּל־אַבְנֵי־כִיס:

*A magic rests on the king's lips;*
*therefore let his mouth not sin in judgment.*
*As just balances and scales are God's,*
*and all the weights in [your] pocket are His work,*

תּוֹעֲבַת מְלָכִים עֲשׂוֹת רֶשַׁע
כִּי בִצְדָקָה יִכּוֹן כִּסֵּא:
רְצוֹן מְלָכִים שִׂפְתֵי־צֶדֶק
וְדֹבֵר יְשָׁרִים יֶאֱהָב:
חֲמַת־מֶלֶךְ מַלְאֲכֵי־מָוֶת
וְאִישׁ חָכָם יְכַפְּרֶנָּה:
בְּאוֹר־פְּנֵי־מֶלֶךְ חַיִּים
וּרְצוֹנוֹ כְּעָב מַלְקוֹשׁ:

*thus let anything evil be an abomination to the king,*
*for by righteousness is a throne established.*
*Lips of righteousness should be the wish of kings,*
*and he should love one who speaks right.*
*If the king's wrath [roars] like death-messengers,*
*may a wise man [be able to] pacify him.*
*Let the light of a king's countenance mean life,*
*and his good will be as a cloud of rain.* (16, 10—15)

The words of a king have extraordinary power. A pronouncement or a
view of his which has filtered through to the public can, like magic, influence the attitude of his people towards right and wrong, to what is
praiseworthy or not. A sovereign should therefore pay heed to his words
far more carefully than an ordinary mortal, to make sure that none of
his utterances infringe upon what is right.

In matters of justice, nothing is too insignificant, even measurements
and scales, for the Name of God to be called over them in protection or
assurance of their legality. In the same way, it should be manifest that
the sovereign abhors any illegal actions and that recognition of the
throne is tantamount to the implementation of justice.

A king can easily promote a general adherence to the law. Once it
becomes known that not one word of disrespect to justice may be uttered in his presence; that, on the contrary, he admires words of
frankness and honesty; and that he allows even his own anger to be ap-
peased by a wise word — then a king's approbation influences
righteousness and goodness as refreshing rain acts on burgeoning seeds.

כְּבֹד אֱלֹהִים הַסְתֵּר דָּבָר
וּכְבֹד מְלָכִים חֲקֹר דָּבָר:
שָׁמַיִם לָרוּם וָאָרֶץ לָעֹמֶק
וְלֵב מְלָכִים אֵין חֵקֶר:
הָגוֹ סִיגִים מִכָּסֶף
וַיֵּצֵא לַצֹּרֵף כֶּלִי:
הָגוֹ רָשָׁע לִפְנֵי־מֶלֶךְ
וְיִכּוֹן בַּצֶּדֶק כִּסְאוֹ:

*The glory of God is the mystery of His rule,*
*but the glory of kings is the unfolding of matters;*
*and yet, as the skies are high and the earth is deep,*
*so the heart of a king is unfathomable.*
*The dross has been separated from the silver*
*if the goldsmith has succeeded in making the vessel.*
*So separate the lawless from the king's surroundings,*
*and his throne shall be established in righteousness. (25, 2—5)*

The reasons and aims of Divine providence are usually beyond human understanding. God is infinitely exalted above the spirit of mortals, and the unfathomable nature of His ways is His glory, before which man bows down in his acknowledged humility. On the other hand, a king's glory, as our Proverbs note, becomes apparent if the motives for his public actions can become clear and intelligible, so that the wisdom and justification for his actions can be appreciated by the knowledgeable among his subjects. The more his people become convinced of the wisdom and justice of his actions, the more they will respect their king. And yet our Proverbs conclude that often the heart of a sovereign is as unfathomable as the depths of the earth and the heights of heaven, in regard to the motives and aims of his decisions. Yet this, as our Proverbs note, is frequently due to his entourage, the close circle of people about him. Through them the clarity of his motives and actions may become blurred. Hence, if his throne is to remain firmly established by justice, let lawless people remain far from it, just as dross must be drawn out from silver if the vessel is to come out pure and shining clear.

רְצוֹן־מֶלֶךְ לְעֶבֶד מַשְׂכִּיל
וְעֶבְרָתוֹ תִּהְיֶה מֵבִישׁ:

*Let the king favor the servant who represents wisdom,*
*and be wrathful to one who betrays his confidence. (14, 35)*

מֹשֵׁל מַקְשִׁיב עַל־דְּבַר־שָׁקֶר
כָּל־מְשָׁרְתָיו רְשָׁעִים:

*If a ruler listens to falsehood,*
*all his servants turn lawless. (29, 12)*

If a ruler wants his court of advisors and assistants to be auspicious for
himself and for his people, his subordinates should have nothing to fear
if they venture to express the truth. On the contrary, his full wrath
should be feared only when there is hypocrisy and flattery. If, however,
a ruler does not like to hear the truth but only what pleases him, then his
court and entourage cannot tolerate honest men; only lawless persons
can approach his person and command his attention.

מֶלֶךְ בְּמִשְׁפָּט יַעֲמִיד אָרֶץ
וְאִישׁ תְּרוּמוֹת יֶהֶרְסֶנָּה:

*By justice, a king establishes his country;*
*but a man who raises levies will ruin it. (29, 4)*

נָגִיד חֲסַר תְּבוּנוֹת וְרַב מַעֲשַׁקּוֹת
שֹׂנֵא בֶצַע יַאֲרִיךְ יָמִים:

*A prince who lacks understanding is rich in oppression;*
*if he is opposed to covetousness, he shall lengthen the days [of his rule].*
*(28, 16)*

Justice is the first and inalienable basis for the life of every community,
be it small or large; and this includes the society of an entire country.
True, the judiciary is not directly in the hands of a king. Nevertheless,

the king can be influential toward the administration of justice in his
country and toward the nomination of men of integrity to administer it.
But this means, first and foremost, that the sovereign himself should
shine in the light of indubitable justice, that he should be free of self-
interest or any private profit-seeking. If that is the case, he will stand out
in highest nobility.

An intelligent ruler does not seek greatness by imposing heavy burdens
upon his subjects. He does not want to be an איש תרומות, a levier of
taxes. He realizes that leniency in the interest of his subjects will
ultimately establish the stability of his reign.

נַהַם כַּכְּפִיר אֵימַת מֶלֶךְ
מִתְעַבְּרוֹ חוֹטֵא נַפְשׁוֹ:

*As the roar of a lion is the fear of a king;*
*he who provokes his anger forfeits his life. (20, 2)*

נַהַם כַּכְּפִיר זַעַף מֶלֶךְ
וּכְטַל עַל־עֵשֶׂב רְצוֹנוֹ:

*As the roar of a lion is a king's wrath,*
*and his favor as dew upon the grass. (19, 12)*

מְזָרֶה רְשָׁעִים מֶלֶךְ חָכָם
וַיָּשֶׁב עֲלֵיהֶם אוֹפָן:

*A wise king scatters the wicked*
*by returning the wheel over them. (20, 26)*

The king's position is so exalted and his power to bring good or woe is
so great, that his wrath is fearful in the same measure as his benevolence
is beneficial. A wise king uses this mighty influence in order to promote

the well-being of his people, to restrain evil and to advance the good and the righteous. True, as the Proverbs point out, dispensation of justice is not among the functions of a king; he is not a judge nor does he sit in judgment. However, inherent in his position is something even higher: he can use his influence in places which the arm of justice cannot reach.

A court is competent to judge only crimes that have been committed and proven. But how many crimes, how much injustice is committed out of sight! Even in a state whose courts are of undoubted incorruptibility and scrupulousness, it is possible for an atmosphere of dishonesty and immorality to flourish, undermining both civil and family life. Whether the seeds of evil are allowed to proliferate in the soil of a nation depends upon public opinion and its attitude toward justice and injustice. Where a general respect towards righteous and good actions prevails, while base and evil deeds are regarded with contempt and condemnation, there the germs of evil, from which crime and injustice on a large scale grow, cannot thrive. But where public opinion condones illegal and immoral behavior, there baseness and evil are allowed to come to the fore; the lawless rise to the top and become the leaders and tonesetters of society. Hence, a wise king considers it his first and most precious prerogative to use his exalted position to influence popular society in a positive way. He is the first citizen; his home is the first one in the country; and he can tune the chords that will vibrate in social and popular life, making it the highest aim of his people to live up to and harmonize with this tune. Royal approval or disapproval is powerful enough to guide affairs in such a direction that those who disregard ethical law will not be entrusted with the portfolio of social life. On the contrary, royal prerogative can weed them out of the influential levels of society and, unless they prefer to join the positive trend, they will be crushed under the wheels of the movement toward justice and morality.

פַּלְגֵי־מַיִם לֶב־מֶלֶךְ בְּיַד־ד'
עַל־כָּל־אֲשֶׁר יַחְפֹּץ יַטֶּנּוּ:

*In the hand of God, the heart of a king is as streams of water: He directs it wheresoever He wills.* (21, 1)

The resolutions of a king are of such far-reaching consequences; they condition the well-being and woe of the community to such an extent that they are bound to be the object of God's special provisional intention. Royal favor or disfavor affects none without God's express dispensation, and in their final effect both the good and the bad derived from a king's actions serve the highest aims of the Master of the Universe, who generates the life of everything and everyone, and has at His service both fools and the lawless (26, 10). Be it royal brother-rivalry, royal temper or royal favor — all such attitudes and policies of sovereigns have been factors to lead our fathers through the school of suffering. The intransigence of a Pharaoh became the iron crucible in which was forged the shining steel of the Jewish nation as an instrument of God.

⊙

The first half of the last chapter in the Book of Proverbs contains admonitions of a queen-mother to her son, the young king. She warns him of enervation by indulging in love for women and luxury, through which kings have often extinguished their career. She warns him of excessive wine-drinking, which in general does not make for happiness, and which is suitable least of all for kings and leaders, since they stand thus to lose their lucidity of mind, knowledge of the law, and judiciousness. She advises him to use his position of power mainly for the benefit of minors, powerless, poor and unprotected people. He should become their advocate, their lawyer and representative. These are her words:

מַה־בְּרִי וּמַה־בַּר־בִּטְנִי
וּמֶה בַּר־נְדָרָי:
אַל־תִּתֵּן לַנָּשִׁים חֵילֶךְ
וּדְרָכֶיךָ לַמְחוֹת מְלָכִין:

*What, my son, and what, son of my womb?*
*and what, son of my vows?*
*Do not give your strength to women,*
*nor your ways to what destroys kings.*

אַל לַמְלָכִים לְמוֹאֵל
אַל לַמְלָכִים שְׁתוֹ־יָיִן
וּלְרוֹזְנִים אֵי שֵׁכָר:
פֶּן־יִשְׁתֶּה וְיִשְׁכַּח מְחֻקָּק
וִישַׁנֶּה דִּין כָּל־בְּנֵי־עֹנִי:
תְּנוּ־שֵׁכָר לְאוֹבֵד
וְיַיִן לְמָרֵי נָפֶשׁ:
יִשְׁתֶּה וְיִשְׁכַּח רִישׁוֹ
וַעֲמָלוֹ לֹא יִזְכָּר־עוֹד:
פְּתַח־פִּיךָ לְאִלֵּם
אֶל־דִּין כָּל־בְּנֵי חֲלוֹף:
פְּתַח־פִּיךָ שְׁפָט־צֶדֶק
וְדִין עָנִי וְאֶבְיוֹן:

*It is not for kings, O Lemuel,*
*not for kings to drink wine;*
*not for leaders is strong drink —*
*lest he drink and forget what is law,*
*and distort justice for all children of misery.*
*Give strong drink to the unfortunate,*
*and wine to the bitter of soul.*
*Let him drink and forget his misery,*
*and forget for the time his misfortune.*
*You, however, open your mouth for the voiceless,*
*in the cause of all who are doomed to disappear.*
*Open your mouth, judge righteously,*
*and plead the cause of the poor and needy. (31, 2–9)*

# XXI

## MATRIMONY

מָצָא אִשָּׁה מָצָא טוֹב
וַיָּפֶק רָצוֹן מֵד':

*He who has found a wife has found great good,*
*and has obtained favor from God.* (18, 22)

The text does not read: "who has found a good wife," but merely "a
wife." Obviously, the concept of "wife" incorporates good; a fault in her
disposition is tantamount to lack of femininity.

בַּיִת וָהוֹן נַחֲלַת אָבוֹת
וּמֵד' אִשָּׁה מַשְׂכָּלֶת:

*A house and riches are an inheritance from fathers,*
*but an understanding wife is from God.* (19, 14)

Someone may own property without necessarily considering this an express Divine favor or dispensation. His parents may have earned it and
have been fortunate enough to be able to leave it to their children. To
have an אשה משכלת, however, a wife of mental and spiritual qualities; a
wife who through an understanding of people and a grasp of circumstances can do justice to her duties — such a blessed gift is a specially intended, specially benevolent dispensation from God.

אֵשֶׁת־חֵן תִּתְמֹךְ כָּבוֹד
וְעָרִיצִים יִתְמְכוּ־עֹשֶׁר:

*A gracious woman finds support in her honor*
*as mighty men find support in riches.* (11, 16)

What constitutes the wealth, support and protection of a gracious woman? It is the awareness of her dignity, the consciousness of her own moral value, held up high and unimpaired. She never acts in a way, nor tolerates anything, which might even remotely prejudice her moral dignity. This mark of her dignity is so manifest upon the conduct, actions, speech and movements of a truly self-respecting and dignified woman, that even the most shameless libertine would not dare permit himself an unseemly expression in her presence.

שְׁתֵה־מַיִם מִבּוֹרֶךָ
וְנוֹזְלִים מִתּוֹךְ בְּאֵרֶךָ:
יָפוּצוּ מַעְיְנֹתֶיךָ חוּצָה
בָּרְחֹבוֹת פַּלְגֵי־מָיִם:
יִהְיוּ־לְךָ לְבַדֶּךָ
וְאֵין לְזָרִים אִתָּךְ:
יְהִי־מְקוֹרְךָ בָרוּךְ
וּשְׂמַח מֵאֵשֶׁת נְעוּרֶךָ:
אַיֶּלֶת אֲהָבִים וְיַעֲלַת חֵן
דַּדֶּיהָ יְרַוֻּךָ בְכָל־עֵת
בְּאַהֲבָתָהּ תִּשְׁגֶּה תָמִיד:
וְלָמָּה תִשְׁגֶּה בְנִי בְזָרָה
וּתְחַבֵּק חֵק נָכְרִיָּה:

*Drink water out of your own cistern*
*and flowing water from your own spring.*
*May your wells be dispersed afield,*
*water-courses into the distance.*
*Let them be your very own*
*and strangers have no part in them.*
*May your source be blessed*
*and you have joy from the wife of your youth:*
*A lovely hind and a graceful doe,*
*may you find satisfaction at her breast at all times,*
*and may you be always caught up in her love.*
*Why should you, my son, let your senses be enticed by a stranger,*
*and embrace the bosom of an alien?*

כִּי נֹכַח עֵינֵי ד׳ דַּרְכֵי־אִישׁ
וְכָל־מַעְגְּלֹתָיו מְפַלֵּס:
עֲווֹנוֹתָיו יִלְכְּדֻנוֹ אֶת־הָרָשָׁע
וּבְחַבְלֵי חַטָּאתוֹ יִתָּמֵךְ:
הוּא יָמוּת בְּאֵין מוּסָר
וּבְרֹב אִוַּלְתּוֹ יִשְׁגֶּה:

*For a man's ways are always directly before God's eyes,*
*and all the circles of his ways are put in the balance.*
*His own devious ways snare lawless man,*
*and by the bonds of his frivolity he shall be fettered.*
*He comes to his end because of his immorality,*
*and because of the excess of his delusion he is caught. (5, 15—23)*

To illustrate happiness by a metaphor of the bestowal of life, it is usual for our Scriptures to speak of refreshing waters. Even the alien prophet [Balaam] described the tents of Jewish family-bliss as "the course of brooks shaped by God" (בנחלים נטיו) and as "water flowing out of His buckets" (יזל מים מדליו; Numbers 24, 6—7). So, too, in the description of our Proverbs, family felicity and matrimonial happiness are pictured in terms of waters: cisterns, in which waters are gathered by human efforts, and springs, in which water naturally wells up.

Marital happiness too is made of elements created by human accomplishments on the one hand, and such as are created by Divine providence, on the other. There is, however, one factor which, according to the wisdom of our Proverbs, constitutes the inalienable basis for marital happiness: faithfulness — not on the part of the wife, which is considered a matter of course, but on the part of the husband. "Yours is the spring, and yours the source"; thus speak our Proverbs to the husband, "from which your joy is drawn." May the love you bear your wife take up all of your affection, and do not pay attention to others, to any זרה, who does not belong to you—not to mention a נכריה, who belongs to another.

The word of God, which established the first marriage, was ודבק באשתו והיו לבשר אחד "let the husband cleave to his wife and become one being". This Divine word retains its validity, and living up to it is the pre-condition of marital and family happiness. However large or small may be the circle in which man and wife move together, to develop it by their common efforts — let their unity, their absolute and exclusive oneness be their goal. Together, by contributing everything noble, good, pure and truthful which a husband and his wife have in them, they build their common life and develop their home. Everything in this home, and especially the children, bear the stamp which characterizes them — so much so that whatever issues from this home, whether its influence be upon the people around it or on the children who stem from it, then even if they come to the farthest distances, they prove to be as פַלְגֵי מִים, unadulterated, unpolluted watercourses from the one parental, prime source. They perpetuate the individual character of their parental home wherever they may go, and testify that nothing alien or strange has been admixed.

Our Proverbs warn the husband in words of the gravest seriousness not to deflect in the slightest way from faithfulness. God's eyes are focused on his ways, and He weighs on the scales of His judgment the devious circles in which he may move. Any way in which a husband seeks his joys by turning his back upon his wife will become a trap and a chain to ultimately ensnare him and lead to the irredeemable ruin of his happiness and joy in life (שגה as per commentary to Genesis 8, 1).

אֵשֶׁת־חַיִל עֲטֶרֶת בַּעְלָהּ
וּכְרָקָב בְּעַצְמוֹתָיו מְבִישָׁה:

*A valiant woman is her husband's crown,*
*but as rot in his bones is one who fails in her calling.* (12, 4)

חַכְמוֹת נָשִׁים בָּנְתָה בֵיתָהּ
וְאִוֶּלֶת בְּיָדֶיהָ תֶהֶרְסֶנּוּ:

*A woman of varied wisdom has built her house,*
*but foolishness tears it down by its own hands.* (14, 1)

הֵלֶךְ טוֹרֵד בְּיוֹם סַגְרִיר
וְאֵשֶׁת מִדְיָנִים נִשְׁתָּוָה:

*A vexing drizzle on a rainy day*
*and a contentious woman are alike.* (27, 15)

טוֹב לָשֶׁבֶת עַל־פִּנַּת־גָּג
מֵאֵשֶׁת מִדְיָנִים וּבֵית חָבֶר:

*Better to dwell on a corner of a housetop*
*than in a pleasant house — with a contentious woman.* (21, 9)

Our Proverbs convey a very high esteem for the activities of an אשת חיל, a woman of spiritual and moral excellence. Scripture values very highly her importance for the happiness of a man and the prosperity of a home — so much so that the Book of Mishlé concludes with a veritable song of praise to an excellent woman, in which the beneficial activity of her whole life is extensively described.

The basic thought of this song is summarized by the verses above: אשת חיל עטרת בעלה an excellent woman is her husband's crown; and חכמות נשים בנתה ביתה, the wisdom of a woman builds her home. A husband can have no greater treasure, nothing which so heightens the value of his own identity, as the possession of a valiant wife. On this our sages say in profound wisdom: בעלה נתעטר בה והיא לא נתעטרה בבעלה—a wife contributes to a far greater extent to the heightening of her husband's value and happiness than the husband to that of his wife. And just as she is the mainstay for her husband's personality, so too for the prospering of the home.

The wife actually is the builder of the home, and this is no simple art. The guidance of domestic life, entrusted to her hands, comprises an abundance of seemingly minor relationships; but the wise or unwise handling of these can be so decisive for the comfort, prospering and happiness of the home that חכמה, simple wisdom, is not sufficient.

Rather חכמות, a whole combination of knowledge, insight, abilities and skills, as well as moral virtue and spiritual excellence, make up the art of the wifely home-builder.

Since the wife plays such a preponderant part in her husband's happiness and domestic prosperity, it follows that a woman who does not meet the expectations held for her and guides the home without wisdom is a misfortune for her husband, and she undermines the happiness of the family. In this connection, our Proverbs emphasize one vice again and again, no doubt in order to impress it upon the hearts of women. This vice, perhaps more a fault of temperament than of character (and therefore an otherwise perfectly virtuous woman may be afflicted with it) is quarrelsomeness. A quarrelsome woman, who always wishes to be in the right; who provokes retorts and yet cannot endure them; who cannot bring herself to a conciliatory silence; or who, even when silent, sulks unforgivingly — such a woman is a direct danger to the harmonious unity of man and wife and brings a blight upon marriage and domesticity. Such discord and strife, as our Proverbs note, can drive a man from his home; and no sociability or companionship which other friends or members of the family might be able to offer can compensate for disharmony between man and wife.

# XXII

## THE VALIANT WIFE

אֵשֶׁת־חַיִל מִי יִמְצָא
וְרָחֹק מִפְּנִינִים מִכְרָהּ׃
בָּטַח בָּהּ לֵב בַּעְלָהּ
וְשָׁלָל לֹא יֶחְסָר׃

*He who finds a valiant wife —*
*her price is far beyond that of pearls.*
*The heart of her husband trusted in her,*
*and he never lacked gain.* (31, 10—11)

The literal meaning of שלל is "booty"; hence it implies a gain to which one had no claim and which he thus never expected, as in ותיתה לך נפשך לשלל. The trust of her husband was not only justified at all times, but actually surpassed by her actions.

גְּמָלַתְהוּ טוֹב וְלֹא־רָע
כֹּל יְמֵי חַיֶּיהָ׃

*She did him good and never evil*
*all the days of her life.* (31, 12)

A person can do another much good, and still cause him moments of chagrin and hurt by personal whims and caprices, and by the manner in which he acts toward him. But the woman to whom this hymn is dedicated gave her husband nothing but happiness and never even a moment of grief all the days of her life.

דָּרְשָׁה צֶמֶר וּפִשְׁתִּ֑ים
וַתַּעַשׂ בְּחֵפֶץ כַּפֶּֽיהָ׃

*She sought out wool and flax*
*and worked it with the willingness of her hands.* (31, 13)

She was industriousness and assiduity incarnate. She sought out
material in order to process it "with the willingness of her hands." It is
significant that the term used here is not חפץ ידיה as we might have expected, but חפץ כפיה. The term כפים denotes not the hand as a working,
creative organ, but actually the "palm of the hand," the hand as an instrument for grasping or enclosing an object. In other words, "chefetz
kapehah" implies that her hands could not bear to be idle, and even if
her palms were folded at rest, they were "willing" and anxious to work.

הָיְתָה כָּאֳנִיּוֹת סוֹחֵר
מִמֶּרְחָק תָּבִיא לַחְמָֽהּ׃

*She was like a merchant ship;*
*she brought her bread from afar.* (31, 14)

She was always busy, and because of her providential planning for even
the remotest contingencies she managed to provide all manner of advantages for her household.

וַתָּקָם בְּעוֹד לַיְלָה
וַתִּתֵּן טֶרֶף לְבֵיתָהּ
וְחֹק לְנַעֲרֹתֶֽיהָ׃
זָמְמָה שָׂדֶה וַתִּקָּחֵהוּ
מִפְּרִי כַפֶּיהָ נָטְעָ כָּֽרֶם׃

*It was still night when she arose*
*and gave food to her household and work to her maids.*
*She saved for [the purchase of] a field and bought it,*
*and she planted a vineyard from the fruit of [the work of] her hands.*
(31, 15–16)

The literal meaning of זמם is "to produce great and far-reaching achievements from small and seemingly humble beginnings." Here it implies
that the woman, through constant thrift, managed to accumulate sav-
ings sufficient to purchase a field.

חָגְרָה בְעוֹז מָתְנֶיהָ
וַתְּאַמֵּץ זְרוֹעֹתֶיהָ:

*She girded herself with might*
*and made her arms strong. (31, 17)*

She was not robust or strong by nature; she "made herself" strong. It
was her zeal and her sense of duty that gave her strength and might.

טָעֲמָה כִּי טוֹב סַחְרָהּ
לֹא־יִכְבֶּה בַלַּיְלָה נֵרָהּ:
יָדֶיהָ שִׁלְּחָה בַכִּישׁוֹר
וְכַפֶּיהָ תָּמְכוּ פָלֶךְ:
כַּפָּהּ פָּרְשָׂה לֶעָנִי
וְיָדֶיהָ שִׁלְּחָה לָאֶבְיוֹן:
לֹא־תִירָא לְבֵיתָהּ מִשָּׁלֶג
כִּי כָל־בֵּיתָהּ לָבֻשׁ שָׁנִים:
מַרְבַדִּים עָשְׂתָה־לָּהּ
שֵׁשׁ וְאַרְגָּמָן לְבוּשָׁהּ:

*She found that her endeavor was good;*
*now her lamp did not go out at night.*
*Now she put her hands to the spindle*
*and her hand held the distaff;*
*but she also opened her hand to the poor*
*and stretched out her hands to the needy.*
*She did not fear frost for her household;*
*all her household was clothed in fine wool;*
*she prepared beds for herself,*
*but her clothing was of linen and purple. (31, 18–22)*

During the winter all the members of her household were dressed in wool, but she needed warm coverings only at night when she rested. During the day when she was busily at work no one ever saw her dressed in anything but linen. Whatever woolen garments she wore served only as ornaments. Her constant activity kept her from feeling the cold.

נוֹדָע בַּשְּׁעָרִים בַּעְלָהּ
בְּשִׁבְתּוֹ עִם־זִקְנֵי־אָרֶץ:

*Her husband was known in the public gatherings*
*when he sat with the elders of the land.* (31, 23)

When her husband sat in the councils of the city or the nation, he was pointed out as the husband of the valiant woman whose moral and spiritual influence was discernible in the words and actions of the man in public life. Thus through the voice of her husband, the fine example she set and her prudent, wise counsel became a beneficial force in the affairs of the community.

סָדִין עָשְׂתָה וַתִּמְכֹּר
וַחֲגוֹר נָתְנָה לַכְּנַעֲנִי:

*She made clcth and sold it,*
*and she gave a belt to the peddler.* (31, 24)

If this verse were meant only to laud her profitable endeavors to provide for the welfare of her household, it would not fit into the present context of the hymn, which now extols the woman's moral and spiritual influence; it would then have been more appropriate at the very beginning, where the thrifty manner in which she managed her household is described. Fortunately the statement וחגור נתנה לכנעני indicates the necessity for a different interpretation of this verse. נתן does not mean "to sell," but denotes the very opposite of "selling" (cf. Deut. 14, 21, לגר תתננה או מכור לנכרי). Accordingly, this sentence seems intended to explain how she managed to procure the means for the charity she practiced:

She wanted to help her fellow-men with her own strength and with the fruit of her own labors. She would spin thread and use it to weave a cloth. As for the thread which was left over, the product of the work of her own hands through which she raised the value of the original raw material, she did not simply give it away in its natural state. Instead, she fashioned it into a belt which she gave as a gift to the poor peddler, who stood to profit by it much more than she had given him to proceeds of the sale or if she had simply given the belt to a beggar. Thus she was conscientious and charitable at the same time, and knew how to make use of the fruits of her labor in such a manner as to give the greatest possible benefit to her fellow-men. Hence the purpose of this verse is to give but one example of how the "valiant woman's" work, her fear of God coupled with prudence, proved to be of practical value and provided a shining example for her husband — who was to apply the same principles in his deliberations in the councils of his community.

עז־וְהָדָר לְבוּשָׁהּ
וַתִּשְׂחַק לְיוֹם אַחֲרוֹן:

*Strength and beauty were her garb,*
*and smiling she faced the last day.* (31,25)

The conscientiousness and kindness which shine forth from the example just given above were basic to her entire personality. These qualities made up the strength (actually the resoluteness) and the beauty, עוז והדר, which constituted her character; and that is the reason why she could face even the last day of her life with a smile.

This is a spendid picture indeed of the life and the work of a Jewish homemaker. Even if from all the past history of our womanhood, the words of the Sacred Scriptures would have preserved for us nothing else but this one glorious testimonial, this one hymn in itself would be a most forceful refutation of the fable fabricated by inconceivable thoughtlessness that the Jewish woman of ancient history had been enslaved and degraded after the fashion of Oriental women. Where is there a European woman of the present century who would not look upon this portrayal from the remote past of Jewish history as a shining ideal which it would be the greatest bliss even only to approximate in her own life?

What, then, is the position of the Jewish woman? She is her husband's trusted friend and she makes him happy. His heart is secure in his trust in her and she is the inspiration behind his greatest achievements.

She enjoys full independence as the manager and director of her household. But she wants to be more than that. She is not content simply to take her husband's earnings and use them for her home, for the maintenance and comfort of her household. Instead, she makes her own economic contribution to the prosperity of her home; and so, of her own free will, she becomes an active partner in her husband's toil and labor.

Constant activity is her element, doing good her delight; wisdom dwells upon her lips, and her every word and action is a lesson in selfless love and devotion.

She is the ever-alert watchman over her own household, and at the same time the quiet wise counselor of her husband in matters affecting the welfare of her entire community.

פִּיהָ פָּתְחָה בְחָכְמָה
וְתוֹרַת חֶסֶד עַל־לְשׁוֹנָהּ:
צוֹפִיָּה הֲלִיכוֹת בֵּיתָהּ
וְלֶחֶם עַצְלוּת לֹא תֹאכֵל:
קָמוּ בָנֶיהָ וַיְאַשְּׁרוּהָ
בַּעְלָהּ וַיְהַלְלָהּ:

*She opened her mouth with wisdom*
*and the teaching of lovingkindness was upon her tongue.*
*She kept constant watch over the ways of her household,*
*and would never eat the bread of idleness.*
*Therefore now her sons rise up and laud her,*
*her husband, and he praises her:*

רַבּוֹת בָּנוֹת עָשׂוּ חָיִל
וְאַתְּ עָלִית עַל־כֻּלָּנָה:
שֶׁקֶר הַחֵן וְהֶבֶל הַיֹּפִי
אִשָּׁה יִרְאַת־ד׳ הִיא תִתְהַלָּל:
תְּנוּ־לָהּ מִפְּרִי יָדֶיהָ
וִיהַלְלוּהָ בַשְּׁעָרִים מַעֲשֶׂיהָ:

*"Many women have done valiantly,*
*but you have excelled them all.*
*Charm is deceit and beauty is vain;*
*a woman who fears God brings praise upon herself.*
*Give her of the fruit of her hands,*
*so that her works may praise her in the gates."* (31, 26—31)

The memory of what she has been will live on forever in the hearts of her husband and her children, who, throughout their lives, will respectfully rise at the remembrance of her and will never tire of praising her. Her memory will live on, too, even outside her immediate family, in the hearts of all her community as an eternal praise and a valiant example to be followed by future generations.

Happy and immortal is the people which can boast of having produced wives and mothers such as these.

# INDEX TO MISHLÉ